Assessment of Teaching and Learning

Assessment of Teaching and Learning

A COMPREHENSIVE GUIDEBOOK FOR LAW SCHOOLS

Kelly Terry
Gerald Hess
Emily Grant
Sandra Simpson

Carolina Academic Press
DURHAM, NORTH CAROLINA

Library of Congress Cataloging-in-Publication Data

Names: Terry, Kelly (Kelly S.), author. | Hess, Gerald, 1952- author. | Grant, Emily (Law professor), author. | Simpson, Sandra (Professor), author.
Title: Assessment of teaching and learning : a comprehensive guidebook for law schools / by Kelly Terry, Gerald Hess, Emily Grant, Sandra Simpson.
Description: Durham, North Carolina : Carolina Academic Press, LLC, [2020]
Identifiers: LCCN 2020038698 (print) | LCCN 2020038699 (ebook) | ISBN 9781611631302 (paperback) | ISBN 9781531015466 (ebook)
Subjects: LCSH: Law--Study and teaching--United States--Evaluation. | Law schools--United States--Evaluation. | Learning--Evaluation.
Classification: LCC KF272 .H463 2020 (print) | LCC KF272 (ebook) | DDC 340.071/173--dc23
LC record available at https://lccn.loc.gov/2020038698
LC ebook record available at https://lccn.loc.gov/2020038699

Carolina Academic Press
700 Kent Street
Durham, North Carolina 27701
Telephone (919) 489-7486
Fax (919) 493-5668
www.cap-press.com

Printed in the United States of America

With gratitude for the support from our colleagues and the administrations at Gonzaga University School of Law, Washburn University School of Law, and the University of Arkansas at Little Rock William H. Bowen School of Law.

Contents

SECTION TWO · ASSESSMENT OF STUDENT LEARNING

INTRODUCTION

What, Why, Who, and How?

1. What?

At the most basic level, assessment is evaluation. It is the process of collecting data about student learning and using that data to improve teaching, learning, and indeed the full functioning of a law school.[1] In that regard, assessment is a tool for schools "to learn something about the effectiveness of the educational program as measured against deliberately chosen benchmark outcomes and to gather and employ evidence that will help the school determine how to achieve those outcomes."[2]

Assessment is not a newfangled educational craze.[3] It has been a vital part of higher education since the 1980s[4] and is grounded in extensive academic research.[5] And although undertaking the assessment process at law schools is a relatively recent endeavor, the research and the ideas have been percolating among legal education scholars for decades.[6] The 2007 report Best Practices for Legal Education suggested, as a guiding principle for law schools, that they "regularly evaluate[] the program of instruction to determine if it is effective at preparing students for the practice of law."[7]

Around that same time, the American Bar Association began a thorough review of the accreditation standards for law schools, and in 2016, a new set of standards relating specifically to assessment took effect:

Table 1.1: ABA Accreditation Standards Relating to Assessment

Standard 301. OBJECTIVES OF PROGRAM OF LEGAL EDUCATION

(a) A law school shall maintain a rigorous program of legal education that prepares its students, upon graduation, for admission to the bar and for effective, ethical, and responsible participation as members of the legal profession.

(b) A law school shall establish and publish learning outcomes designed to achieve these objectives.

Standard 302. LEARNING OUTCOMES

A law school shall establish learning outcomes that shall, at a minimum, include competency in the following:

(a) Knowledge and understanding of substantive and procedural law;

(b) Legal analysis and reasoning, legal research, problem-solving, and written and oral communication in the legal context;

(c) Exercise of proper professional and ethical responsibilities to clients and the legal system; and

(d) Other professional skills needed for competent and ethical participation as a member of the legal profession.

Standard 314. ASSESSMENT OF STUDENT LEARNING

A law school shall utilize both formative and summative assessment methods in its curriculum to measure and improve student learning and provide meaningful feedback to students.

Standard 315. EVALUATION OF PROGRAM OF LEGAL EDUCATION, LEARNING OUTCOMES, AND ASSESSMENT METHODS

The dean and the faculty of a law school shall conduct ongoing evaluation of the law school's program of legal education, learning outcomes, and assessment methods; and shall use the results of this evaluation to determine the degree of student attainment of competency in the learning outcomes and to make appropriate changes to improve the curriculum.

In short, a law school must establish a program of legal education and identify specific learning outcomes, or goals, that it is seeking to achieve (Standard 301). Those learning outcomes should include, at the very least, the topics listed in Standard 302. The law school should use both formative and summative assessment methods when evaluating students (Standard 314). And Standard 315 brings it all together: the law school administration and faculty "shall conduct ongoing evaluation" of the school and should use the results of that evaluation to make decisions about the future.

2. Why?

Most law schools have undertaken the assessment process, or at least have begun thinking about it, in response to these new directives from the ABA. Nonetheless, the underlying purpose of the entire endeavor is to improve legal education.[8] The process is designed to help law schools ensure that they, as institutions, are accomplishing their goals and that their students are taking away the things that are most important. It is also an opportunity for law schools to gather empirical evidence about their strengths and to continue and encourage curricular growth in those areas.[9]

Assessment can feel very detail-oriented and technical, full of numbers and spreadsheets and charts. It is easy, in the midst of filling out forms and creating graphs and gathering data, to get wrapped up in a numbers game where the entire focus becomes just checking boxes on a form to submit to the ABA. But the goal of engaging in assessment is not to just "pass" and satisfy the ABA, though that hope most definitely exists. Instead, the whole point, the big picture focus of assessment, is for an institution to honestly evaluate itself and to make necessary improvements. Law school faculty and administration will be making decisions about curriculum and strategic planning and hiring; the information gleaned from the assessment process can help inform those decisions and ultimately lead to improved student learning.[10]

3. Who?

Assessment occurs at various levels within a law school. Institutional assessment, as mandated by Standards 302 and 315, focuses on the law school's overall effectiveness as a provider of education.[11] At this level, the assessment process looks at the collective performance of students as a measure of whether the law school as a whole is accomplishing its big-picture goals.

Program-level assessment evaluates various programs within the law school—clinics, externships, certificate or other specialty programs, the legal writing program, the library.[12] It can also include co-curricular activities like moot court or law review. And it may even extend to less academic departments in the building, such as the admissions office or the career services office.

Course-level assessment allows professors to analyze their own courses with an eye toward whether the desired content is being absorbed by the students.[13] In addition to professors data gathering and analyzing the course, law school administration may wish to devise methods for reviewing and evaluating an individual professor's teaching effectiveness.

The results of the assessment process at each level work together to provide law schools with a cohesive, "whole-building" approach to improvement. The efforts of individual faculty members and separate departments in the building blend into an overall assessment of the institution, where "faculty as a whole use assessment of student learning to improve learning systematically and collaboratively."[14]

One challenge for law schools will be to create a building-wide culture of assessment. A "majority of law teachers must be committed to data-driven continuous improvements in teaching and learning,"[15] rather than placing the burden on a small group of people. Creating a pervasive culture of assessment takes time, but it is vital to the success of the endeavor.[16]

Additionally, the fundamentals of assessment can be used to evaluate teaching, as an activity separate and apart from student learning. This process can be useful for encouraging more effective teaching methods and for making personnel decisions.

4. How?

In general, the assessment process will look similar at each level, and this book will discuss these steps in a variety of contexts:

1. Creating student learning outcomes and ensuring that the curriculum aligns with the outcomes.
2. Designing and administering assessment instruments to measure student achievement of those outcomes.
3. Reviewing and analyzing data that assessment instruments produce.
4. Making changes based on the data to improve student learning.
5. Repeating the process to evaluate the impact of the changes and whether they made any difference in student learning.

Assessment is a cyclical process; it's iterative in that the data leads to information, which can lead to changes in curriculum and instruction, which produces new data to analyze. Institutions that merely gather data in spreadsheets will wind up being data rich but information poor. Instead, law schools must use the data "to determine whether they are delivering an effective educational program."[17] The assessment process is meaningful only when schools use the data "to improve [themselves], to change the curriculum, to change teaching and learning methods, and even to change the assessment methods themselves."[18]

Assessment in law schools can be viewed as a prism. Contained within the prism are principles and practices that apply to various aspects of legal education, including institutional assessment, programmatic assessment, and course-level assessment of student learning, as well as assessment of teaching effectiveness. This book is structured to be a resource in all of those areas. Section 1 begins with a thorough overview of the assessment process generally, and it includes a chapter about how to build a culture of assessment throughout the institution. Section 2 turns to the specifics of assessing student learning in a variety of contexts: at the institutional level, at the course level, and in the context of other programs in the law school, including experiential learning, legal writing, centers and concentrations, co-curricular activities, and non-academic units. Section 3 focuses the assessment lens on teaching, with a discussion of the fundamentals and suggestions for both summative and formative assessment of teaching performance.

Endnotes

1. Barbara E. Walvoord, Assessment Clear and Simple: A Practical Guide for Institutions, Departments, and General Education 2 (2010).
2. Judith Welch Wegner, *Assessment Plans that Support Student Learning*, in Building on Best Practices: Transforming Legal Education in a Changing World 26 (Deborah Maranville et al. eds., 2015).
3. Gregory S. Munro, Outcomes Assessment for Law Schools 5 (2000).
4. *Id.* at 3; *see generally id.* at 21–25.
5. *Id.* at 5.
6. *Id.* at 25–29.
7. Roy Stuckey et al., Best Practices for Legal Education: A Vision and a Road Map 265 (2007).
8. Lori E. Shaw & Victoria L. VanZandt, Student Learning Outcomes and Law School Assessment: A Practical Guide to Measuring Institutional Effectiveness 31 (2015); Andrea Susnir Funk, The Art of Assessment: Making Outcomes Assessment Accessible, Sustainable, and Meaningful 6 (2017).
9. Shaw & VanZandt, *supra* note 8, at 32.
10. Walvoord, *supra* note 1, at 11; Funk, *supra* note 8, at 14.
11. Shaw & VanZandt, *supra* note 8, at 6.
12. Funk, *supra* note 8, at 28.
13. *Id.*
14. Barbara Glesner Fines, *An Institutional Culture of Assessment for Student Learning*, in Building on Best Practices: Transforming Legal Education in a Changing World 416 (Deborah Maranville et al. eds. 2015).
15. *Id.* at 418.
16. Funk, *supra* note 8, at 9.
17. Stuckey, *supra* note 7, at 272.
18. *Id.* at 273.

Assessment of Teaching and Learning

Section One: Assessment Fundamentals

CHAPTER ONE

Fundamentals of Assessment at All Levels of Legal Education

Assessment takes place at three levels within a law school: the institutional level, the program level, and the course level. The focus of the process becomes more particularized as it moves from the macro (institutional) level to the micro (course) level. Assessment at the institutional level examines whether a school's graduates as a whole have achieved competency in broad areas of knowledge, skills, and values that the faculty have deemed essential to the practice of law.[1] Program-level assessment, in turn, evaluates whether students who complete a distinct academic program within the curriculum, such as a lawyering-skills program, a legal-writing program, or a concentration, have developed competencies that the program faculty have identified as the intended learning from that program.[2] Course-level assessment operates at the most granular level and focuses on whether the students who complete an individual course have learned the specific knowledge, skills, and values that the instructor intended for them to learn.[3]

While the focus, methods, and interested parties may change from one level to the next, the assessment process "is fundamentally the same at all levels."[4] Educational theorists typically divide the assessment process into a series of steps, such as these articulated by assessment expert Mary Allen:

1. Develop learning outcomes;
2. Ensure alignment between the curriculum and the outcomes;
3. Develop an assessment plan;
4. Collect the assessment data;
5. Evaluate the assessment data;
6. Use results to improve the program; and
7. Routinely examine the assessment process and correct, as needed.[5]

Similarly, the process may be depicted in visual form, such as this illustration created by the University of Tennessee, Knoxville:[6]

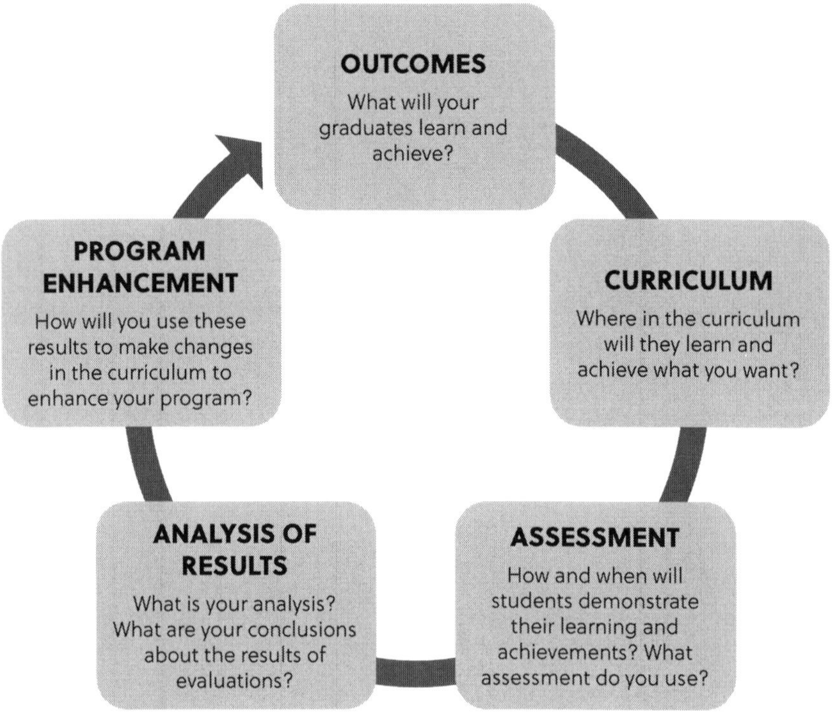

Figure 1.1: Assessment Cycle

This chapter explains each of the steps of a typical assessment process for any level of legal education, as well as necessary decisions that must be made along the way. Subsequent chapters will discuss how to implement this process specifically at the institutional, program, and course levels.

1. Developing Learning Outcomes

a. A General Process for Writing Learning Outcomes

A learning outcome is simply a statement that describes "what we want the result of obtaining an education at our institution to be: what our graduates will know, what they will be able to do, and what they will value."[7] Educational experts have identified several characteristics of effectively written outcome statements. First, an outcome statement should focus on what students will learn and be able to do, and not on what professors will do or the material they will cover.[8] Second, "[t]he outcomes should also reflect what is important in a particular area of law or for law practice, and focus on those skills or the knowledge that will endure."[9] Finally, outcomes should be "general enough to capture important learning but clear and specific enough to be measurable."[10] In this context, "measurable" does not mean "decimal-point accuracy"; rather, it means "a general judgment of whether students know, think, and can do most of what we intend for them."[11]

With these principles in mind, faculty can use a basic formula to draft outcome statements for the entire program of legal education, for distinct programs within the curriculum, and for individual courses. "Under this formula, each learning outcome should have a *stem*, an *action verb*, and *outcome*."[12] The outcome statement starts with the stem, which is "the part of the outcome that focuses on the students and when or what they should be able to do or know."[13] For example, the stem for an institutional outcome might state something like: "Upon graduation, students will be able to...." Similarly, a learning outcome for an experiential-learning program might state, "Upon completing this program, students will be able to...." Finally, a learning outcome for an individual course would state, "Upon completing the Civil Procedure I course, students will be able to...."

The remaining parts of an outcome statement are comprised of a description of the type of learning that students should achieve and a verb that identifies actions students will take to demonstrate their learning. Educational theorists generally recognize three types (or "domains") of learning:

- "the cognitive domain (increasingly complex sorts of understandings and analytical processes),
- the psychomotor or performance domain (complex patterns of physical or motor activity such as lawyering activities), and
- the affective or feeling domain (values, attitudes, and beliefs)."[14]

The chart on the following page provides examples of learning within each of these domains.

Table 1.1: Domains of Learning

Learning Within the Cognitive Domain
• Recalling legal principles in a particular area of law • Synthesizing cases and statutes • Spotting legal issues in a fact pattern • Identifying relevant facts • Applying governing legal principles to facts to reach a conclusion
Learning Within the Psychomotor/Performance Domain
• Interviewing a client • Arguing a pre-trial motion • Conducting settlement negotiations • Conducting a direct examination of a fact witness • Making a closing argument
Learning Within the Affective/Feeling Domain
• Demonstrating respect for students, staff, and faculty • Developing an attitude of cooperation with students, faculty, lawyers, and judges • Identifying values conflicts in representing clients • Formulating one's own version of the moral lawyer • Demonstrating honesty, reliability, judgment, and hard work

Learning outcomes are not exclusive to one domain, however, and overlap often occurs. For example, the ability to argue a pre-trial motion in court necessarily will depend on the cognitive ability to understand and recall the governing legal principles and apply them to the facts of the case. In adopting learning outcomes, experts recommend choosing a combination of outcomes from each of these domains.

Finally, the action verb should align with the type of learning that the outcome addresses and describe some observable act that students will perform to demonstrate their development in that area. Learning taxonomies can be helpful in selecting appropriate action verbs. A learning taxonomy is simply a system that classifies educational objectives and usually includes guidelines for developing them.[15] The most well-known learning taxonomy is probably Bloom's Taxonomy, which includes categories of learning outcomes within the cognitive domain.[16] These outcomes are organized along a continuum that reflects the degree to which a learner has developed certain cognitive abilities and thinking skills.[17] The lowest level of the taxonomy is knowledge, which is simply the ability to remember and recall information, followed by comprehension, application, analysis, synthesis, and evaluation.[18] Using this taxonomy, educators have developed lists of action verbs that correlate with the various levels of cognitive learning and can be used in writing outcome statements. For example, below is a list of action verbs prepared by the New York

University Steinhardt School of Culture, Education, and Human Development that corresponds to the levels of the cognitive-domain taxonomy:[19]

Table 1.2: Actions Verbs for Cognitive-Domain Taxonomy

Definitions	Knowledge	Comprehension	Application	Analysis	Synthesis	Evaluation
Bloom's Definition	Remember previously learned information.	Demonstrate an understanding of the facts.	Apply knowledge to actual situations.	Break down objects or ideas into simpler parts and find evidence to support generalizations.	Compile component ideas into a new whole or propose alternative solutions.	Make and defend judgments based on internal evidence or external criteria.
Verbs	• Arrange • Define • Describe • Duplicate • Identify • Label • List • Match • Memorize • Name • Order • Outline • Recognize • Relate • Recall • Repeat • Reproduce • Select • State	• Classify • Convert • Defend • Describe • Discuss • Distinguish • Estimate • Explain • Express • Extend • Generalize • Give example(s) • Identify • Indicate • Infer • Locate • Paraphrase • Predict • Recognize • Rewrite • Review • Select • Summarize • Translate	• Apply • Change • Choose • Compute • Demonstrate • Discover • Dramatize • Employ • Illustrate • Interpret • Manipulate • Modify • Operate • Practice • Predict • Prepare • Produce • Relate • Schedule • Show • Sketch • Solve • Use • Write	• Analyze • Appraise • Break down • Calculate • Categorize • Compare • Contrast • Criticize • Diagram • Differentiate • Discriminate • Distinguish • Examine • Experiment • Identify • Illustrate • Infer • Model • Outline • Point out • Question • Relate • Select • Separate • Subdivide • Test	• Arrange • Assemble • Categorize • Collect • Combine • Comply • Compose • Construct • Create • Design • Develop • Devise • Explain • Formulate • Generate • Plan • Prepare • Rearrange • Reconstruct • Relate • Reorganize • Revise • Rewrite • Set up • Summarize • Synthesize • Tell • Write	• Appraise • Argue • Assess • Attach • Choose • Compare • Conclude • Contrast • Defend • Describe • Discriminate • Estimate • Evaluate • Explain • Judge • Justify • Interpret • Relate • Predict • Rate • Select • Summarize • Support • Value

Using the three-part formula of stem, action verb, and intended learning, the chart below illustrates the components of example learning outcomes at the institutional, program, and course levels.

Table 1.3: Learning Outcomes Components

Outcome Level	Stem	Action Verb	Intended Learning
Institutional	Graduates will be able to	demonstrate	effective problem-solving skills
Program	Students who complete this program will be able to	write	an effective litigation document
Course	Students who complete this course will be able to	identify	relevant legal issues in a fact pattern

Since 2016, the American Bar Association (ABA) has required U.S. law schools to establish and publish institutional learning outcomes that, at a minimum, include competency in the following:

a) Knowledge and understanding of substantive and procedural law;

b) Legal analysis and reasoning, legal research, problem-solving, and written and oral communication in the legal context;

c) Exercise of proper professional and ethical responsibilities to clients and the legal system; and

d) Other professional skills needed for competent and ethical participation as a member of the legal profession.[20]

The ABA also requires course-level learning outcomes,[21] although it has not mandated learning outcomes at the program level. Subsequent chapters provide specific guidance for drafting learning outcomes at the institutional, program, and course levels.

b. Using Institutional-, Program-, and Course-Level Outcomes to Create a Cohesive Curriculum

While the ABA does not require law schools to establish program-level learning outcomes, they are beneficial because they provide a bridge between institutional- and course-level outcomes and help to ensure curricular alignment. Assessment expert Peggy Maki explains how institutional-, program-, and course-level learning outcomes should integrate with one another to create a coherent curriculum:

> In a cohesive curricular and co-curricular design, these institution-level outcomes are seeded into program or department-level outcomes; in turn, institution and program or department-level outcomes are seeded into the courses and educational experiences that altogether contribute to students' major program of study and to their institution-wide learning. Institution- and program- or department-level outcomes become more specifically stated as they are adapted to the context of courses; modules; [and] educational experiences.[22]

Thus, program- and course-level outcomes should follow from the institutional learning outcomes and be consistent with them. The diagram below illustrates how a learning outcome related to written communication skills could be integrated across the levels of an institution, an experiential-learning program, and an individual clinical course:

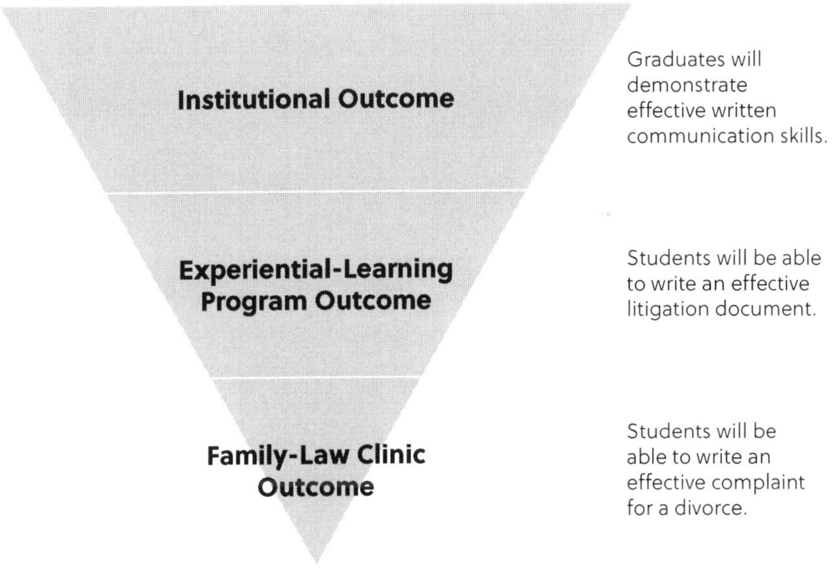

Figure 1.2: Integration of Outcomes Across Institutional, Program, and Course Levels

Through this integration, the outcomes build on one another from the institutional level to the course level, and the curriculum becomes a "pathway[] for learning" rather than just a collection of independent courses.[23]

2. Ensuring Alignment Between Outcomes and the Curriculum, Programs, and Courses

"For students to learn what is expected of them, the relevant subject matter must be addressed and reinforced in the curriculum."[24] This principle applies to subject matter at the institutional, program, and course levels. Students can be expected to learn the knowledge, skills, and values described in an outcome statement only if they are exposed to that content and provided the opportunity to apply and practice it. Thus, faculty must check the content of their curriculum, programs, and courses to ensure that they are addressing and reinforcing the intended subject matter.

At the institutional level, this "check" typically is accomplished through curriculum mapping, which is a process for taking an inventory of the curriculum. To undertake this process, a school's assessment coordinator, committee, or task force should create and complete a chart (the "map") that compares the school's institutional learning outcomes to the content of its required courses. In making this comparison, the required courses should be examined to determine which, if any, of them addresses the learning outcomes.[25] By creating this map, educators obtain a broad view of students' progress through the curriculum and are able "to see how frequently students have or have had opportunities to hone a particular ability."[26]

A curriculum map for institutional outcomes should include only required courses. Elective courses should be excluded because "the purpose of the curriculum map is to make sure that *every* student, regardless of curricular choices, has ample opportunity to achieve key learning goals. By definition, electives aren't taken by everyone."[27] If the curriculum offers clusters of courses and requires students to take one or more of those courses, those courses may be included in the curriculum map if the courses all address at least one shared learning outcome.[28] The table below illustrates how a curriculum map comparing institutional learning outcomes to a typical required curriculum might be formatted:

Table 1.4: Sample Form for Curriculum Map

	Contracts	Torts	Prop.	Legal Writing	Crim. Law	Civ. Pro.	Evidence	Con. Law	Trial Adv.	Prof. Resp.	Req'd Clinic or Externship
Knowledge Outcome 1											
Knowledge Outcome 2											
Knowledge Outcome 3											
Skills Outcome 1											
Skills Outcome 2											
Skills Outcome 3											
Values Outcome 1											
Values Outcome 2											
Values Outcome 3											

To complete the map, the assessment coordinator or committee must review the content of each listed course to determine if it addresses each of the listed learning outcomes.[29] Before reviewing that content, however, those completing the map must decide the depth of coverage that they seek for each outcome. For example, in a basic curriculum map, the reviewers might just place a checkmark in the box for each course that touches on or addresses an outcome in some fashion. However, many experts recommend that the map state the level of depth at which the course focuses on the outcome. According to *Best Practices for Legal Education*, "[f]or each outcome, a curriculum map identifies where in the curriculum students will be ***introduced*** to the skill, value, or knowledge; where in the curriculum the students will ***practice*** it; and at what point in the curriculum students can be expected to have attained the desired level of ***proficiency.***"[30] Other scholars recommend using the levels of Introduction, Competency, and Proficiency,[31] or Introduced, Practiced, and Demonstrated.[32] The faculty as a whole should decide the levels of depth that the curriculum map will specify. Using the sample map in Table 1.4 above, with the levels of Introduced, Practiced, and Demonstrated, a completed curriculum map might look like this:[33]

Table 1.5: Sample Completed Curriculum Map

	Contracts	Torts	Prop.	Legal Writing	Crim. Law	Civ. Pro.	Evidence	Con. Law	Trial Adv.	Prof. Resp.	Req'd Clinic or Externship
Knowledge Outcome 1	I	I	I		I	I	P, D	P, D		P, D	
Knowledge Outcome 2				I					P		D
Knowledge Outcome 3				I					P		D
Skills Outcome 1	I	I	I		I	I	P, D	P, D		P, D	
Skills Outcome 2				I					P, D		D
Skills Outcome 3				I					P, D		D
Values Outcome 1										I, P	D
Values Outcome 2				I						P, D	
Values Outcome 3	I	I		I					P, D	D	D

Examining the required courses to determine the level at which they address the outcomes can be accomplished in a variety of ways. For example, the reviewers might read faculty members' course descriptions and syllabi, or they might attend particular class sessions to observe how the outcomes are addressed in those classes. In addition, many experts recommend surveying the faculty to ask them about the learning outcomes for their courses, the level at which particular outcomes are developed, and their methods for assessing particular outcomes.[34] An important point to remember is that a curriculum map will not remain static once it is completed. For example, faculty may change their course descriptions and syllabi, or they may alter the depth at which they treat an outcome in their courses. Similarly, new faculty who join the law school may design their courses in ways that differ from the ways that previous faculty taught the courses. Thus, assessment leaders must stay abreast of changes like these and update the curriculum map accordingly.

Once this information is gathered and the curriculum map is completed, the reviewers must analyze what it reveals about the treatment of the school's institutional outcomes. In particular, they should look for gaps and patterns.[35] For example, is the law school actually providing all students with the opportunity to learn the knowledge, skills, and values encompassed in its outcomes? Is there an outcome that is not addressed in any of the required courses in the curriculum? Are the outcomes merely introduced in courses, but not subsequently practiced or treated with enough depth to allow students to achieve competency in them?[36] Are some outcomes over-emphasized and addressed in multiple courses, while others are under-emphasized and hardly covered?[37]

This process should produce a great deal of information about the content of a school's curriculum and how the curriculum aligns with the institutional outcomes. Using this information, faculty should be able to make thoughtful decisions about the outcomes themselves, the sequence of the curriculum, the design of individual courses, and teaching methods. For example, if the school has adopted an institutional outcome that is not addressed anywhere in its curriculum, it must ask if that outcome is truly critical to its graduates' education. If it is, then the school must change its curriculum to incorporate that outcome in one or more of its required courses or create a new course to address it. If it is not, then the school must discard the outcome. Similarly, curricular changes must be made if an outcome is merely introduced in certain courses, but students do not have subsequent opportunities to practice or achieve competency in it. In that situation, opportunities should be created in later courses for students to practice the outcome and demonstrate competency. If a faculty cannot or will not create such opportunities, then the outcome should be abandoned.

A similar mapping process should be carried out for program and course learning outcomes. Faculty who teach courses within a particular program should inventory the courses that comprise the program to ensure that they provide students sufficient opportunities to develop competency in the program learning outcomes. If there are gaps between the courses and the program learning outcomes, then changes in either the program content or program outcomes should be made.

The mapping at the course level is the least complicated of the three. At this level, the instructor of the particular course should simply examine the course design, content, teaching methods, and learning activities to ensure that students are receiving sufficient opportunities to achieve the course learning outcomes that the instructor has identified. If students are not receiving those opportunities, then the instructor must decide whether to change the learning outcomes or to make changes in the course design.

3. Developing Assessment Plans

Conducting an assessment process at any level involves identifying, collecting, managing, and evaluating a significant amount of information over an extended period of time. To organize this information, faculty who are involved in assessment efforts—whether at the institutional, program, or course level—should create an assessment plan, which is simply a written document setting out the process to be followed in determining whether students are achieving the stated learning outcomes.[38] The plan typically includes the learning outcomes at issue, the curriculum or content map for those outcomes, a schedule specifying when and how often each outcome will be assessed, the types of evidence of student learning that will be used to evaluate student attainment of each outcome, and the number of measures of student learning that will be considered. These components of an assessment plan are discussed individually in the sections that follow. For reference, the assessment plans that the University of Arkansas at Little Rock William H. Bowen School of Law and the Washburn University School of Law have adopted for their institutional learning outcomes are included in the Appendix.

a. Creating an Assessment Schedule

According to Professor Andrea Susnir Funk, the first rule of assessing institutional learning outcomes is that "you cannot assess every learning outcome every year."[39] Given the amount of work required, trying to assess every outcome every year is simply not feasible, and it would make the assessment process unsustainable.[40] Rather, faculty should create a cycle for assessing each outcome every few years on a repeating basis. Most educational programs, for example, "are subject to periodic review cycles, with formal program review every five to seven years"; these program review schedules often are used as a basis for an assessment cycle.[41]

The ABA, however, has recently changed its accreditation schedule to conduct site visits only every ten years,[42] and it has not stated how often it expects law schools to assess their learning outcomes. Accordingly, schools must determine on their own how often to assess them. When the period between ABA site visits was seven years, Professors Lori Shaw and Victoria VanZandt suggested that schools should complete the assessment cycle for each learning outcome at least once or twice during that period.[43] Since the period between site visits is now even longer, law schools should assess their institutional outcomes a minimum of two times between site visits, and more if possible.[44] Shaw and VanZandt recommend adopting a schedule for measuring each outcome at least once every four years.[45] The diagram below illustrates a possible timeline for assessing twelve institutional outcomes over the course of nine years:

Table 1.6: Sample Assessment Schedule

Learning Outcomes	2021–2022	2021–2022	2021–2022.	2021–2022	2021–2022	2021–2022	2021–2022	2021–2022	2021–2022
Knowledge Outcome 1									
Knowledge Outcome 2									
Knowledge Outcome 3									
Skills Outcome 1									
Skills Outcome 2									
Skills Outcome 3									
Values Outcome 1									
Values Outcome 2									
Values Outcome 3									

It likely will be feasible to assess program and course outcomes on a more frequent basis, since programs and courses often have fewer learning outcomes than the law school as a whole and examine the work of only students in the program or course, rather than the entire student body. For example, if a program has four learning outcomes, then the program leaders might assess two of the outcomes each year. Similarly, instructors should be able to complete their assessment of student learning in a course immediately after the course ends. Thus, instructors or program leaders can create a schedule for assessing course and program outcomes every year or every other year.

b. Deciding the Types of Assessment Measures to Use

1) Direct and Indirect Measures

Law schools also must decide the types of measures they will use to assess whether students are achieving competency in their institutional, program, and course outcomes. Assessment measures (also known as "instruments" or "tools") are simply the "means by which one gathers evidence to demonstrate learning or the achievement of learning outcomes; they are indicators of performance."[46] Educational experts typically categorize assessment instruments as either "direct measures" or "indirect measures."

Direct measures are based on actual student work or performance and require students to display their knowledge and skills to a trained evaluator.[47] Examples of direct assessment measures include exams, quizzes, papers, drafting assignments, presentations, skills performances, portfolios, and evaluations by externship and clinical supervisors. "Direct assessment tools tend to be viewed with great favor because they do not involve guesswork. What the students can and cannot do or do and do not know is right there in front of the assessor and any 'outside' constituency, such as an accreditor, who wishes to review the work product."[48] Assessment experts also suggest that direct measures are "more likely to yield meaningful data because we are evaluating students based on work they are heavily invested in, and for which they have incentives to do their best."[49]

Indirect measures, on the other hand, "are based upon opinion, either the student's opinion or any other observer's opinion."[50] Forms of indirect assessment include surveys and focus groups of students and graduates asking them about their learning and the value of their educational experience; surveys and focus groups of employers asking for their perceptions about the knowledge, skills, and values of the school's students or graduates; and students' or graduates' self-assessment of their own knowledge, skills, and values.[51] While indirect evidence can provide useful information, it is based on opinions and self-reporting and therefore is less reliable than direct evidence. Accordingly, "*no assessment of knowledge, understanding, or thinking or performance skills should consist of indirect evidence alone*."[52] For an assessment program to have credibility, schools must include direct assessment measures.[53]

When determining the assessment measures to use, faculty must decide whether to use "embedded" assessments or "add-on" assessments. Embedded assessments are assignments or learning activities that students complete as part of a regular course or program; in addition to professors evaluating the assignments for their specific courses, a school's assessment leaders also can review these same assignments for evidence of student learning with respect to the school's institutional and program outcomes.[54] Conversely, add-on assessments are instruments, such as surveys or exit interviews, that are administered solely to obtain information for assessment purposes and are not part of a regular course or program.[55] Experts recommend using embedded assessments whenever possible because they allow the gathering of assessment information from assignments that already have been created for other purposes, which saves faculty time and energy.[56] Since embedded assessments already exist, "it may take little or no time, money, or effort for the assessment task force to use them. It may be as simple as looking at the product of an activity (*e.g.*, an exam answer) in a different way."[57] In addition, students are motivated to complete the course assignments on which their grades depend, so embedded assessments likely produce more accurate information about student learning than add-on assessments.[58]

Embedded assessments for measuring institutional outcomes can be identified through the curriculum-mapping process. When mapping the curriculum to determine which courses address the institutional learning outcomes, assessment leaders also should identify the assignments and activities that students complete in those courses and decide whether student performance on those assignments and activities can be used to evaluate achievement of the school's institutional outcomes. Assessment leaders then can review those assignments, or a representative sample of them, to determine if students are achieving the learning set forth in the institutional outcomes.

A similar process can be used for identifying embedded assessments that can be used to evaluate program learning outcomes. Assignments from courses within the program can be identified and reviewed to assess student attainment of the program outcomes. For course-level outcomes, professors will review the assignments from their own courses. Thus, it is possible that an assessment from a single course could serve three purposes, providing evidence of student learning at the course, program, and institutional level.

To gather indirect evidence about students' learning, law schools have a variety of tools from which to choose. For example, they might administer self-assessments in which they ask students to evaluate their own growth and progress toward the school's stated outcomes. These self-assessments could be administered at a single point in the educational process, such as at graduation, or they could be administered longitudinally, such as during the first year, second year, and third year, to track student progress over time. Other instruments for gathering indirect evidence include focus groups and surveys of employers, current students, and graduates. Employers, for example, could be asked for their opinions about whether the school's graduates who work for them possess the various competencies that make up the school's learning outcomes.

An existing survey that also can provide useful data is the Law School Survey of Student Engagement (LSSSE), which was created by the Indiana University Center for Postsecondary research. Since 2004, participating law schools nationwide have administered the survey to their students on an annual basis.[59] The survey questions focus on student engagement and are designed to measure the effects of legal education on students.[60] Thus, faculty should review their school's LSSSE data to determine if it provides any relevant information regarding student achievement of institutional, program, and course learning outcomes.

2) Formative and Summative Assessments

In selecting which direct and indirect measures to include in an assessment plan, educators also should consider whether the purpose of the assessment instrument was formative or summative.[61] The ABA Standards mandate that a law school must use "both formative and summative assessment methods in its curriculum to measure and improve student learning and provide meaningful feedback to students."[62] An assessment is formative if its primary purpose is to provide feedback to students and faculty on student performance. ABA Standard 314 defines formative assessments as "measurements at different points during a particular course or at different points over the span of a student's education that provide meaningful feedback to improve student learning."[63] Formative assessments often are ungraded, but teachers may choose to assign grades to them.

Summative assessments, on the other hand, are used for assigning a grade or otherwise indicating a student's level of achievement at the end of a course or unit of study. ABA Standard 314 defines summative assessments as "measurements at the culmination of a particular course or at the culmination of any part of a student's legal education that measure the degree of student learning."[64] "In contrast to formative evaluation, which looks forward to ways in which students might continue to learn, *summative* evaluation looks back and judges how much students have learned."[65] Since summative assessments typically are graded, students likely will be more motivated to prepare for them and put forth their best efforts, so summative assessments may be more accurate measures of student learning than assessments that are purely formative.

3) Course Grades Are Not Acceptable Outcome Measures

When deciding the types of assessment measures to use, faculty must understand that "[a]ssessment and grading are not synonymous."[66] While assessment and grading are related in that both involve review of student work product and performance, they are distinct processes that should not be conflated or viewed as interchangeable. There are several crucial differences between assessing student learning and assigning course grades, which render course grades of limited, if any, value in an assessment process.

First, assessing student learning and awarding grades serve entirely different purposes. Grading "is evaluative — designed to sort and classify students, to confer distinction or channel students," while "assessment is ameliorative — designed to improve student learning and faculty teaching."[67] To accomplish its sorting function, law-school grading often is based on a mandated curve that requires a specific and pre-determined distribution of grades.[68] So, students graded on a curve are evaluated in relationship to one another, rather than against absolute standards. Grades assigned on a relative scale, however, "do not really provide information on the absolute level of student performance (except perhaps for very strong or very weak performance)."[69] Moreover, when schools employ a mandatory curve, "the overall course grades are essentially the same from year to year, regardless of student performance."[70] Thus, professors are not able to track ups and downs in student performance from curved grades.[71] An assessment process, on the other hand, identifies specific learning outcomes and then measures student work against established performance levels, typically ranging from "weak" to "exemplary," to determine whether students have achieved competency in the outcomes. Through this process, professors can identify the areas in which students are attaining the outcomes and the areas in which they are falling short, which allows professors to take steps to improve learning in the areas of deficiency.

Second, the focus of assessment is collective, while the focus of grading is individual. Assessment "focuses on entire cohorts of students, and it often considers how effectively many people, not just an individual faculty member, are collectively helping them learn."[72] Assessment examines patterns and trends in student learning across multiple courses to evaluate the program of legal education as a whole and identify areas for improvement. Conversely, a professor's assignment of a course grade to an individual student provides only that professor's summary measure of the performance of that one particular student.[73] In addition, grades may be based on "inconsistent, imprecise, and idiosyncratic criteria,"[74] rather than the pre-established criterion-referenced standards that are applied consistently to all student work in a well-executed assessment process.

Third, assessment focuses on student learning with respect to individual learning outcomes, while grades reflect student performance with respect to multiple outcomes. In an assessment process, each learning outcome is analyzed separately and independently. The learning outcome is identified, the evidence relating to that outcome is gathered, that evidence is evaluated, and a conclusion is reached regarding the level of student learning achieved with respect to that outcome. Thus, there is a laser-like focus on one outcome at a time that allows faculty to pinpoint specific areas of strength and weakness.[75]

Assigning a course grade, however, does not have this singular focus. Professors typically weigh several factors in determining course grades, such as multiple assessments keyed to different learning outcomes, or a single assessment administered at the end of the semester to evaluate all of the course's learning outcomes. In addition, professors often base grades on factors unrelated to students' mastery of course learning outcomes, such as attendance, class participation, punctuality, penalties for late assignments, and opportunities for extra credit.[76] Thus, a grade is an aggregation based on a combination of inputs, and it does not provide disaggregated information regarding student learning in any particular area. A student's grade of "B" in an Ethics course, for example, implies that the student probably learned a good deal about the course's subject matter, but it does not show which learning outcomes were mastered and which were not. The final grade does not indicate whether or how well the student can spot ethical issues, apply the governing rules of professional conduct to a set of facts, or internalize professional values such as honesty and integrity.[77] An assessment process focusing on each of those competencies as a discrete learning outcome, however, would provide that information.

In sum, a grade is "essentially an artificial construct designed to compare the performance of one student to another and rank them accordingly."[78] Thus, while grades may provide some indirect evidence about student learning, they "are not acceptable outcome measures."[79]

c. Deciding the Number of Assessment Measures to Use

With a variety of available direct and indirect measures from which to choose, assessment leaders must decide how many assessments they will consider in evaluating whether students are achieving competency in the learning outcomes. Assessment expert Barbara Walvoord recommends using a minimum of two measures for each outcome—one direct measure and one indirect measure.[80] Multiple measures are essential because no single assessment instrument, even if it is very well designed and executed, "can provide the comprehensive view needed to determine whether a criterion is being achieved."[81] Students may perform better on one type of assessment than another, so using multiple assessments provides students with more opportunities to demonstrate their learning and produces a more accurate picture of whether students are achieving learning outcomes.[82] Using multiple measures also enhances credibility in the assessment process by allowing faculty to compare results from multiple methods.[83] When multiple methods of assessment produce similar findings, greater confidence may be placed in the results.[84]

An assessment process must be sustainable to be effective. Collecting a mountain of assessment data that faculty members do not have sufficient time to consider and analyze is a waste of effort. Accordingly, law schools are advised to start with a manageable number of assessment measures, such as two embedded direct measures, or Dr. Walvoord's recommendation of one direct measure and one indirect measure. If faculty determine that they would like to have even more information about student learning, and they have adequate time to evaluate it, then more assessment measures can be added to the school's assessment plan as the process progresses.

d. Effective Assessment Measures Are Valid, Reliable, and Fair[85]

Assessment leaders must design their assessment instruments to ensure that they are valid, reliable, and fair.[86] Validity means that the assessment measures the knowledge, skills, or values that the teacher taught and intended for students to learn.[87] If an assessment measures something other than that, then it is not valid. Thus, an assessment that purports to measure students' ability to spot legal issues in a fact pattern must actually measure and provide information regarding students' development of that competency. If an instrument actually measures students' knowledge of substantive law or their ability to synthesize cases, then it is not a valid measure for issue-spotting.

Reliability means that the assessment instrument is consistent and "yields the same results on repeated trials."[88] An assessment is reliable if a teacher can evaluate a student's performance on it multiple times and award the same or a similar score each time. For example, assume that an upper-level seminar paper is used to gauge students' writing skills. If one inserted three copies of the same student paper into the pile of papers being reviewed by an evaluator, the assignment would demonstrate reliability if the evaluator gave all three of the copies the same or a similar score.[89] Thus, reliability reduces the impact of subjective influences in the assessment process, such as whether a student's performance is assessed first or last. Assessment instruments that do not yield consistent results lack reliability and are "of no value in an assessment program."[90]

Finally, fairness in assessment means that "students are given equitable opportunities to demonstrate what they know"[91] and can do. To ensure fairness, assessments should have clear instructions that are easily understood, and they should not include cultural references that reflect biases or favor students from a particular background.[92] Fairness also is enhanced when teachers administer multiple assessments of different types, so all of the assessments do not favor students with a particular set of skills.[93] For example, a teacher might include both writing tasks and class presentations as assessments, so that students who excel at writing and students who excel at speaking both have equal opportunities to demonstrate their learning.

4. Collecting the Assessment Data

a. Determining the Amount of Data to Collect

1) Using Representative Samples

Once assessment leaders decide the type and number of assessment instruments they will use, they need to determine how many students will be asked to complete them. How many students need to be assessed in order to draw reliable conclusions about whether students are achieving institutional, program, and course learning outcomes? No hard and fast rule exists to answer this question. The reliability of results usually increases as larger numbers of students are assessed and more data are collected.[94] Assessment at the course level usually will involve the fewest number of students since it is limited to a single course; thus, it should be feasible to assess the learning of all the students in a course with respect to each course learning outcome.

Program and institutional assessment, however, typically will involve larger numbers of students. While schools should strive to assess as many students as possible at the program and institutional levels, it may not be possible to review and evaluate assessments completed by each student in the cohort being assessed. Assume for example, that a school has decided to use client-engagement letters submitted in a second-year lawyering skills simulation course to assess students' written communication skills. Assume further that the second-year class consists of 300 students. It simply may not be feasible for an assessment committee to review all 300 letters for institutional assessment purposes. Institutional assessment, however, does not require the measurement of each and every student's development.[95] Rather, reviewing a representative sample of student work is an acceptable method for drawing conclusions about student learning as a whole.[96]

If assessment leaders are going to use a representative sample, they must determine an appropriate sample size. While there is no established rule for determining an appropriate size, "[t]he sample must be representative and complete."[97] Some commentators have suggested as a rule of thumb that, at a minimum, the sample "should be **the greater of 10 students or 10 percent of the student population being measured**."[98] So, if 80 students submit an upper-level seminar paper that is being used to assess critical-thinking skills, faculty would assess at least 10 of the papers, but if 300 students submitted papers, then the faculty would assess at least 30 of the papers.

Other experts suggest deciding the sample size based on the margin of error that is acceptable.[99] Using a formula, experts have calculated the following error margins based on sample size:[100]

Table 1.7: Error Margins Based on Sample Size

Random Sample Size	Error Margin
9604	1%
2401	2%
1067	3%
600	4%
384	5%
264	6%
196	7%

Thus, sample size depends in large part on the error margin that faculty are willing to tolerate. According to assessment expert Linda Suskie, "[w]hile professional pollsters often aim for sample sizes of about 1,000 people, with an error margin of three percent, unless your assessments may lead to major (read expensive) changes, a sample of no more than 300 or 400 is probably sufficient."[101] If a sample that size is still too large to be practical, faculty may use a smaller sample that is more feasible, so long as they recognize that the error margin will increase.[102] According to Suskie, "[i]f the assessment will likely lead to only minor changes, such as adjusting the curriculum in a course or two, a smaller sample may be fine."[103]

2) Methods for Choosing Representative Samples

A variety of methods exists for choosing representative samples, including simple random samples, cluster random samples, and stratified random samples.[104] Simple random sampling requires that every student in the population being assessed has an equal chance to be selected for the sample.[105] When using simple random sampling, it is important to use methods that will reduce bias in the selection of students.[106] One method for reducing bias is to use a random number generator to select students based on their exam numbers and then assess the work product of those students.[107]

Cluster random sampling "involves randomly selecting subgroups/sections and assessing everyone in that section."[108] For example, assume that a law school decided to use essay exams from its required legal ethics course to assess professional-identity learning outcomes, and there were multiple sections of the course. If the school used cluster random sampling, it would choose one or more of those sections and review all of the exams from the selected sections.[109]

Stratified random sampling involves dividing the student population into subgroups based on significant characteristics of interest to the school, such as gender, race, or grade-point average, and selecting a representative sample from each subgroup.[110] This method would not be appropriate for assessing an entire student body's achievement of learning outcomes, but it could be useful if a school wanted to obtain disaggregated data regarding how well certain subgroups of students are achieving the outcomes. Stratified sampling tends to be used when concerns exist about how a certain segment of the student population is doing.[111]

If these sampling methods are not possible, information often is collected from what is known as a "convenience sample."[112] This type of sample occurs when faculty "cannot comply with the rules for appropriate sampling and have simply done the best they can in locating individuals to participate in the assessment."[113] In-class quizzes, for example, are completed only by those students who attend the class on the day the quiz is given, and the characteristics of those students may not be representative of the entire student population.[114] This same concern exists for surveys administered to students, since they are completed only by students who voluntarily participate. Assessment data, however, do not have to comply with empirical-research protocols, and information of this type is still quite meaningful and useful.[115]

b. Methods for Gathering the Assessment Data

Once the amount of data to collect has been decided, assessment leaders at the various levels should design systems for gathering, storing, and protecting that data. Otherwise, the information may be inadvertently destroyed or discarded, or simply not made available in a timely manner. The leader for an institutional assessment process may be an assessment coordinator, an associate dean for academic affairs, an assessment committee, or an assessment task force. Program-level assessment likely will be led by the program leader, such as the director of a legal-writing program, an associate dean for experiential learning, or the library director. Course-level assessment will be conducted by the course instructor. The designated leader, whether an individual or a committee, should create the process for gathering and maintaining the assessment data. When designing these processes, assessment leaders must ensure that they comply with the Family Educational Rights and Privacy Act (FERPA), which is a federal law that limits the disclosure of personally identifiable information in educational records.[116]

The nature of the assessment instruments likely will determine the method for collecting them. For example, if the assessment data consist of embedded assessments, such as exams or seminar papers (or rubrics completed for such assignments), the assessment leader will need to set up a process to work with the faculty administering the assessments to collect copies of them, a representative sample of them, or the rubrics used to evaluate them. That process could require the faculty member to provide the information directly to the assessment leader or to provide it to another member of the law school staff, such as the associate dean for academic affairs or the registrar, who then submits the information to the assessment leader.

Assessment data that originate outside of the law school may need to be obtained from the dean or another law school administrator. For example, entities external to the law school generate bar exam data and LSSSE data and then report that data to the law school. Law schools also may hire consultants to conduct focus groups or surveys of employers and alumni. If a school's assessment plan calls for review of data that is produced outside of the law school, the assessment leader should identify the administrator who receives that information and set up a process for obtaining the data from that person.

Finally, assessment leaders also should decide how long they will retain assessment data after they have reviewed it. Data from institutional- and program-level assessment typically is summarized in a written assessment report, which also includes conclusions drawn from the data and recommendations for improvement. So the question really is how long to retain the underlying raw data, such as the rubrics, survey instruments, and student work products. For guidance on this question, assessment leaders can look to the records-retention policy of their school or parent institution. Another suggestion is to keep the data until at least the next ABA accreditation inspection, in case any members of the site-inspection team ask to see it.

5. Evaluating the Assessment Data

Once the evidence of student learning has been gathered, faculty must evaluate it to determine what it demonstrates regarding student learning. The fundamental question faculty must answer is, "On what basis do we decide that a sufficiently high percentage of our students have been shown to have learned a sufficient amount for us to say, 'This is good enough'?"[117] Answering this question is a subjective process that requires informed judgment.[118] In the context of legal education, the "good enough" is "competence," since that is the requirement set by ABA Standard 302. The Standard, however, does not define "competence," so schools must establish their own definition of competence for each of their learning outcomes at the institutional, program, and course levels.[119]

Defining competence requires faculty to answer three interrelated questions:

- What kind of standard will be used to evaluate student performance? For example, a criterion-referenced standard, an external standard, or a value-added standard?
- What is the minimum score for competence on an assessment instrument?
- How many students from the group being assessed must achieve that minimum score in order to declare that the institutional, program, or course learning outcomes have been successfully achieved?[120]

The process for answering each of these questions is explained in turn below.

a. Deciding the Standard for Measuring Student Performance

In isolation, a student's score on an assessment instrument, such as an exam, a paper, or a skills performance, is meaningless. A score of 80 on a test, for example, tells one nothing about how well the student did. For the score to have meaning, there must be a standard against which to compare it, such as an internal grade scale set by the school administering the test or scores achieved by other students on the same test at peer schools.[121] Faculty must establish these standards[122] for the assessment instruments they use to measure student learning. There are several types of standards from which to choose, including criterion-referenced standards, norm-referenced standards, external standards, value-added standards, and historical trends standards.[123] The standards should be selected when faculty are planning the assessment process, not when they have collected evidence and are ready to review it.[124] Each type of standard, along with its advantages, disadvantages, and typical uses, is discussed below.

1) Criterion-Referenced Standards

Criterion-referenced standards, also known as local standards, measure competency by comparing student performance against a set of absolute criteria that are established by those teaching at the institution, in the program, or in the course.[125] Institutional assessment almost always uses local, criterion-referenced standards for measuring competency[126] because the purpose "is to learn something about the effectiveness of the educational program as measured against deliberately chosen benchmark outcomes and to gather and employ evidence that will help the school determine how to achieve those outcomes."[127] When a criterion-referenced standard is used, in theory at least, "every student could be found competent or every student could be found to be incompetent."[128] Suskie recommends that faculty start by establishing a local, criterion-referenced standard to articulate the qualities of what they consider minimally competent student performance.[129] Local standards have the added advantage of faculty ownership, because faculty "pay much closer attention to assessment results when they have played a role in establishing performance expectations."[130]

The performance expectations typically are set forth in a rubric,[131] which is a set of detailed written criteria that describe what students should learn and how they will be evaluated.[132] While rubrics vary considerably in complexity and design, they typically "divide an assignment into its component parts and provide a detailed description of what constitutes acceptable or unacceptable levels of performance for each of those parts."[133] Reviewing a set of completed rubrics for a group of students will identify patterns in student learning, revealing areas of strength and weakness with respect to the stated learning outcomes.[134] Thus, law schools that use criterion-referenced standards for an assessment process will need to create rubrics for each of the assessment instruments. For institutional learning outcomes, faculty should create rubrics that capture the knowledge, skills, or values of each outcome and also work in conjunction with the embedded assessments that professors are already using in their courses.[135] Professors will grade the course assessments as they normally do to assign course grades, and then either the professor or an assessment committee can apply the rubric to the assessments to evaluate them for institutional assessment purposes.

A rubric can be created for any type of assessment instrument. Professors Dannelle Stevens and Antonia Levi provide an excellent step-by-step guide for designing rubrics in their book *Introduction to Rubrics: An Assessment Tool to Save Grading Time.*[136] According to Stevens and Levi, "[r]ubrics are composed of four basic parts in which the professor sets out the parameters of the assignment."[137] Those four parts, which are set out in a grid, are a task description, the dimensions of the assignment, a scale of performance levels, and specific descriptions for each level of performance.[138]

The task description is simply the assignment itself that involves some sort of student performance, whether in the form of a paper, a presentation, or a skills demonstration.[139]

The dimensions of the assignment are the skills and knowledge that are required and are being assessed.[140] "Dimensions should actually represent the type of component skills students must combine in a successful scholarly work, such as . . . content, technique, citation, examples, analysis, and a use of language appropriate to the occasion."[141] Dividing the assignment into such distinct dimensions allows "the components of the task [to be] clearly identified."[142]

The performance scale sets out the levels of achievement that students may attain on each dimension of the assignment, such as "exemplary," "competent," or "unacceptable."[143] Since institutional and program assessment focus on measuring competence, these three levels typically are all that is needed in a rubric for institutional and program assessment. For course-level assessment that has a more formative purpose, instructors may want to make finer distinctions among student work and divide the rubric into additional levels of performance.[144]

Finally, the performance descriptions set out the qualities that comprise each level on the scale. For example, in a scale that includes levels of exemplary, competent, and unacceptable, the rubric should describe the elements of a performance that is exemplary, a performance that is competent, and a performance that is unacceptable.[145] The performance elements should be described as specifically as possible so the evaluators using the rubric can apply it accurately and consistently across the student work they review.

On the next two pages is an example of a rubric for a client letter, created by the University of New Hampshire School of Law, that illustrates the rubric components discussed above.[146]

Additional discussion and examples of rubrics for institutional-, program-, and course-level assessment are included in the subsequent chapters that specifically address assessment processes at those levels.

Figure 1.3: Sample Rubric

Performance Levels

	Exemplary Advanced work for first year law student in LW I at this time in the course—on a job, the work would need very little revision for a supervising attorney to use	**Competent** Proficient work for a first-year law student in LW I at this time in the course—on a job, the work would need to be revised with input from supervising attorney	**Developing** Work needs additional content or skills to be competent—on a job, the work would not be helpful and supervising attorney would need to start over
Summary Paragraph The purpose of the summary is to let the client know the most essential points of the analysis. This is what you might want the client to read as the client is waiting to meet with you.	□ **Clearly communicates** most important legal analysis in layperson's terms □ **Includes recommended** course of action—what are the next steps? □ **Applies** law to facts to show support for the recommended course of action	□ **Analysis is generally clear**; may contain portions where there is too much legalese or where the language is too formal □ **Includes somewhat clear** recommended course of action □ **Somewhat applies** law to facts to show support for the recommended course of action but may lack clear connections	□ **Analysis is unclear** because legalese or language or writing mechanics and grammar make it too difficult to follow □ **Refers to** course of action but client would be confused about what she is being counseled to do □ **Minimally applies** law to client facts OR relies too much on law OR relies entirely on facts to summarize the explanation
Facts Facts should be stated specifically in letters to avoid confusion by the client. Facts that are unknown, but critical to the case, are often identified.	□ **Clearly states** dispositive facts in an organized way, notes absence of necessary facts (if applicable) □ **Clearly states** that opinion was formed based on facts in letter □ **Asks client to review closely** and report any discrepancies □ **Clearly identifies additional facts** that might be helpful or facts that need further development	□ **Facts are identified** but may include **minimal irrelevant** facts or **omit a couple** dispositive facts □ **States** that opinion was formed based on facts in letter □ **Asks client to review facts** □ **Some reference** to developing additional facts	□ **Facts are identified but include** several **irrelevant** facts **or omit several** dispositive facts or are overly general □ **Omits** that opinion was formed based on facts in letter □ **Does not ask client to review** facts closely and report any discrepancies □ **Little reference** to developing additional facts

continued on next page

Figure 1.3: Sample Rubric *continued*

Performance Levels

	Exemplary	Competent	Developing
Legal Analysis (Explanation) Client letters must include the relevant legal analysis necessary to answer the client's question.	□ **Identifies** all relevant steps in legal analysis in a way that the client can easily understand □ **Clearly articulates** applicable rule □ **Client's facts** are woven into analysis **so that client can clearly understand** how lawyer made prediction □ **Notes any uncertainty** or unsettled aspects of the law, and weaknesses, and resolves them	□ **Identifies** the most relevant steps in legal analysis in a way that the client can understand □ **Articulates** applicable rule **somewhat clearly** □ **Client's facts** are woven into analysis but may have **one area** where relationship between law and facts **is unclear** □ **Notes some uncertainty** or unsettled aspects of the law, as well as weaknesses, but may not resolve them	□ **Identifies** some of the legal analysis but omits important points □ **Unclearly or inaccurately** articulates rules and/or tests □ **Client's facts** are woven into analysis **but relationship** between law and facts **is** unclear or client's facts not woven into analysis □ **Fails to note uncertainty** or unsettled aspects of the law, as well as weaknesses, or notes them but ineffectively resolves them
Organization Like all legal writing, client letters require organization around central points of analysis.	□ **Large-scale organization is evident** in clearly written, plain English, concise topic sentences □ **Organization** within paragraphs **is evident** in clear, concise sentences logically ordered □ **Sentences are clear** and concise □ **Headings** are **effective**	□ **Large-scale organization is somewhat evident** in clearly written, plain English, concise topic sentences □ **Organization** within paragraphs **is mostly evident** but some sentence sequences may be difficult to follow □ **Sentences are mostly clear** and concise □ **Headings** are **somewhat effective**	□ **Large-scale organization is hard to follow**; topic sentences mostly lacking □ **Organization** within paragraphs **is confusing** □ **Sentences are unclear** and fail to communicate efficiently or logically □ **Headings are mostly ineffective**
Writing Mechanics	□ **Uses correct** grammar, punctuation, and spelling	□ **There are some errors** to fix, but generally uses correct conventions	□ **Errors distract** the reader and make letter difficult to read

2) Norm-Referenced Standards

Norm-referenced standards, also known as peer or comparative standards, measure competency by comparing one student's performance against the performance of other students.[147] This type of standard answers the question, "How do our students compare to peers at our school or at other schools?"[148] A norm-referenced standard can be used only if the students who are being compared are all given the same assessment.[149] This requirement makes the use of norm-referenced standards highly unlikely for law schools conducting institutional assessment, because schools do not use the same exams or other types of assessment instruments. Moreover, Shaw and VanZandt contend that norm-referenced assessment cannot be used "when undertaking an institutional assessment because no matter how well or how poorly the students do as a group, the performance numbers will look the same. For example, if your school's curve is based on a requirement that the overall GPA for the class is 3.00, the mean will be 3.00 in years when your students are brilliant and in years when your students are mediocre."[150]

3) External Standards

An external standard measures competency by comparing student performance against criteria set by experts outside of the law school.[151] "External standards most often come from tests required for certification or licensure."[152] Thus, the bar exam and the Multistate Professional Responsibility Examination (MPRE) are assessment instruments that can provide external standards for measuring student competency in the subjects they test. An advantage of external standards derived from a test like the bar exam or the MPRE is that the exam creators have already established the standards for minimum competence (*i.e.*, the passing score), so law schools do not have to invest the time and effort to make that determination. That "advantage," however, also can be a disadvantage because the bar examiners' definition of minimum competence may differ from a law school's definition, and the knowledge and skills tested on the bar exam may not align well with a law school's particular learning outcomes.[153] Accordingly, external standards such as the bar exam and the MPRE should be used only if they are congruent with a law school's stated learning outcomes and accurately measure the intended learning.[154]

4) Value-Added Standards

Value-added standards, also known as longitudinal or growth standards, measure competency by comparing students' performance on an assessment instrument, such as a test, to their subsequent performance on the same instrument after they have completed some additional portion of their education.[155] Thus, this standard answers the question of whether students are improving[156] and tries to "determine whether there has been value added by the students' progression through the curriculum."[157]

Using a value-added standard, however, doubles the workload because the same assessment must be administered and scored twice.[158] In addition, value-added standards are imprecise because determining the cause of any demonstrated improvement is difficult; the improvement may be the result of external forces such as outside employment or normal maturation, rather than a particular pedagogical approach or curriculum.[159] Value-added standards also do not provide the information that outside constituencies, such as accreditors, potential employers, and prospective law students, typically want. Those audiences usually are not interested in whether students have learned "something" over the course of their education; rather, they want to know whether students have learned "enough" to be competent lawyers.[160] Thus, value-added standards are rarely used for institutional assessment,[161] although they may be useful for assessment at the program or course level.

5) Historical Trends Standards

Historical trends standards measure student competency by comparing students against peers in prior classes.[162] This standard seeks to identify whether a program is improving over time, as reflected by improving student performance. "The historical trends perspective differs from the value-added perspective because it looks at changes in *successive* groups of students rather than change within *one* group or *one* student."[163] A school might use a historical trends standard, for example, to compare the scores of successive groups of students on a rubric used to evaluate upper-level writing papers. An increase in the rubric scores over successive groups of students would provide good evidence that changes made in the legal-writing program have been effective. Similarly, if a school has decided to use the bar exam as an external standard to measure student competency, it might also use a historical trends standard to determine whether higher scores of successive groups of students on the various components of the exam indicate an increase in student learning. A possible shortcoming of the historical trends standard is that the historical data necessary to make these comparisons are not always available.[164] So schools that want to use this type of standard should create a process for collecting and maintaining this historical data.

b. Setting Minimum Scores for Competence on Assessment Instruments

Once the type of standard is decided, faculty then must set a minimum score for each assessment instrument that denotes competence in the knowledge, skills, or values that are being measured. Often referred to as "benchmarks," "cutoff scores," or "cutscores,"[165] these scores set the "minimally acceptable" level for student achievement or performance on an assessment.[166] Setting benchmarks is a subjective process that requires the use of informed judgment,[167] and there is no error-free approach.[168] Nonetheless, experts in the field have identified best practices to follow, which are discussed below.

According to assessment expert Linda Suskie, the most important rule to remember in setting benchmarks is that they must be justifiable.[169] "You must be able to convince your stakeholders that your standards are appropriately rigorous. You must be able to explain not only *what* minimally acceptable student achievement is but *why* you consider that level minimally acceptable."[170] To ensure this level of rigor, Suskie recommends that faculty setting benchmarks ask the following questions:

- What achievement level would earn the lowest possible passing grade at this point in the student's studies?
- What is the lowest achievement level that would nonetheless adequately prepare students for success in what comes next in their lives: the next course in a sequence, more advanced study, or employment?
- What is the lowest achievement level that wouldn't embarrass you, if people learned that a student passed this course or graduated performing at that level?[171]

Questions such as these are useful because they help identify the performance level for minimum competence, which is what the benchmark reflects. Analogizing to grades, the benchmark score is similar to the minimum score for awarding credit in a pass/fail course; it is not the level achieved by typical B students.[172]

Another factor to consider in setting benchmarks is how the evidence regarding student achievement of them will be used.[173] If the evidence will be used to identify areas for improvement in student learning, then Suskie recommends setting a relatively high measure so faculty can increase the chances of identifying the areas that need improvement.[174] Similarly, if faculty will use the evidence to determine whether graduates are competent in the school's learning outcomes upon completing their degree program, then they should set a relatively high bar to ensure that their graduates are indeed competent.[175] This factor weighs in favor of relatively high benchmarks in legal education, since the mission of law schools is to produce competent lawyers.

The harm resulting from setting benchmarks too high or too low also should be taken into consideration. When benchmarks are set too high, which results in large numbers of students not reaching them, they may not accurately represent whether students actually are minimally competent. Thus, faculty may spend time and effort working to improve student learning when that is not actually necessary.[176] When benchmarks are set too low, however, the risk is that schools will graduate students who are not competent for practice. Graduates who are not competent for practice present a danger to their future clients and to the legal profession itself. Graduates who do not possess minimum competence also are likely to fail the bar exam, which could jeopardize a law school's accreditation.[177] These risks weigh in favor of law schools setting benchmarks that are higher rather than lower.

The process for setting benchmarks typically involves convening a group of experts to discuss the assessment instruments being administered and identify the level of minimally competent performance for them. Ideally, either a faculty expert in the subject matter, or the law school's assessment committee, will create a draft of a rubric for the assignment, as discussed in Section 5a(1) above. Then, the assessment committee, task force, or other appropriate group charged with setting the benchmark would meet to discuss the elements of the rubric, whether it includes all of the essential performance criteria (*i.e.*, knowledge, skills, values) for the assignment, and the minimum score that a student should achieve on the rubric to demonstrate minimum competence. The goal of the discussion is to "decide what skill level is required of an entry-level lawyer."[178] In addition to law faculty, it can be helpful to include local attorneys in the group who can contribute a real-world perspective from practice. Practicing attorneys can provide insights on the abilities that the profession realistically expects from new lawyers, since faculty often have unrealistic expectations for their students and may initially set the cut-off level too high.[179]

In determining the benchmarks, several types of resources are available to inform the group's thinking. A good starting point is for the group to review samples of student work, compare them against the rubric for the assignment, and identify examples that it considers excellent, adequate, and inadequate. From these examples, the group can articulate the qualities that differentiate the excellent examples from the ones that are merely adequate and the adequate examples from the ones that are inadequate. With these specific qualities in mind, the group can determine whether the excellent examples should set the benchmark for minimum competence, or whether the adequate examples more accurately reflect minimum competence.[180]

For assessment instruments based on external standards, there may be pre-existing benchmark scores that law schools can use. For example, each state sets its own passing score for its bar exam, and the MEE and MPT portions of the exam are graded locally by the states that administer them.[181] Each jurisdiction also sets its own passing score for the MPRE.[182] If schools are using the bar exam, components of the bar exam, or the MPRE to assess their learning outcomes, they could look to these pre-existing scores for guidance as they set the benchmark scores for the exam or exam components they are using in their assessment process.

In addition, many law schools ask their students to participate in the Law School Survey of Student Engagement (LSSSE). Many of the LSSSE questions ask students to evaluate, on a scale from one to four, the knowledge, skills, and values they have gained from their classes and other experiences in law school. Law school administrators then receive the mean scores of their students' responses. If a school is using its LSSSE scores as indirect evidence to assess its learning outcomes, it could compare its LSSSE scores to those of peer schools to set benchmarks. For example, the LSSSE asks students to rate the degree to which their law school experience has contributed to their ability to think critically and analytically, with a response of one being "very little" and a response of four being "very much." If the average score of a school's students in response to this question is a 2.5, while the average scores of peer schools are 3.0 or higher, a school could establish 3.0 as the benchmark it wants to achieve on this question. A score lower than that would indicate that corrective action is needed because students are reporting that their legal education is not sufficiently developing their ability to think critically and analytically.

Faculty also may look to benchmarks set by other law schools as examples to follow. As law schools engage more deeply in assessment, many have developed rubrics for assessing their institutional outcomes. Professor Andrea Curcio has written about and provided examples of rubrics that the Georgia State University College of Law has developed to measure its institutional learning outcomes.[183] The Holloran Center for Ethical Leadership in the Professions at the University of St. Thomas School of Law has created rubrics for assessing learning outcomes related to the formation of professional identity.[184] The American Association of Colleges and Universities has designed rubrics for sixteen different learning outcomes, including teamwork, problem-solving, and intercultural competence.[185] Examples of law school rubrics also are available on the website of the Institute for Law Teaching and Learning.[186] Assessment leaders may be able to adapt the benchmarks set in these rubrics for use at their own schools.

The type of assessment that is being used also should be considered in determining an appropriate benchmark for competence. Professors cannot realistically expect the same level of performance on a timed, in-class essay exam as they would on a seminar paper for which a student produced multiple drafts, received the professor's feedback, and had an entire semester to write. Thus, the benchmark for minimum competence on an essay exam likely will be set lower than the benchmark for a seminar paper.[187]

Once these factors have been taken into consideration, faculty should reach agreement on the benchmarks that will constitute minimum competence for particular assessments. Then, faculty must test the benchmarks by applying them to the assessments to determine if they set accurate expectations for minimum competence.[188] For example, if only 40% of students achieve the benchmark score for minimum competence on an upper-level seminar paper, does that mean that the students lack adequate writing skills, or does it mean that the benchmark score was set too high? To answer this question, faculty will need to think carefully about the assignment itself and the expectations they set for student performance. Subsequent modification of the benchmark may be necessary, because "[a]fter a trial exercise, many educators will find that the initial cut-off score or rating level needs adjusting to account for too high or too low expectations."[189]

Finally, this process for setting benchmarks can have varying levels of formality. It can be as simple as convening a group of informed participants, having them consider and discuss the factors explained above, and then asking them to reach a consensus on benchmark scores. Alternatively, it could take the form of an official "cutscore study," in which experts in educational measurement and testing use an empirical research method to determine benchmark scores.[190] For law schools, the simpler process should suffice, because the

ABA has not indicated that formal cutscore studies are necessary for purposes of institutional assessment and accreditation. A discussion of the process for an official cutscore study is beyond the scope of this book, but many resources are available on this topic for those who would like to learn more about it.[191]

c. Setting Performance Thresholds

Once the benchmarks for competence have been set for each assessment instrument, assessment leaders then must determine the percentage of students who must achieve that benchmark in order to declare that the learning outcomes have been met. This percentage is known as a "target"[192] or a "performance threshold."[193] These percentages describe the expectations for students' collective performance on direct or indirect assessment instruments in a quantifiable way.[194] For example, if a school is using a rubric to assess students' writing skills on an upper-level seminar paper, the faculty might set the performance threshold at 75%, which means that if 75% of the papers assessed achieve the rubric's benchmark for minimum competence, then the school can declare that its institutional learning outcome for writing skills has been met. Conversely, if fewer than 75% of the papers achieve that score, then the outcome has not been met, and the school must investigate to determine the cause of the shortcoming.[195]

In setting these percentages, Suskie recommends making a distinction between whether learning outcomes are essential or aspirational. For critical learning outcomes, faculty should aim for almost all student work to meet the benchmark. According to Suskie, "[s]ome learning goals are so basic, essential, or vital to health and safety that we want absolute assurance that *every* student graduates with minimally adequate achievement of them."[196] Suskie and other experts recognize, however, that a performance threshold of 100% is likely unrealistic.[197] Regardless of how well an assessment instrument is designed, it is "an imperfect, incomplete sample of what students have learned."[198] Moreover, it is possible for students who actually have mastered important learning outcomes to perform poorly on any given assessment because they misunderstand it, are ill, or are distracted by a personal issue.[199] Thus, Suskie asserts that for outcomes that have "grave consequences for students who don't achieve them at a minimally adequate level—a target close to, but not quite at 100 percent is often appropriate."[200]

Clients certainly can suffer grave consequences if their lawyers are not minimally competent, which argues in favor of law schools setting high performance thresholds for the learning outcomes they deem essential. The question is how high. The ABA has not set a performance threshold that law schools must achieve for their learning outcomes.[201] Accordingly, law schools must set these performance thresholds for themselves at the level the faculty deem acceptable. Shaw and VanZandt state that schools should adopt thresholds that are "aggressive but attainable."[202] A threshold "should be something that pushes or stretches both the students and the school a bit, but it should not be impossible to achieve."[203]

To set performance thresholds for assessment instruments like exams, papers, and skills performances that faculty have designed and administered locally, schools can look to past student performance for a baseline.[204] For example, assume that a school is using a rubric to evaluate students' upper-level seminar papers for competency in its learning outcome for writing skills, and that it has set a score of 75 points (out of a possible 100 points) as the benchmark score for minimum competence. Assume further that the school has used the rubric for two years. In the first year of using the rubric, 70% of the students in the graduating class achieved the benchmark score. In the second year of using the rubric, 80% of the students achieved the benchmark score. In setting a performance threshold for this assessment, the school has several options. First, it could simply set the threshold at 70%, since it has evidence that its students can meet that threshold. Second, it could set the threshold at 75%, since that is the average percentage for the two years for which it has used the rubric. Third, it could set the threshold at 80% or even higher, since that percentage seems attainable in light of past performance and the school likely wants to have high standards for its graduates. Strong writing skills are crucial for lawyers, which is a factor that weighs in favor of setting a high threshold for this learning outcome. However, there is no "perfect" threshold, so this question must be decided by the faculty's informed judgment and its expectations regarding the percentage of its graduates who should demonstrate competency in its learning outcomes.

For assessment instruments based on external standards, there may be pre-existing performance thresholds that a law school can adopt. For example, the ABA Standards require that 75% of a law school's graduates must pass a bar exam within two years of graduation for the school to maintain its accreditation.[205] This 75% pass rate is a performance threshold, and a law school could adopt this percentage as its performance threshold for any learning outcomes that it is using the bar exam to assess.

Some commentators suggest setting a performance threshold of 80% for assessment instruments, based on noted educational psychologist Benjamin Bloom's Mastery Learning theory.[206] Bloom's Mastery Learning, however, is an intensive instructional strategy that divides course content into units that last one to two weeks, uses formative assessments at the end of each unit to determine if students have mastered desired concepts and skills, and then provides either corrective assignments and individualized feedback for students who do not achieve mastery, or special enrichment activities for students who do demonstrate mastery.[207] This process is then repeated for subsequent instructional units. Bloom posited that, if instructors follow this process of frequent formative assessments, feedback, and correction of individual learning errors, nearly all students should be able to learn a subject to a high level of mastery, which he defined as an "A" level.

There are at least two problems with applying an 80% performance threshold derived from Bloom's Mastery Learning theory to legal education. First, law professors typically do not employ the multiple formative assessments, individualized feedback, and corrective measures that Bloom's Mastery Learning requires. In the absence of those pedagogical techniques, it is not reasonable to expect the high percentage of students achieving mastery that Bloom projected. Second, Bloom's approach focuses on an instructional method for helping students achieve "mastery" of learning outcomes, which he defined as an "A" level of performance. Law schools, however, must demonstrate only that their graduates have achieved "competence" in learning outcomes, which is a lower standard than Bloom's mastery level. This difference between mastery and competence makes it difficult to draw parallels between Bloom's expectations for student learning and law schools' expectations for the learning of their graduates. Thus, while law schools are certainly free to set performance thresholds for their assessment instruments at 80%, they should base that percentage on a rationale other than Bloom's Mastery Learning approach.

As noted above, Suskie distinguishes between essential and aspirational learning outcomes when setting performance thresholds. She describes aspirational learning outcomes as those that "we hope students make progress with…, but we don't expect all students to achieve them. No one expects every college graduate to be an inspirational leader or a compelling public speaker, for example."[208] Accordingly, Suskie recognizes that it is acceptable to set lower performance thresholds for learning outcomes that are aspirational. However, she recommends that the performance threshold for aspirational learning goals should be set at a minimum of 50%.[209] If more than half of students are not achieving an aspirational goal, it suggests there is a problem not with the students but with teaching methods, curriculum design, or the particular assessment instrument that is being used.[210]

Finally, faculty should understand that setting benchmarks and performance thresholds is an iterative process. Once the benchmarks and thresholds have been established, they must be applied to student work to gauge both how students are performing and whether the benchmarks and thresholds seem appropriate in light of that performance. Since this process is new for most law schools, it may take some time and a few cycles of applying the benchmarks and thresholds to identify the levels that are right for a particular school. Thus, setting benchmarks and performance thresholds is "a perpetual work in progress, something to be adjusted as you learn more about your goals, the assessment tools you're using, and your students' performance."[211]

6. Using Data to Improve Student Learning at the Institutional, Program, and Course Levels

The ultimate goal of assessment is not simply measurement; it is informed, continuous improvement in the curriculum and student learning. Thus, once the benchmarks and performance thresholds discussed above have been applied to determine whether students are achieving the stated learning outcomes, faculty then must use the information gleaned from that analysis to identify improvements that can produce learning gains at the institutional, program, and course levels. This step often is referred to as "closing the loop," because it is the point at which assessment data "feed back into the curriculum or program of legal education and contribute to conversation about change."[212] This section offers suggestions for presenting the assessment data, facilitating conversations about it, and identifying changes that can lead to improvement.

a. Presenting the Assessment Data and Facilitating Conversations About It

Law schools have an array of audiences with varying interests in their assessment efforts and results. Audiences include administrators, faculty, current students, alumni, the ABA, regional accreditors, parent university leaders, governing boards, employers, prospective students, the public, and other law schools.

To decide how best to communicate with each audience about assessment, law schools should begin by determining the nature of their interests. Some interests will be common among most audiences, while others will be specific to a particular group. Next, law schools should decide what types of information are appropriate for each audience. The level of depth and detail of information will vary from audience to audience. Then, law schools should decide how best to present that content. Potential methods include text, slides, graphs, charts, and tables. Finally, schools must decide what medium to use to communicate with each audience. Possible media include reports, accreditation documents, oral presentations, the law school website, and articles in alumni publications, bar magazines, and scholarly journals.

Law school administrators and faculty. The primary audience for a law school's assessment data is its deans and faculty members, who have responsibility for designing, delivering, assessing, and revising the school's learning outcomes, curriculum, and assessment scheme. To carry out those responsibilities, faculty and deans need detailed reports, including the list of learning outcomes, curriculum maps that illustrate how the curriculum provides opportunities for students to achieve the outcomes, methods of assessing student achievement of each outcome, and a summary of the results of those assessments. Depending on the issue the deans or faculty are addressing, access to both raw data and analyses of the data may be appropriate.

To ensure engagement with this information, it should be presented in a forum where faculty and administrators can review and discuss it together, such as a regular faculty meeting or a meeting designated specifically to discuss assessment results. At the University of Arkansas at Little Rock William H. Bowen School of Law, for example, annual assessment reports are due at the end of the spring semester. Then, once the faculty return after the summer break, the chair of the Assessment Committee presents the assessment results at a faculty meeting early in the fall semester and leads a discussion of them. Structured conversations that include specific, planned questions about the faculty's reactions to the data can be helpful. "Sharing and discussing assessment findings paves the way for important conversations about teaching approaches, the need for course or curriculum modifications, and, ultimately, improving student learning."[213] When recommendations emerge from these discussions, they should be documented in the assessment plan as next steps to implement.[214]

Current students. Current students have a personal stake in the effectiveness of the law school curriculum. Their level of achievement of the school's learning outcomes is the ultimate measure of the curriculum. The list of learning outcomes and curriculum map should be directly communicated to students via a student handbook and the law school's website. Further, student surveys may play a role in the assessment and revision of the curriculum. Students should receive a summary of the results of those surveys and be informed about what steps, if any, the school plans to take in light of the results.

Alumni. Alumni often have an interest in the continued improvement of the law school and its reputation. Presentations by faculty or deans at alumni events and articles in alumni magazines are appropriate vehicles to inform alumni of updates in the school's learning outcomes, its curriculum, and its efforts to publicize its curricular innovations. In addition, some alumni may play a role in the revision of the learning outcomes and curriculum through their participation in a focus group or a law school advisory board; in that case, they should have access to reports with more detailed assessment data and analysis.

ABA, regional accreditors, parent universities, and governing boards. All U.S. law schools are governed by the ABA and regional accrediting bodies. In addition, most law schools are accountable to parent universities or governing boards. Reports to those entities should contain the list of student outcomes, curriculum map, a summary of the assessment scheme, a summary of student achievement of learning outcomes, and the process the school employs for continuous improvement. Parent universities often create forms for assessment plans and annual reports that their various colleges and departments, including law schools, must use to submit their assessment findings.

Employers, prospective students, and the public. Law schools communicate with these audiences primarily though their websites. Employers, prospective students, and the public may be most interested in the extent to which graduates are prepared for practice. Consequently, law schools should include their learning outcomes on their websites and make choices about what types of assessment results to summarize on their websites as well.

Other law schools. Law schools can assist one another by sharing their experiences with outcomes assessment. Law school websites can publish their student learning outcomes, curriculum maps, and assessment scheme. Articles in scholarly journals can provide detailed descriptions of assessment data, analysis, results, subsequent curricular revisions, and assessment of the effectiveness of the curricular changes.

b. Identifying Changes That Can Lead to Improvement

Concrete recommendations for changes to improve student learning should emerge from this review and discussion of the assessment findings. Recommendations might include changes in a law school's learning outcomes, curriculum, course design, and assessment instruments.

- **Learning outcomes.** After gathering and assessing data on student achievement of learning outcomes, the school should make appropriate adjustments to its list of learning outcomes. Some outcomes may not adequately define the knowledge, skill, or value the school wants students to achieve. Other outcomes may be redundant. The school's list of outcomes may be missing knowledge, skills, or values that assessment revealed as important learning goals. Conversely, the outcomes may include an area that assessment reveals is not crucial to students' competence to enter practice.

- **Curriculum.** Assessment analysis may provide a basis to add courses, eliminate courses, change credit allocations, change the learning outcomes a course is to address, add or subtract co-curricular activities, or modify academic support programs.
- **Course design.** Analysis of the extent to which students are achieving learning outcomes is important feedback for faculty members. That information can show faculty members which portions of their courses are most and least effective. Thoughtful faculty members will make appropriate design changes in their courses to maximize student learning.
- **Assessment instruments.** If students are failing to meet learning outcomes, faculty should re-examine their assessment instruments to ensure that they are accurate measures of student learning. If the instruments are poorly designed, confusing, or not in alignment with the intended learning outcomes, then they must be corrected.

7. Regularly Examining the Assessment Process and Making Corrections, as Needed

Continuous improvement should include the assessment scheme itself. As schools gain experience and expertise in assessment, they should evaluate their data collection and analysis practices and revise them accordingly. Through this evaluation, they should be able to identify ways to make the assessment process more reliable, efficient, and sustainable.

Endnotes

1. *See, e.g.*, ANDREA SUSNIR FUNK, THE ART OF ASSESSMENT: MAKING OUTCOMES ASSESSMENT ACCESSIBLE, SUSTAINABLE, AND MEANINGFUL 41 (2017); PEGGY L. MAKI, ASSESSING FOR LEARNING: BUILDING A SUSTAINABLE COMMITMENT ACROSS THE INSTITUTION 90 (2d ed. 2010).

2. *E.g.*, FUNK, *supra* note 1, at 28; LORI E. SHAW & VICTORIA L. VANZANDT, STUDENT LEARNING OUTCOMES AND LAW SCHOOL ASSESSMENT: A PRACTICAL GUIDE TO MEASURING INSTITUTIONAL EFFECTIVENESS 14 (2015).

3. *E.g.*, Funk, *supra* note 1, at 28; Shaw & VanZandt, *supra* note 2, at 14.

4. Mary E. Huba & Jann E. Freed, Learner-Centered Assessment on College Campuses: Shifting the Focus from Teaching to Learning 8 (2000).

5. Mary J. Allen, Assessing Academic Programs in Higher Education 10 (2004).

6. *See Programmatic Assessment at UT*, Office of Inst. Research & Assessment, Univ. of Tenn. Knoxville, https://oira.utk.edu/assessment/programmatic%20assessment/ (last visited July 8, 2020). This illustration is reprinted with the express authorization of the University of Tennessee, Knoxville Office of Institutional Research and Assessment.

7. Shaw & VanZandt, *supra* note 2, at 8; *see also* Building on Best Practices: Transforming Legal Education in a Changing World 28 (Deborah Maranville et al. eds., 2015) (hereinafter "Building on Best Practices") ("Learning outcomes emphasize the knowledge, skills, and attitudes to be evidenced by students at the end of a particular period, and use a clear, active verbal framework about what students can be expected to do (analyze, explain, produce) rather than more passive ones (understand, appreciate).").

8. Anthony Niedwiecki, *Law Schools and Learning Outcomes: Developing a Coherent, Cohesive, and Comprehensive Law School Curriculum*, 64 Clev. St. L. Rev. 661, 679 (2016); Huba & Freed, *supra* note 4, at 98–99.

9. Niedwiecki, *supra* note 8, at 679.

10. Huba & Freed, *supra* note 4, at 116.

11. Roy Stuckey et al., Best Practices for Legal Education: A Vision and a Road Map 49 (2007) (hereinafter "Best Practices for Legal Education") (quoting James O. Nichols, The Departmental Guide and Record Book for Student Outcomes Assessment and Institutional Effectiveness 22 (1995)).

12. Niedwiecki, *supra* note 8, at 679 (emphasis in original).

13. *Id.*

14. Best Practices for Legal Education, *supra* note 11, at 167; *see also* Trudy W. Banta & Catherine A. Palomba, Assessment Essentials: Planning, Implementing, and Improving Assessment in Higher Education 67 (2d ed. 2015) ("Educators distinguish between cognitive, affective, and psychomotor learning outcomes—what students know, value, and can do.").

15. *E.g.*, Huba & Freed, *supra* note 4, at 112; Shaw & VanZandt, *supra* note 2, at 66; *see also* Maki, *supra* note 1, at 91 ("Taxonomies also help educators identify the verbs that describe what students should chronologically represent or demonstrate.").

16. *See* Taxonomy of Educational Objectives, Book 1: Cognitive Domain (Benjamin S. Bloom ed., 1956). Other learning taxonomies that also can be helpful in crafting learning outcomes include Fink's "Taxonomy of Significant Learning"; Marzano, Pickering, and McTighe's "Dimensions of Learning"; and Marzano and Kendall's "Taxonomy of Educational Objectives." Linda Suskie, Assessing Student Learning: A Common Sense Guide 52–53 (3d ed. 2018); *see also* Maki, *supra* note 1, at 104 (citing other learning taxonomies); Michael Hunter Schwartz, *Teaching Law by Design: How Learning Theory and Instructional Design Can Inform and Reform Law Teaching*, 38 San Diego L. Rev. 347, 395–98 (2001) (discussing Professor Robert Gagné's five domains of learning).

17. *E.g.*, Shaw & VanZandt, *supra* note 2, at 66–67.

18. *Id.*

19. *See Bloom's Taxonomy Action Verbs*, N.Y.U. Steinhardt Sch. of Culture, Educ., & Human Dev., https://research.steinhardt.nyu.edu/scmsAdmin/media/users/VerbsforStudentLearningObjectives.pdf (last visited July 10, 2020).

20. ABA Standards and Rules of Procedure for Approval of Law Schools 2020–2021, Standard 302.

21. ABA Section of Legal Educ. & Admissions to the Bar, Managing Director's Guidance Memo: Standards 301, 302, 314, and 315, at 4 (June 2015), https://www.aals.org/wp-content/uploads/2015/06/ABA-Guidance-Stds-301-302-314-315-June-2015.pdf.

22. Maki, *supra* note 1, at 90; *see also* Huba & Freed, *supra* note 4, at 107 ("Intended learning outcomes at the program level should reflect the type of knowledge and skills expected in members of the program's discipline, but they should be compatible with and support institutional outcomes.").

23. Best Practices for Legal Education, *supra* note 11, at 95 (quoting *Principles of Good Practice in the New Academy, in* Ass'n of Am. Coll. & Univ., Greater Expectations: A New Vision for Learning as a Nation Goes to College 30 (2002)).

24. Banta & Palomba, *supra* note 14, at 71.

25. *See, e.g.*, Maki, *supra* note 1, at 62 (Curriculum maps "provide an overview of students' learning journey—a place to locate where educational opportunities are specifically designed to address institutional and program-level expectations.").

26. *Id.* at 61; *see also id.* (Curriculum maps "reveal the distribution of opportunities to learn across an institution.").

27. Suskie, *supra* note 16, at 79 (emphasis in original); *see also, e.g.*, Susan Hanley Duncan, *They're Back! The New Accreditation Standards Coming to a Law School Near You—A 2018 Update, Guide to Compliance, and Dean's Role in Implementing*, 67 J. Legal Educ. 462, 471 (2018) ("For example, if negotiation is offered only in an elective class, then many students may not achieve that learning outcome and the negotiation skill is really an 'orphan' outcome.").

28. Suskie, *supra* note 16, at 79. If the courses in the cluster are included in the curriculum map, they should be grouped together in the same column or row, depending on how the map is designed. *Id.*

29. *See, e.g.*, Banta & Palomba, *supra* note 14, at 72 ("Filling in the grid or matrix allows faculty to see the outcomes covered in each course.").

30. Best Practices for Legal Education, *supra* note 11, at 93 (emphasis added).

31. Shaw & Van Zandt, *supra* note 2, at 78–79.

32. Allen, *supra* note 5, at 42–43; *see also* Janet W. Fisher, *Putting Students at the Center of Legal Education: How an Emphasis on Outcome Measures in the ABA Standards for Approval of Law Schools Might Transform the Educational Experience of Law Schools*, 35 S. Ill. U. L.J. 225, 232 (2011) (noting that the curriculum map should indicate "where students first encounter the outcome, where students practice the outcome, and at what point the students can be expected to have achieved the outcome").

33. It might be possible for students to be introduced to and achieve the faculty's desired level of proficiency in a particular area before their final year of law school. "For example, a law school may decide that legal research skills can be introduced, practiced, and mastered by the end of the first year of law school." Best Practices for Legal Education, *supra* note 11, at 93.

34. *See* Funk, *supra* note 1, at 47; Shaw & VanZandt, *supra* note 2, at 78–79, 209–212; *see also* Debra Moss Curtis & David M. Moss, *Curriculum Mapping: Bringing Evidence-Based Frameworks to Legal Education*, 34 Nova L. Rev. 473, 491–92 (2010) (describing survey of faculty used in curriculum-mapping process).

35. *See, e.g.*, Maki, *supra* note 1, at 61 (Curriculum maps "identify gaps in student learning opportunities or identify concentrations of learning experiences without further opportunity for students to transfer, build on, or apply learning.").

36. *See generally* Shaw & VanZandt, *supra* note 2, at 79 (discussing questions to consider in analysis of curriculum map).

37. *See, e.g.*, Banta & Palomba, *supra* note 14, at 72 ("If a particular outcome is getting too much coverage or too little, the curriculum map will reveal the imbalance.").

38. *See, e.g.*, *id.* at 20 ("An assessment plan captures agreement about what matters, gives direction for actions, and provides a means to determine if progress is being made."); *see also* Funk, *supra* note 1, at 30 (describing assessment plan); Shaw & VanZandt, *supra* note 2, at 54–57 (same).

39. Funk, *supra* note 1, at 55.

40. *See, e.g.*, *id.* at 55; Shaw & VanZandt, *supra* note 2, at 83–84.

41. ALLEN, *supra* note 3, at 6; *see also* BANTA & PALOMBA, *supra* note 14, at 21–22 (citing examples of schools that use three to five-year assessment cycles).
42. ABA STANDARDS AND RULES OF PROCEDURE FOR APPROVAL OF LAW SCHOOLS 2020–2021, RULE 4(b)(1).
43. SHAW & VANZANDT, *supra* note 2, at 83.
44. *See, e.g.*, SUSKIE, *supra* note 16, at 99 (suggesting that key learning outcomes should be assessed at least every three years and preferably every two years.). *But cf., e.g.*, CARWINA WENG ET AL., LEARNING LAW THROUGH EXPERIENCE & BY DESIGN 9 (2019) ("As the cycle for accreditation has lengthened to ten years, the program assessment cycle will probably follow suit. The ABA has assured schools that they need not assess each program outcome every year . . . but must assess all of the outcomes and demonstrate appropriate adjustment to the program within an accreditation cycle.").
45. SHAW & VANZANDT, *supra* note 2, at 83–84; *see also id.* at 83 ("When the ABA comes to town, you want to be able to say that you have thoughtfully evaluated the degree of student attainment of competency as to each outcome.").
46. *Id.* at 183.
47. *Id.* at 104; *see also* BANTA & PALOMBA, *supra* note 14, at 23.
48. SHAW & VAN ZANDT, *supra* note 2, at 105.
49. Docia L. Rudley, *Bridging the Divide Between Assessment and Accreditation*, 62 N.Y.L. SCH. L. REV. 35, 45 (2017–2018).
50. SHAW & VAN ZANDT, *supra* note 2, at 104.
51. BANTA & PALOMBA, *supra* note 14, at 23; HUBA & FREED, *supra* note 4, at 11; SHAW & VANZANDT, *supra* note 2, at 106–108.
52. SUSKIE, *supra* note 16, at 26 (emphasis in original).
53. BANTA & PALOMBA, *supra* note 14, at 23.
54. *See, e.g., id.* at 25; SHAW & VANZANDT, *supra* note 2, at 185; SUSKIE, *supra* note 16, at 156–157.
55. SUSKIE, *supra* note 16, at 157.
56. BANTA & PALOMBA, *supra* note 14, at 25; FUNK, *supra* note 1, at 29; SUSKIE, *supra* note 16, at 156.
57. SHAW & VANZANDT, *supra* note 2, at 101.
58. *See id.* at 100 ("Using embedded tools is preferable because students tend to take assignments more seriously (and hence perform better) in the context of a class. Therefore, embedded tools may provide better evidence of student learning."); *see also, e.g.*, Rudley, *supra* note 49, at 45 ("When possible, use assessment that is already embedded in the curriculum to ensure that students are invested in their performance and that the results are genuinely of interest to them and to faculty members."); SUSKIE, *supra* note 16, at 279 ("Grades are a powerful incentive for students to participate in an assessment and to give it serious thought and effort.").
59. *See Who We Are*, LSSSE, https://lssse.indiana.edu/who-we-are/ (last visited July 8, 2020).
60. *See LSSSE Surveys*, LSSSE, https://lssse.indiana.edu/about-lssse-surveys/ (last visited July 8, 2020).
61. This discussion of formative and summative assessment is adapted from Kelly S. Terry, *Embedding Assessment Principles in Externships*, 20 CLIN. L. REV. 467, 476–78 (2014).
62. ABA STANDARDS AND RULES OF PROCEDURE FOR APPROVAL OF LAW SCHOOLS 2020–2021, STANDARD 314.
63. ABA STANDARDS AND RULES OF PROCEDURE FOR APPROVAL OF LAW SCHOOLS 2020–2021, STANDARD 314, INTERPRETATION 314-1.
64. *Id.*
65. Lynn M. Daggett, *All of the Above: Computerized Exam Scoring of Multiple Choice Items Helps to: (A) Show How Exam Items Worked Technically, (B) Maximize Exam Fairness, (C) Justly*

Assign Letter Grades, and (D) Provide Feedback on Student Learning, 57 J. Legal Educ. 391, 397 (2007) (emphasis in original). Some assessments can be both formative and summative. For example, a midterm exam is summative in that it evaluates a student's learning up to a certain point in the semester, but it also is formative in that it provides students with feedback on their knowledge and skills that they can use to improve their learning during the remainder of the semester.

66. Shaw & VanZandt, *supra* note 2, at 12; *see also* Building on Best Practices, *supra* note 7, at 94 ("Probably the single greatest confusion in vocabulary is that which equates *assessment* with *grading*.") (emphasis in original).

67. Building on Best Practices, *supra* note 7, at 94.

68. This is known as norm-referenced or norm-based grading. Best Practices for Legal Education, *supra* note 11, at 243–244; *see also* Building on Best Practices, *supra* note 7, at 422.

69. Building on Best Practices, *supra* note 7, at 422 n.2. Mandatory grade curves also fail to recognize that different cohorts of students can have differing abilities. "Consider, for example, how a teacher might perceive an unusually strong or an unusually weak class. If a mandatory grading curve is in effect, student performance in each class will be forced into nearly the same distribution." *Id.*

70. Shaw & VanZandt, *supra* note 2, at 13.

71. *Id.*

72. Suskie, *supra* note 16, at 10; *see also* Shaw & VanZandt, *supra* note 2, at 13 ("[W]hen assessing institutional achievement of outcomes, data is typically culled across courses, professors, and dates using a variety of tools.")

73. Banta & Palomba, *supra* note 14, at 53.

74. Suskie, *supra* note 16, at 10; *see also* Building on Best Practices, *supra* note 7, at 94 ("[G] rades do not explicitly reference any clear criteria.").

75. *See* Shaw & VanZandt, *supra* note 2, at 13.

76. Thus, when factors such as these are considered in a final grade, students who do not achieve the course learning outcomes might still receive a fairly high grade by attending classes and participating in discussions, submitting their assignments on time, and taking advantage of opportunities for extra credit. Conversely, students who do achieve the course learning outcomes may receive a lower grade if they miss classes, fail to participate in discussions, or submit late assignments. *See, e.g.*, Suskie, *supra* note 16, at 10.

77. *See, e.g.*, Allen, *supra* note 5, at 11 ("Grades do indicate something about student learning, but at a level too broad for meaningful assessment. If the average GPA of program graduates is 2.89, which learning objectives are being mastered and which require faculty attention?").

78. Shaw & VanZandt, *supra* note 2, at 13.

79. *Id.* at 13; *see also* Building on Best Practices, *supra* note 7, at 422 ("[T]raditional grading practices do not inform the law school in evaluating the effectiveness of its program.").

80. Barbara E. Walvoord, Assessment Clear and Simple: A Practical Guide for Institutions, Departments, and General Education 59–60 (2010).

81. Shaw & VanZandt, *supra* note 2, at 112.

82. *See* Maki, *supra* note 1, at 157.

83. Banta & Palomba, *supra* note 14, at 31; *see also* Suskie, *supra* note 16, at 327 ("Comparing evidence from various assessments against one another is called *corroboration* or *triangulation*.") (emphasis in original).

84. Duncan, *supra* note 27, at 477 ("Greater accuracy and authority are achieved when several methods of assessment produce similar findings."); Funk, *supra* note 1, at 74 n.3 ("Taken together, information gleaned from multiple sources will strengthen your confidence in your observations and conclusions.").

85. This discussion of validity, reliability, and fairness is adapted from Terry, *supra* note 61, at 480–82.

86. Best Practices for Legal Education, *supra* note 11, at 239.

87. Steven Friedland, *A Critical Inquiry Into the Traditional Uses of Law School Evaluations*, 23 Pace L. Rev. 147, 158 (2002); *see also* Gregory S. Munro, Outcomes Assessment for Law Schools 106 (2000) ("In law school courses, validity means the test or other assessment of student performance measures whether the course goals and objectives have been met. This is content validity.").

88. Best Practices for Legal Education, *supra* note 11, at 239.

89. *See, e.g.*, Munro, *supra* note 87, at 108.

90. *Id.* at 107.

91. Linda Suskie, *Fair Assessment Practices: Giving Students Equitable Opportunities to Demonstrate Learning*, AAHE Bulletin 52(9) (May 2000).

92. Suskie, *supra* note 16, at 30–31.

93. Suskie, *supra* note 91.

94. *E.g.*, Funk, *supra* note 1, at 37.

95. Shaw & VanZandt, *supra* note 2, at 114. Some parent universities, however, may require the assessment of all students. Accordingly, law schools should determine whether they are subject to any such policies.

96. The same time concerns apply to indirect assessments like interviews and focus groups. While the financial costs of these assessment instruments typically are low, the time and effort required to conduct them with all students may be prohibitive. Suskie, *supra* note 16, at 158.

97. Shaw & VanZandt, *supra* note 2, at 114.

98. *Id.* (emphasis in original).

99. Suskie, *supra* note 16, at 159–160.

100. This table is reproduced from *id.* at 159.

101. *Id.*

102. *Id.* at 159–160.

103. *Id.* at 160.

104. Shaw & VanZandt, *supra* note 2, at 115.

105. *Id.*

106. Maki, *supra* note 1, at 258.

107. Shaw & VanZandt, *supra* note 2, at 115.

108. *Id.*

109. *See, e.g.*, *id.*

110. *Id.*

111. *Id.*

112. Banta & Palomba, *supra* note 14, at 90.

113. *Id.*

114. *E.g.*, *id.* at 90–91.

115. *See* Funk, *supra* note 1, at 73–74.

116. 20 U.S.C. § 1232g; 34 C.F.R. Part 99.

117. Cecilia L. López, *A Decade of Assessing Student Learning: What We Have Learned, and What Is Next*, *in* Outcomes Assessment in Higher Education: Views and Perspectives 67–68 (Peter Hernon & Robert E. Dugan eds., 2004); *see also* Suskie, *supra* note 16, at 288 ("Defining successful outcomes means having a clear sense of what is good enough.").

118. Suskie, *supra* note 16, at 290.

119. *See* Shaw & VanZandt, *supra* note 2, at 126 ("To date, the ABA has not set a threshold other than to state that students should be 'competent' in the learning outcomes. So, it will be up to you and your faculty to define 'competency' for your students."); *see also* Margaret Martin Barry, *Reflections on Identifying and Mapping Learning Competencies and Outcomes: What Do We Want Law Students to Learn?*, 62 N.Y.L. Sch. L. Rev. 131, 147 (2017–2018) ("Another aspect

of adopting student learning outcomes and competencies is deciding what level of accomplishment should be achieved for each. Every competency should be learned at a level that the faculty believes is sufficient.").

120. Faculty and administrators must "ask what percentage of students completing a program should perform at what level and against what (or whose) standards for them to be satisfied with the evidence of students' learning generated by assessment practices across the academic program or major." López, *supra* note 117, at 67.

121. *See, e.g.*, Suskie, *supra* note 16, at 288–290.

122. Some commentators use the term "benchmark" rather than standard to describe this frame of reference. *See, e.g.*, Shaw & VanZandt, *supra* note 2, at 92–93. There is no consensus on terminology, so this book uses the term "standard."

123. Suskie, *supra* note 16, at 290–96. No particular standard is perfect, and none provides a complete picture of success or failure regarding student learning. Accordingly, experts recommend using more than one standard to evaluate assessment data, if that is possible and feasible. *Id.* at 297.

124. *Id.* at 290.

125. *Id.*

126. Shaw & VanZandt, *supra* note 2, at 93; *see also* Allen, *supra* note 5, at 158 ("Faculty generally set their own standards when they do program assessment.).

127. Building on Best Practices, *supra* note 7, at 26.

128. Shaw & VanZandt, *supra* note 2, at 93.

129. Suskie, *supra* note 16, at 297.

130. *Id.* at 290 (quoting Suzanne L. Pieper et al., *What Do I Do with the Data Now?": Analyzing Assessment Information for Accountability and Improvement*, 3 Research & Practice in Assessment 4, 7 (2008), http://www.rpajournal.com/dev/wp-content/uploads/2012/05/A11.pdf).

131. This discussion of rubrics is adapted from Terry, *supra* note 61, at 493–98.

132. Sophie Sparrow, *Describing the Ball: Improve Teaching by Using Rubrics — Explicit Grading Criteria*, 2004 Mich. St. L. Rev. 1, 6 (2004); *see also* Best Practices for Legal Education, *supra* note 11, at 244 ("Criteria-referenced assessments rely on detailed, explicit criteria that identify the abilities students should be demonstrating (for example, applying and distinguishing cases) and the bases on which the instructor will distinguish among excellent, good, competent, or incompetent performances."); Dannelle D. Stevens & Antonia J. Levi, Introduction to Rubrics: An Assessment Tool to Save Grading Time, Convey Effective Feedback, and Promote Student Learning 3 (2005) (hereinafter "Introduction to Rubrics") ("At its most basic, a rubric is a scoring tool that lays out the specific expectations for an assignment.").

133. Introduction to Rubrics, *supra* note 132, at 3; Sparrow, *supra* note 132, at 7 (noting that rubrics typically include benchmarks describing varying levels of student performance).

134. Maki, *supra* note 1, at 219.

135. Andrea A. Curcio, *A Simple, Low-Cost Institutional Learning-Outcomes Assessment Process*, 67 J. Legal Educ. 489, 493 (2018).

136. Introduction to Rubrics, *supra* note 132, at 5–15. For other helpful explanations of the process for creating rubrics, see Sparrow, *supra* note 132, at 32–37; Suskie, *supra* note 16, at 190–203. Resources for creating rubrics also are available online. *See, e.g.*, *Resources*, Inst. for L. Teaching & Learning, http://lawteaching.org/resources/ (last visited July 8, 2020); *Rubrics*, Ga. State U., https://oie.gsu.edu/assessment-and-review-academic-and-adminstrative/academic-assessment-and-review/assessment-manual/choosing-appropriate-assessment-methods/rubrics/ (last visited July 8, 2020).

137. Introduction to Rubrics, *supra* note 132, at 5.

138. *Id.* at 5–6.

139. *Id.* at 6.

140. *Id.* at 6, 9–10.
141. *Id.* at 10.
142. *Id.*
143. *Id.* at 8. For ease of reading and grading, Stevens and Levi also recommend that rubrics should not exceed one page. *Id.* at 7.
144. *Id.* at 8–9. Stevens and Levi recommend limiting a rubric to just three levels of performance when initially constructing it, and, if necessary, expanding it to include additional levels after it has been used on an actual assignment. *Id.* at 8.
145. *Id.* at 10–11.
146. The authors thank Professor Sophie Sparrow of the University of New Hampshire School of Law for sharing this rubric with the Institute for Law Teaching and Learning.
147. Shaw & VanZandt, *supra* note 2, at 93; Suskie, *supra* note 16, at 291.
148. Suskie, *supra* note 16, at 296.
149. *Id.* at 292.
150. Shaw & VanZandt, *supra* note 2, at 93.
151. *Id.*; Suskie, *supra* note 16, at 291.
152. Suskie, *supra* note 16, at 291.
153. *Id.*
154. *See, e,g.*, Shaw & VanZandt, *supra* note 2, at 13 ("To put it simply, what the bar exam tests does not directly correlate with what we teach.").
155. *Id.* at 93; Suskie, *supra* note 16, at 293–95.
156. Suskie, *supra* note 16, at 296.
157. Shaw & VanZandt, *supra* note 2, at 93.
158. Suskie, *supra* note 16, at 295.
159. *Id.* at 294.
160. Shaw & VanZandt, *supra* note 2, at 93.
161. *Id.*
162. Suskie, *supra* note 16, at 295.
163. *Id.* (emphasis in original).
164. *Id.*
165. *Id.* at 290; *see also* T. Dary Erwin, Assessing Student Learning and Development: A Guide to the Principles, Goals, and Methods of Determining College Outcomes 113–14 (1991); Michael J. Zieky, Marianne Perie, & Samuel A. Livingston, Cutscores: A Manual for Setting Standards of Performance on Educational and Occupational Tests 1, 9–11 (2008).
166. Suskie, *supra* note 16, at 290.
167. *Id.* at 290, 298–99.
168. Erwin, *supra* note 165, at 114.
169. Suskie, *supra* note 16, at 299.
170. *Id.* (emphasis in original).
171. *Id.* at 297–98.
172. Erwin, *supra* note 165, at 115.
173. Suskie, *supra* note 16, at 298.
174. *Id.*
175. *Id.*
176. *Id.*
177. ABA Standards and Rules of Procedure for Approval of Law Schools 2020–2021, Standard 316.
178. Shaw & VanZandt, *supra* note 2, at 143.
179. Erwin, *supra* note 165, at 114.

180. Suskie, *supra* note 16, at 299–300.
181. *See Multistate Essay Examination*, Nat'l Conference of Bar Examiners, http://www.ncbex.org/exams/mee (last visited July 8, 2020); *Multistate Performance Test*, Nat'l Conference of Bar Examiners, http://www.ncbex.org/exams/mpt/ (last visited July 8, 2020).
182. *See Multistate Professional Responsibility Examination*, Nat'l Conference of Bar Examiners, http://www.ncbex.org/exams/mpre/ (last visited July 8, 2020).
183. Curcio, *supra* note 135, at 515–29.
184. *See Holloran Competency Milestones*, Holloran Ctr., Univ. of St. Thomas, https://www.stthomas.edu/hollorancenter/hollorancompetencymilestones/ (last visited July 8, 2020).
185. *See VALUE Rubric Development Project*, Ass'n of Am. Coll. & Univ., https://www.aacu.org/value/rubrics (last visited July 8, 2020).
186. See Inst. for L. Teaching & Learning, *supra* note 136.
187. Suskie, *supra* note 16, at 299–300.
188. *Id.* at 300.
189. Erwin, *supra* note 165, at 114 ("Most faculty set the cutoff level too high initially, often having unrealistic expectations for their students.").
190. *See, e.g.*, Setting Performance Standards: Foundations, Methods, and Innovations (Gregory J. Cizek ed., 2d ed. 2012); Zieky et al., *supra* note 165.
191. *Id.*
192. Suskie, *supra* note 16, at 300; *see also id.* at 290 (A target is "the proportion of students that should achieve at least that minimally acceptable level.").
193. Shaw & VanZandt, *supra* note 2, at 125 (defining performance thresholds as "minimum expectation levels for the group as a whole").
194. *Id.*
195. *E.g.*, *id.*
196. Suskie, *supra* note 16, at 301 (emphasis in original).
197. *Id.*; *see also* Shaw & VanZandt, *supra* note 2, at 126.
198. Suskie, *supra* note 16, at 301.
199. *Id.*
200. *Id.*
201. ABA Standard 302 states that graduates should be competent in their school's learning outcomes, but it does not specify the percentage of students who must achieve competence.
202. Shaw & VanZandt, *supra* note 2, at 126.
203. *Id.*
204. Monica Stitt-Bergh, *What's Good Enough? Setting Standards* 34–36 (2014) (presentation at the 2014 Annual Conference of the Association for Assessment of Learning in Higher Education) (presentation materials on file with author).
205. ABA Standards and Rules of Procedure for Approval of Law Schools 2020–2021, Standard 316.
206. Shaw & VanZandt, *supra* note 2, at 126 ("As a rule of thumb, some experts argue for an 80% standard for thresholds. This threshold is based in large part on Bloom's mastery learning standard.").
207. Benjamin S. Bloom, *Learning for Mastery*, Evaluation Comment, 1, no. 2 (1968); Benjamin S. Bloom, *Mastery Learning*, *in* Mastery Learning: Theory and Practice 47–63 (James H. Block ed., 1971); Thomas R. Guskey, *Closing Achievement Gaps: Revisiting Benjamin S. Bloom's 'Learning for Mastery'*, J. Advanced Acad., Vol. 19, No. 1, 12–21 (2007).
208. Suskie, *supra* note 16, at 301.
209. *Id.*
210. *Id.*
211. *Id.* at 303.

212. Docia L. Rudley, *Organizing Program Level Assessment to Foster Dialogue About Improving Student Learning*, 95 U. Det. Mercy L. Rev. 393, 404 (2018).
213. *Id.*
214. *Id.*

CHAPTER TWO

Creating a Culture of Assessment

Creating a culture of assessment is integral to any successful organization in higher education. And just saying the law school has a healthy assessment culture does not make it materialize. There are fifteen elements needed for an institution to claim it has a legitimate culture of assessment. Those fifteen are: "clear general educational goals, common use of assessment related terms, faculty ownership of assessment programs, ongoing professional development, administrative encouragement of assessment, practical assessment plans, systematic assessment, the setting of student learning outcomes for all courses and programs, comprehensive program review, assessment of co-curricular activities, assessment of overall institutional effectiveness, informational forums about assessment, inclusion of assessment in plans and budgets, celebration of successes, and, finally, responsiveness to proposals for new endeavors related to assessment."[1] An institution must be heavily engaged in all fifteen of these elements to establish that it has created a culture of assessment.[2]

As this new era of assessment is just barely upon law schools, it is unlikely any law school is fulfilling all fifteen criteria at this time. Despite the new focus on accountability and the changes to the ABA standards, few law schools have actually created a culture of assessment. The reasons for this disconnect are too numerous to fully discuss in this chapter. Briefly, however, this disconnect is due, in part, to the failure of administrators and faculty to see assessment as anything but a "box-checking exercise" performed for ABA accreditation.[3] Also, for many faculty and administrators, programmatic assessment goes against the belief in academic freedom, independence, and shared governance.[4] This hijacking of assessment as solely an accreditation task robs the institution of the full value and purpose of assessment, which is improving student learning.[5] Evolving into a learning organization is a difficult step. There is good news, though; a culture of assessment can be built if an institution focuses on just a few elements, such as creating buy-in from the faculty, building faculty engagement (shifting focus from compliance to improving student learning), increasing administrative support (including resource allocation and celebrating assessment successes), building trust (by utilizing assessment data appropriately), and emphasizing assessment as the scholarship of teaching and learning.[6]

Before diving into creating a culture of assessment, it is important to define what a culture of assessment is in order to provide a target for law schools to reach for. A culture of assessment goes far beyond simply assessing students.[7] "A culture of assessment means that the concept of assessment is widely and clearly understood and faculty and staff share a belief in a systematic process for continuous improvement."[8] Organizations that value assessment understand that its culture is an "environment in which decisions are based on facts, research, and analysis, and where services are planned and delivered in ways that maximize positive outcomes and impacts for [students]."[9] Organizations maintain their culture of assessment by cultivating staff and faculty who care to know about the results their teaching is producing and whether students are really learning what is being taught, as assessment is data driven.

The culture of assessment revolves around doing what is best for student learning, and in order to accomplish that, departments and professors need to be continually assessing students to ascertain where they are in their learning. Too often, universities (and law schools) begrudgingly "assess" student learning to "check the box" for accreditation by conducting surveys of various stake holders and thereby miss the point, which is that "too little learning" is taking place in higher education.[10] Tragically, most law schools are really good at knowing what they teach their students but are lacking in understanding what students are learning. Thus, creating a culture of assessment shifts the focus from teaching to learning, which puts students and their learning back "at the top of each institution's priorit[y]."[11] Creating this new culture will require a shift from reliance on summative assessment (which students rarely pick up or review) to frequent formative assessment in each class giving students feedback and opportunities to interact with their professor.[12] Ultimately, "the overall long-term goal of the law school should be to create a culture of assessment in which 'the predominating attitudes and behaviors that characterize the functioning of an institution support the assessment of student learning outcomes.'"[13] This chapter will look at the history of assessment in colleges and cover ideas on how to create this culture in law schools.

1. The Cycle and History of Assessment in Higher Education

To change to a culture of assessment that focuses on student learning, an institution must understand the cycle of assessment. Assessment in higher education has been around for 25 years or more as a requirement for both regional and national accreditation.[14] Originally, faculty had very little to say in or very little involvement in the assessment process, as it was mainly run by deans, provosts, and administrators.[15] The next phase moved into programmatic level assessment, which had more faculty input but which was again mostly run by administrators collecting secondhand information from surveys and large national studies.[16] The next phase in this process, however, related to assessment pointing to the need for change in a curriculum or program, which required at least small groups of faculty working on the proposed changes to present to the full faculty.[17] Even in this phase, though, the changes and the assessments tended to be rudimentary and not large-scale changes, thereby requiring very little faculty effort or buy-in.[18]

Accreditation teams at the higher education level (and likely soon at the law school level) are now looking not only for the measurement of student learning but also for a sustained and serious effort being made by the institution to close the loop and improve the curriculum to ensure that the learning outcomes are being met.[19] This last phase will cause problems in law school faculties across the country if a culture of assessment is not created and promoted. The experts and articles written on the subject of creating and managing this last cycle of assessment (closing the loop and utilizing data-driven decisions to support student learning) all point to similar necessities: strong leadership supporting assessment, faculty buy-in, incentives and rewards for participation, explicit responsibilities, focus on student learning and measuring what is valued, and permission to fail and experiment.

2. Steps to Creating the Culture of Assessment

Emphatically, a successful assessment system relies on strong leadership of the dean of the law school and the main campus administration to effectuate a change to a culture of assessment. Those leaders must understand the steps of assessment: establishing learning outcomes, providing learning opportunities, assessing the student learning, and using the results to improve student learning. All change in any organization is difficult. An organization's culture is made up of the beliefs of the organization's members, and "the essence of culture is the values, beliefs, and assumptions that, over time become shared and taken for granted through a continuous, collaborative learning and influencing process."[20] The culture of the organization will determine the faculty's attitude about what is important and if assessment fits into that category.[21] Failure to change typically stems from lack of consensus building and lack of support for the change.[22] Also, this failure could be a result of the strength of the law school's culture against assessment and how well the law school typically deals with change.[23] To effectuate change to culture or to establish a new culture, the organization must believe that if it doesn't change, it may not survive, or the change must be seen as a strong positive change which will help the organization grow.[24] Therefore, to accomplish transformation in any organization, a dean and the university leadership should:

- establish a sense of urgency,
- form a guiding coalition,
- create and communicate a vision,
- involve the entire faculty, staff, and other stakeholders in the assessment process,
- set up a reward system that supports assessment,
- consolidate data collection, and
- institutionalize new approaches.[25]

a. Establish a Sense of Urgency

The change in the ABA standards went a long way in establishing the urgency of creating learning outcomes and assessing those outcomes. In an accreditation year, urgency is automatically created. This, however, is not enough to actually create a culture of assessment that will sustain a law school and effect permanent change using the data collected to improve student learning. Once the accreditation team is on the plane leaving the law school, the sense of urgency to use assessment data will recede unless a culture of assessment is created. To provide permanency, creating a sense of urgency should not induce fear in faculty and staff, but rather urgency should be created by a "sense of possibility."[26] A leader, who has a clearly communicated vision on assessment and who can convey confidence in the faculty's ability to improve student learning, can create the needed urgency. The dean of the law school and the administration must truly understand the faculty and be able to speak to their shared vision and passion.

At Gonzaga University School of Law, for instance, the faculty is very committed to doing what is in the best interest of the students. The best way to create a culture of assessment at Gonzaga would be to focus the message on how guided and effective assessment can and will improve student learning which is in the best interest of students. Thus, a leader can create a sense of urgency by focusing the assessment message on how it can improve bar passage rates, open up doors for student employment, and provide a sense of accomplishment for students through feedback. Lastly, urgency can be created through funding. A leader can offer potential increases in funding for departments or courses which include various types of assessments which feed into the learning outcomes.[27] This sense of urgency and importance can be created by funding programs and courses which can show though their documentation that students are meeting targets and benchmarks.

b. Form a Guiding Coalition

To create change, the dean and the administration must form a support group or "guiding coalition" to help push for change. A leader cannot be effective, motivate faculty to change, and create the culture of assessment if he or she has not formed trust in the faculty.[28] To build this trust and the coalition of leaders to help guide the change in culture, a leader must identify a group of people who share the vision of assessment, have credibility among the faculty, and possess good communication skills. [29] This coalition of people must also understand their colleagues, have good listening skills, and exercise a lot of patience. Change is difficult, and push-back should be expected. Faculty members will question the value of assessment, the value of identifying learning outcomes, the use of the data, the effect on academic freedom, etc. All of these concerns are valid and should be handled by listening to faculty concerns and addressing them. Consequently, it is important for the dean to form a coalition so that he or she has support, including others with whom to share the burden of initiating the necessary changes.

c. Create and Communicate a Vision

The dean and the coalition also must develop and communicate a vision for assessment which reflects an understanding of the law school's unique culture and what the law school values.[30] It is essential for the dean and the coalition to create and communicate a clear vision to help anticipate and engage with the inevitable resistance from faculty; understanding the source of this resistance is important to the success of the assessment vision.[31] This resistance can come from many sources: academic freedom, concerns about "busy work," discord between faculty and administration, under-staffing, feeling watched, worry that assessment results will be used to punish faculty, lack of resources (money, time, energy), etc. Therefore, to create a culture of assessment, the coalition and the dean must understand the sources of the resistance to change and shape the vision to assuage the resistance.

At most schools the coalition created by the dean to carry out the vision is the "assessment committee," but perhaps the vision would be better understood and reflected if the committee was named the "improving student learning committee" or the "curricular innovations committee." This small change in messaging may go a long way in helping the administration forward its vision. After the committee works through its first outcome and makes recommendations to the faculty, the committee should also meet with the dean (and administration team) to revisit the vision and make necessary changes to that vision. Often once the assessment committee makes its way through one cycle, it may be clear that the vision needs to change or be revised.

Once the vision is created, the dean and the coalition must communicate the vision in a straightforward way. An effective vision will tell the faculty and staff how the law school world is changing and the compelling reasons to set goals, assess student achievement, and make necessary changes.[32] Further, successful communication of the assessment vision and goals should be couched in terms of a "sustainable culture of inquiry."[33] This message must make clear that assessment's goal is not to "check a box" and is not being done "because main campus is making us," but rather because the law school is choosing to invest time, resources, money, and personnel in assessment to inquire as to how the students are learning and to make necessary improvements that are data based. Strong leadership with a clear message of the importance of assessment and its role in improving student learning is essential to the success of any assessment program. This is also essential to creating a culture of assessment.

d. Involve the Entire Faculty, Staff, and Other Stakeholders in the Assessment Process

As the case has already been made for strong leadership, vision, and communication, it is now appropriate to look at utilizing and engaging faculty and staff in the assessment process. As mentioned above, the dean must have a coalition of supporters of assessment, but equally important is involving the entire faculty and staff in this process so that assessment is not just what "so-and-so" does. One person or a small group of faculty and staff cannot successfully carry the assessment load. If the law school goes down this road, a culture of assessment is not created, and assessment becomes a "box checking" exercise; in other words, it becomes a waste of time and resources and fails to improve student learning. Whereas the coalition (the main committee members) will be in charge of the assessment process, the whole faculty and staff should be involved in the work.

For instance, let's assume the outcome being assessed is "students should understand the rules of ethics and demonstrate that understanding though their dealings with colleagues, professors, employers, and the community." It seems pretty obvious the committee would work with the professors who teach professional responsibility. If the school, however, wants to create a culture of assessment and wants to improve student learning, the committee should reach out to the clinicians, students, librarians, externship directors, staff (including janitors, on-site baristas, food providers, etc.), employers, and other professors who discuss and assess ethics. In this way, the faculty, staff, students, and other stakeholders feel empowered to make changes and feel heard. This process of inclusion will go a long way to creating a culture of assessment.

e. Set up a Reward System That Supports Assessment

Creating a culture of assessment necessarily requires setting up a system of rewards and celebrations of success (and failures). Rewards can take many forms, but any reward speaks volumes as to the importance of assessment at the law school. The dean can provide small stipends for faculty members willing to be part of the committee. Time is also a resource that is always in short supply for faculty and staff. A course release for meaningful assessment work would send a message as to the importance of the process of assessment. Further, some law schools have hired staff dedicated solely to identifying, collecting, and analyzing assessment data. It seems clear the dean can send a message of the importance of this assessment endeavor if he or she dedicates finances, time, and personnel to it. The less time faculty and staff have to devote to assessment, the less meaningful the results will be.[34]

Related to the dedication of resources, the dean can encourage the promotion and retention committee and the faculty as a whole to recognize assessment and its methodology as a scholarly endeavor in its own right. Doing this sends a message to the law school that assessment is important. A study done in the Midwest at a liberal arts college measured the attitude of faculty regarding assessment; the study clearly showed faculty members were willing to put in the time to take assessment seriously if they saw assessment as a scholarly activity. [35] The dean, the promotion and retention committee, and the university can recognize that publishing, presenting, and attending workshops in the area of assessment is legitimate scholarship that can lead to the granting of tenure. If the law school and its accompanying parent organization fund and recognize assessment as its own scholarship area, it would send a clear message of the importance of assessment and help enforce the culture of assessment.

f. Consolidate Data Collection

To cultivate a successful culture of assessment, the committee in charge or the associate dean's office should investigate and find a platform to collect data. A comprehensive search of such platforms is beyond this book's reach, but it is safe to say, platforms exist (for a price) which will help faculty and the data collectors see the value in the collected data. Many of the platforms allow the data collectors to see in real time the syllabus for each course, the quizzes given in each course, and the grades of all the students. The data collector can then see where outcomes are being measured and how the students are doing overall. This investment by the law school will send a message of the importance of collecting and analyzing the data to facilitate student learning. Once the stakeholders see the value of the data collected and the ease with which it can be collected through these commercial platforms, the culture of assessment is cemented.

g. Institutionalize New Approaches

The literature and the studies in this area of creating an assessment culture drive home the point that all new hires should be trained on assessment techniques, and all proposals for new courses or programs must come with an assessment matrix showing how assessment will be utilized in measuring their outcomes.[36] This requirement works to communicate to newcomers and to existing staff and faculty the importance of assessment in the everyday life of the law school. New members of the law school team and existing faculty members should be sent to teaching workshops that focus on assessment techniques to help them understand the value of assessment of learning outcomes.

This will help professors be better teachers, help students learn, and help make data-driven curricular decisions.

3. Conclusion

To truly create a culture of assessment, the law school's mission and formal documents should reflect the most important concern: student learning. These documents and the mission should explicitly refer to the outcomes for the students and the expectation of assessment.[37] The focus of the law school should be on "doing assessment rather than just using assessment"[38] to build a culture of bettering the law school through the use of evidence. This is not just using evidence from the students but also using evidence from other stakeholders including the community to improve learning outcomes, teaching strategies, and support systems.[39] This culture of assessment cannot just be a burst of activity before the ABA visits; rather, assessment should be part of everyday life at the law school. Using evidence to inform teaching and institutional decisions should be part of the fabric of the law school.[40]

To get there, a law school will need strong leaders who believe in the value of data-based decision making, can communicate that belief, and can get buy-in from the stakeholders, particularly faculty. Leadership must provide time and financial support to help faculty and staff to adopt the assessment mindset while understanding the existing culture. If the law school's stakeholders can see the benefits of data-based decisions that come from assessment methods, change can happen. The best approach is to continue to focus on what is important to all law school employees: student learning. To facilitate the long-term change in culture at any institution, policies and formal documents should reflect the importance of assessment to the everyday life of the law school. Without that, it is likely the stakeholders will return to old habits once the urgency has subsided.[41]

Endnotes

1. Wendy F. Weiner, *Establishing a Culture of Assessment*, Am. Ass'n of Univ. Professors (July–Aug. 2009), https://www.aaup.org/article/establishing-culture-assessment (last visited July 12, 2020).
2. *Id.*
3. Meredith G. Farkas, *Building and Sustaining a Culture of Assessment: Best Practices for Change Leadership*, 41 Reference Servs. Rev. 13 (2013), https://doi.org/10.1108/00907321311300857 (last visited July 12, 2020).

4. *Id.*
5. *Id.*
6. Larry Cunningham, *Building a Culture of Assessment in Law Schools*, 69 Case W. Reserve L. Rev. 395, 407–411 (2018).
7. *Id.*
8. Michael R. Lane et al., *Improving Assessment: Creating a Culture of Assessment with a Change Management Approach*, 4 J. of Case Studies in Accreditation & Assessment 1, 4 (2014).
9. Amos Lakos & Shelley Phipps, *Creating a Culture of Assessment: A Catalyst for Organizational Change*, 4 Libraries & the Academy 345, 352 (2004), https://muse.jhu.edu/article/170684 (last visited July 12, 2020).
10. Richard H. Hersh & Richard P. Keeling, *Changing Institutional Culture to Promote Assessment of Higher Learning*, Nat'l Inst. for Learning Outcomes Assessment (Feb. 2013), https://www.learningoutcomeassessment.org/documents/occasionalpaperseventeen.pdf (last visited July 12, 2020).
11. *Id.*
12. *Id.*
13. Janet W. Fisher, *Putting Students at the Center of Legal Education: How an Emphasis on Outcome Measures in the ABA Standards for Approval of Law Schools Might Transform the Educational Experience of Law Students*, 35 S. Ill. U. L.J. 225, 234 (2011).
14. Lane, *supra* note 8.
15. *Id.*
16. *Id.*
17. *Id.*
18. *Id.*
19. *Id.*
20. Lakos, *supra* note 9, at 348.
21. *Id.*
22. Farkas, *supra* note 3.
23. Lakos, *supra* note 9, at 349.
24. *Id.*
25. *See generally* Farkas, *supra* note 3.
26. *Id.*
27. Lane, *supra* note 8.
28. Farkas, *supra* note 3.
29. *Id.*
30. *Id.*
31. *Id.*
32. Lane, *supra* note 8.
33. Cunningham, *supra* note 6, at 409.
34. Farkas, *supra* note 3.
35. Cunningham, *supra* note 6, at 415.
36. Farkas, *supra* note 3.
37. Lakos, *supra* note 9, at 352.
38. Linda Suskie, Assessing Student Learning: A Common Sense Guide 118 (3d ed. 2018).
39. *Id.*
40. *Id.*
41. Farkas, *supra* note 3.

Section Two: Assessment of Student Learning

CHAPTER THREE

Assessment at the Institutional Level

Chapter 1 explained fundamental principles that should guide an assessment process at any level of a law school's educational program. This chapter demonstrates how to apply those principles in the specific context of assessment at the institutional level.

1. Developing Institutional Learning Outcomes for a School's J.D. Program

Institutional learning outcomes became a requirement for U.S. law schools in 2016 when the ABA implemented new accreditation standards.[1] Those standards now mandate that law schools establish and publish learning outcomes designed to prepare their students, "upon graduation, for admission to the bar and for effective, ethical, and responsible participation as members of the legal profession."[2] At a minimum, law schools must establish learning outcomes that include competency in the following:

a) Knowledge and understanding of substantive and procedural law;

b) Legal analysis and reasoning, legal research, problem-solving, and written and oral communication in the legal context;

c) Exercise of proper professional and ethical responsibilities to clients and the legal system; and

d) Other professional skills needed for competent and ethical participation as a member of the legal profession.[3]

These categories outline just the bare minimum for institutional learning outcomes, and schools are free to adopt additional outcomes that are consistent with their unique mission. Indeed, the mission statement, which every law school must have,[4] is a good starting point for developing institutional learning outcomes, since the mission statement "communicates a broad vision of the fundamental purposes and values of the program, providing an important view of what matters most to faculty."[5] Distinct mission statements "will inform varying 'learning outcomes' appropriate to each school."[6]

To illustrate this concept, consider the following mission statements from three different law schools:

> Gonzaga University School of Law: "To provide an excellent legal education informed by our humanistic, Jesuit, and Catholic traditions and values."[7]
>
> University of Arkansas at Little Rock William H. Bowen School of Law: "[Providing] a high quality legal education that equips students with the knowledge, skills, and ethical concepts to not only function as competent attorneys, public officials, business persons, and other professionals, but also to think critically about the efficacy of the law and legal institutions and to work for their improvement."[8]
>
> Washington University in St. Louis School of Law: "WashULaw's mission is to equip students with knowledge and skills to ethically and effectively practice law and pursue justice in a dynamic and globally interconnected legal environment. We strive to foster a vibrant intellectual culture characterized by rigorous exchange of views and the production and dissemination of influential research. Our school cultivates a collaborative and supportive community of students, faculty, staff, and alumni that prizes diversity and values connection to, and service in, broader civic and professional communities."[9]

These mission statements reflect the distinctive identities and purposes of, respectively, a Jesuit law school, a public law school in a small city, and a private law school in a large, metropolitan area. Those identities and purposes, in turn, will shape each school's institutional learning outcomes.

In addition to aligning with its mission, a law school's institutional outcomes "must consist of clear and concise statements of knowledge that students are expected to acquire, skills students are expected to develop, and values that they are expected to understand and integrate into their professional lives."[10] Thus, institutional outcomes necessarily are broad statements that describe in general terms all of the types of learning a school intends for its graduates to accomplish. Those broad terms, however, "can make it far too easy to create a list of outcomes that mean absolutely nothing. For instance, of course a law graduate should be able to communicate, but what does that mean in real terms?"[11] To prevent this sort of confusion, and to ensure that institutional learning outcomes can be measured, each outcome should be broken down into performance criteria, "which are the more specific characteristics students must demonstrate to establish a particular outcome has been satisfied."[12] "The performance criteria are intended to address the ambiguities found in the learning outcomes. They force you to describe in concrete terms what each outcome requires."[13] These criteria, in turn, will form the basis for the rubrics that will be created to evaluate the assessments used for measuring students' achievement of the learning outcomes.

To illustrate the relationship between institutional learning outcomes and performance criteria, below are Washburn University School of Law's six institutional learning outcomes, which include the performance criteria for each outcome:

Table 3.1: Washburn University School of Law Learning Outcomes

1. **Graduates will demonstrate knowledge of the law and the legal system.**
    - 1.1. Students will demonstrate an understanding of the terms, rules, and principles of law.
    - 1.2. Students will read authority, identify the rules within the authority, and synthesize those rules into a logical framework for analysis.
    - 1.3. Students will demonstrate an understanding of organization, hierarchy, and relationships within the legal system.
    - 1.4. Students will demonstrate an understanding of primary and secondary sources of law and the ways in which they relate to one another.

2. **Graduates will demonstrate analytical and problem-solving skills.**
    - 2.1. Students will apply controlling legal principles to legal problems.
    - 2.2. Students will use analogical reasoning to solve legal problems.
    - 2.3. Students will use policy-based reasoning to solve legal problems.

3. **Graduates will communicate effectively.**
    - 3.1. Students will write in a clear, concise, well-organized, professional manner that is appropriate to the audience and the circumstances.
    - 3.2. Students will speak in a clear, concise, well-organized, professional manner that is appropriate to the audience and the circumstances.
    - 3.3. Students will demonstrate active listening in communications with others, including legal professionals and laypersons.

4. **Graduates will demonstrate competency in legal practice skills.**
    - 4.1. Students will demonstrate the ability to conduct legal research.
    - 4.2. Students will demonstrate the ability to conduct a factual investigation.
    - 4.3. Students will demonstrate the ability to interview and counsel a client.
    - 4.4. Students will demonstrate the ability to negotiate and advocate on behalf of a client in appropriate circumstances.
    - 4.5. Students will demonstrate the ability to draft documents used in legal practice.

continued on next page

Table 3.1: Washburn University School of Law Learning Outcomes *continued*

5. Graduates will possess the requisite skills to recognize and resolve dilemmas in an ethical and professional manner.

5.1 Students will articulate the sources, structure, and substance of the laws governing the ethics of the legal profession.

5.2. When presented with a dilemma drawn from case-based or hypothetical facts, students will articulate the relevant and applicable ethical standards, apply those ethical standards, and propose one or more resolutions that result in an ethical outcome.

5.3. Students will consistently exercise professional and ethical responsibilities.

6. Graduates will demonstrate knowledge of the importance of service to the profession and to the community at large, both nationally and internationally.

6.1. Students will demonstrate an awareness of and a willingness to contribute to the profession's responsibility to ensure access to justice.

6.2. Students will demonstrate a willingness to contribute to serving the underserved and traditionally marginalized communities.

6.3. Students will understand comparative perspectives on law, whether from international or foreign legal systems, other academic disciplines, or other critical viewpoints, and will use those perspectives as tools for critiquing or challenging the role of law in society.

6.4. Students will recognize the existence and value of diversity both within the legal profession and among the clients it serves.[14]

The ABA does not mandate a particular process that law schools must follow in generating institutional learning outcomes for their graduates. It likely will be easier and more efficient for a law school committee or task force to create the first draft of a set of learning outcomes, rather than trying to have the entire faculty write them together. The task of generating the initial draft might be assigned to a curriculum committee, an assessment committee, or a special committee appointed specifically for the task. Once the committee has completed its draft, it should submit the draft to the entire faculty for review and comment, and the faculty as a whole should reach consensus on the final version of outcomes after discussion and deliberation.[15] Outcomes imposed by the administration are unlikely to be effective in shaping and assessing law school curricula.

In addition to these principles, the following guidelines are offered to help law schools efficiently develop appropriate institutional learning outcomes:

1. Institutional learning outcomes should address the three broad types of learning identified above: knowledge (*e.g.*, substantive law, procedural

law, legal theory), skills (*e.g.*, analysis, research, writing, advocacy, negotiation), and values (*e.g.*, professional ethics, cultural awareness, pro bono).

2. Input from the bench and bar can help the faculty articulate learning outcomes that prepare students for the practice of law.
3. The set of institutional learning outcomes should be realistic and achievable in light of the law school's strengths, challenges, and resources. Law schools typically should limit themselves to six to twelve outcomes, with three to seven performance criteria per outcome.[16]
4. Appropriate guiding questions for the faculty include: What do our students do after they graduate? What do our students most need to succeed in those pursuits? What makes our graduates attractive to employers? What capabilities would our ideal graduate have?
5. Law schools need not develop institutional learning outcomes from scratch. Examples of learning outcomes for law schools are widely available.

Resources for law schools engaged in creating or revising their institutional learning outcomes include *Educating Lawyers*,[17] the *MacCrate Report*,[18] *Best Practices for Legal Education*,[19] Shultz and Zedeck's list of 26 lawyering-effectiveness factors,[20] the Foundations for Practice Report,[21] and outcomes adopted by other law schools. *Educating Lawyers*, for example, provides a helpful conceptual framework through its three apprenticeships: (1) cognitive, which focuses on academic knowledge of the profession and analytical thinking; (2) practice, including the practical skills shared by competent professionals; and (3) identity, encompassing the purposes, values, roles, and responsibilities of the profession.[22]

The *MacCrate Report* sets out a Statement of Fundamental Lawyering Skills and Professional Values designed to describe what it takes to practice law effectively and responsibly. *MacCrate*'s list of fundamental lawyering skills includes problem solving, legal analysis, legal research, fact investigation, oral and written communication, counseling, negotiation, litigation process, alternative dispute resolution procedures, organization and management of legal work, and recognizing and resolving ethical dilemmas.[23] The fundamental values of the profession include providing competent representation; striving to promote justice, fairness, and morality; striving to improve the profession; and professional self- development.[24]

Best Practices for Legal Education contains a chapter on student learning outcomes, including a detailed list of outcomes law schools can consider when articulating their own set of learning outcomes. The list includes:

- Graduates demonstrate at the point of admission the ability to solve legal problems effectively and responsibly, including the ability to:
  - work with clients to identify their objectives, identify and evaluate the merits and risks of their options, and advise on solutions;
  - progress civil and criminal matters towards resolution using a range of techniques and approaches;
  - draft agreements and other documentation to enable actions and transactions to be completed;
  - plan and implement strategies to progress cases and transactions expeditiously and with propriety.
- Graduates have and are able to demonstrate at the point of admission to practice the attributes of effective, responsible lawyers, which include the following knowledge, understandings, skills, and abilities:
  - self-reflection and lifelong learning skills,
  - intellectual and analytical skills,
  - core knowledge of the law,
  - core understanding of the law,
  - professional skills, and
  - professionalism.
- Graduates demonstrate self-reflection and lifelong learning skills.
- Graduates demonstrate the intellectual and analytical skills required to:
  - apply methods and techniques to review, consolidate, extend, and apply knowledge and understanding and to initiate and carry out projects; and
  - critically evaluate arguments, assumptions, abstract concepts, and data to make judgments and to frame appropriate questions to achieve a solution, or identify a range of solutions to a problem.
- Graduates demonstrate practical judgment.

- Graduates demonstrate analytical skills.
- Graduates demonstrate self-efficacy.
- Graduates demonstrate core knowledge of the law:
    - the jurisdiction, authority, and procedures of the legal institutions and the professions that initiate, develop, interpret, and apply the law of relevant jurisdictions, including knowledge of constitutional law and judicial review;
    - the rules of professional conduct (including the accounts rules); and
    - the regulatory and fiscal framework within which business and other legal transactions and financial services are conducted.
- Graduates demonstrate core understanding of the law:
    - the law of contract and tort and of parties' obligations, rights, and remedies;
    - criminal law;
    - the legal concept of property and the protection, disposal, acquisition, and transmission of proprietary interests;
    - equitable rights, titles, and interests;
    - the range of legal protections available to the individual in society in civil and criminal matters and with regard to their human rights;
    - legal personality and business structures; and
    - the values and principles on which professional rules are constructed.
- Graduates demonstrate professional skills:
    - the application of techniques to communicate effectively with clients, colleagues, and members of other professions;
    - the ability to recognize clients' financial, commercial, and personal constraints and priorities;
    - the ability to advocate a case on behalf of others, and to participate in trials to the extent allowed upon admission to practice;
    - effective use of current technologies and strategies to store, retrieve, and analyze information and to undertake factual and legal research;

- an appreciation of the commercial environment of legal practice, including the market for legal services;
- the ability to recognize and resolve ethical dilemmas;
- effective skills for client relationship management and knowledge of how to act if a client is dissatisfied with the advice or service provided;
- employment of risk management skills;
- the capacity to recognize personal and professional strengths and weaknesses, to identify the limits of personal knowledge and skill, and to develop strategies that will enhance professional performance;
- the ability to manage personal workload and to manage efficiently, effectively, and concurrently a number of client matters; and
- the ability to work effectively as a member of a team.

- Graduates demonstrate professionalism:
    - appropriate behaviors and integrity in a range of situations;
    - the capacity to deal sensitively and effectively with clients, colleagues, and others from a range of social, economic, and ethnic backgrounds, identifying and responding positively and appropriately to issues of culture and disability that might affect communication techniques and influence a client's objectives.
- Graduates strive to seek justice.
- Graduates foster respect for the rule of law.
- Graduates embody honor, integrity, and fair play and are truthful and candid.
- Graduates deal sensitively and effectively with diverse clients and colleagues.
- Graduates nurture quality of life.[25]

In 2011, professors Marjorie Shultz and Sheldon Zedeck published the results of an empirical research study identifying 26 factors that predict lawyer effectiveness.[26] These factors provide a list of traits that law schools can consider incorporating into their institutional learning outcomes. The 26 effectiveness factors include:

Table 3.2: 26 Lawyering Effectiveness Factors

Analysis and Reasoning	Organizing and Managing Others (Staff/ Colleagues)
Creativity/Innovation	Negotiation Skills
Problem Solving	Able to See the World Through the Eyes of Others
Practical Judgment	Networking and Business Development
Researching the Law	Providing Advice and Counsel and Building Relationships with Clients
Fact Finding	Developing Relationships within the Legal Profession
Questioning and Interviewing	Evaluation, Development, and Mentoring
Influencing and Advocating	Passion and Engagement
Writing	Diligence
Speaking	Integrity/Honesty
Listening	Stress Management
Strategic Planning	Community Involvement and Service
Organizing and Managing One's Own Work	Self-Development

In addition, a recent national survey of more than 24,000 lawyers identified characteristics, professional competencies, and legal skills that practicing attorneys deem the most important for new lawyers to have when they enter the profession.[27] The table below shows the competencies, characteristics, and skills that at least 75% of the survey respondents identified as necessary at the start of practice:[28]

Table 3.3: Competencies, Characteristics, and Skills from Foundations for Practice Study

Listen attentively and respectfully	Regulate emotions and demonstrate self-control	Take individual responsibility for actions and results	Arrive on time for meetings, appointments, and hearings	Conscientiousness
Promptly respond to inquiries and requests	Exhibit tact and diplomacy	Understand when to engage supervisor or seek advice in problem-solving	Understand and apply legal privilege concepts	Common sense
Speak in a manner that meets legal and professional standards	Effectively research the law	Honor commitments	Integrity and trustworthiness	Intelligence
Write in a manner that meets legal and professional standards	Have a strong work ethic and put forth best effort	Keep information confidential	Diligence	Strong moral compass
Treat others with courtesy and respect	Show initiative	Adhere to proper timekeeping and billing practices	Attention to detail	Energy

Law schools could consider including some or all of these competencies, qualities, and skills in their institutional learning outcomes.

In addition to the learning outcomes for Washburn University School of Law listed in Table 3.1, examples of statements of institutional learning outcomes from three other law schools follow below. Indiana University Robert H. McKinney School of Law has adopted these learning outcomes for its J.D. program:

Table 3.4: Indiana University Robert H. McKinney School of Law Learning Outcomes

A McKinney graduate will be prepared to:

Build upon an existing base of legal knowledge and skills to succeed in the graduate's chosen career path.
Exercise sound professional judgment and fulfill ethical responsibilities.

Exhibit a high degree of competence in legal analysis, reasoning, research, and writing.
Demonstrate acumen in oral communication in the legal context.
Serve as a leader or contributing team member in professional settings.
Transition readily to law practice or other government, non-profit, or private sector employment.
Leverage a network of professional relationships.
Appreciate that excellence as a lawyer requires individual, life-long effort.[29]

The University of the Pacific McGeorge School of Law identifies institutional learning outcomes focused on knowledge, skills, and values:

Table 3.5: University of the Pacific McGeorge School of Law Learning Outcomes

Each student will:

Demonstrate the ability to identify and understand key concepts in U.S. substantive law, legal theory, and procedure.
Apply knowledge and critical thinking skills to perform competent legal analysis, reasoning, and problem solving.
Demonstrate the ability to strategize, develop, and conduct efficient legal research in U.S. law.
Demonstrate the ability to identify and understand foundational concepts in international law and to perform international legal research.
Demonstrate communication skills, including effective listening and critical reading, writing in objective and persuasive styles, and oral advocacy and other oral communications.
Demonstrate professional judgment, ethics, and professionalism through conduct consistent with the legal profession's values, standards, and discipline.
Demonstrate the ability to understand, collaborate, and engage with people of diverse backgrounds and experiences in a variety of legal settings and contexts.
Demonstrate understanding of the legal profession's commitment to access to justice.
Demonstrate understanding of career options and steps toward defining and achieving career goals in light of personal values.[30]

The University of Memphis Cecil C. Humphreys School of Law has adopted learning outcomes reflecting "the knowledge, skills, and values that the faculty believes are essential to the practice of law."[31] Thus, its outcomes state that:

Table 3.6: University of Memphis Cecil C. Humphreys School of Law Learning Outcomes

Learning Outcome 1: Graduates will demonstrate knowledge and understanding of the law and the American legal system. Graduates will demonstrate achievement of this learning outcome by:

- Criterion 1: Identifying, defining, and explaining the foundational terms, rules, principles, and policies of the following fundamental areas of law: civil procedure, constitutional law, contracts, criminal law, criminal procedure, torts, property, evidence, and professional responsibility.
- Criterion 2: Identifying, defining, and explaining the fundamental terms, rules, principles and policies of two of the following areas of law: corporate tax, fair employment practices, income taxation, labor law, legislation, sales, or secured transactions.
- Criterion 3: Identifying, defining, and explaining the fundamental terms, rules, principles and policies of two of the following areas of law: administrative law, business organizations, decedents' estates, family law, conflict of laws, and remedies.
- Criterion 4: Describing the organization, hierarchy, and relationships within the American legal system.
- Criterion 5: Identifying the sources of primary law and describing their relationships to each other.

Learning Outcome 2: Graduates will demonstrate competency in legal analysis and legal reasoning. Graduates will demonstrate achievement of this learning outcome by:

- Criterion 1: Critically reading the applicable authority, including identifying the key rules within each authority, applying fundamental statutory construction principles when engaging with enacted law, and recognizing the role of policy in the authorities.
- Criterion 2: Synthesizing the relevant rules of law into a logical framework for analysis, including harmonizing apparently conflicting authorities and recognizing genuinely conflicting authorities.
- Criterion 3: Where rules conflict, analyzing which rule a court is likely to apply.
- Criterion 4: Identifying legal issues in factual situations that differ from those in which the knowledge was first encountered.
- Criterion 5: Identifying legal rules relevant to each legal issue implicated by the facts.
- Criterion 6: Identifying the legally significant facts relevant to each applicable legal rule.
- Criterion 7: Applying the identified rules to the facts to formulate and evaluate potential arguments and counterarguments regarding the outcome of the issue.
- Criterion 8: When appropriate, analogizing the facts to and distinguishing the facts from those of precedent cases to determine the likely outcome of the case.
- Criterion 9: Evaluating and criticizing the quality of legal analysis in terms of both reasoning and support in sources of law.

Learning Outcome 3: Graduates will demonstrate competency in legal problem solving. Graduates will demonstrate achievement of this learning outcome by:

- Criterion 1: Identifying and exploring their clients' goals.
- Criterion 2: Identifying and diagnosing problems as they relate to their clients' goals.
- Criterion 3: Formulating and evaluating legal and non-legal solutions and strategies, taking into account the client's interests, goals, and objectives.
- Criterion 4: Articulating practical considerations, such as cost and effects on other people.
- Criterion 5: Developing and implementing plans of action to advance the client's goals.

Learning Outcome 4: Graduates will demonstrate competence in effective and efficient research. Graduates will demonstrate achievement of this learning outcome by:

- Criterion 1: Articulating the hierarchical structure of the law and the difference between binding and persuasive authority.
- Criterion 2: Explaining the difference between primary sources of law and secondary sources.
- Criterion 3: Developing an effective research strategy.
- Criterion 4: Employing effective research methodologies to locate and, as appropriate, update authorities relevant to the specific legal issue.
- Criterion 5: Accurately assessing the weight of authorities.

Learning Outcome 5: Graduates will communicate effectively in the legal context. Graduates will demonstrate achievement of this learning outcome by:

- Criterion 1: Writing documents that are clear, concise, well-reasoned, organized, professional in tone, appropriate to the audience and the circumstances, and, if appropriate, contain proper citation to authority.
- Criterion 2: Speaking in a clear, concise, well-reasoned, organized, and professional manner that is appropriate to the audience and the circumstances.
- Criterion 3: Actively listening to clients, colleagues, judges, and others to acquire and preserve the information communicated.
- Criterion 4: Critically reading written communications to acquire and preserve the information communicated.

Learning Outcome 6: Graduates will recognize and understand the ethical and professional responsibilities of lawyers to clients and the legal system. Graduates will demonstrate achievement of this learning outcome by:

- Criterion 1: Identifying and explaining the applicable law governing lawyers.
- Criterion 2: Using the law governing lawyers to recognize ethical and other professional dilemmas.
- Criterion 3: Applying the law governing lawyers to help resolve ethical and other professional dilemmas.
- Criterion 4: Exercising professional judgment to help resolve ethical and other professional dilemmas.

continued on next page

Table 3.6: University of Memphis Cecil C. Humphreys School of Law Learning Outcomes *continued*

Learning Outcome 7: Graduates will demonstrate competency in those other professional skills and values necessary for legal practice. Graduates will demonstrate achievement of this learning outcome by:

- Criterion 1: Capably managing a legal project (*e.g.*, case, memorandum, mediation) from its inception to its conclusion.
- Criterion 2: Effectively planning and controlling their use of time.
- Criterion 3: Being prepared for and attending to scheduled obligations, whether through timely submission of work product or in-person appearance.
- Criterion 4: Exhibiting civility, awareness of cultural differences, and respect and consideration of others.
- Criterion 5: Exhibiting integrity, diligence, honesty, and good judgment.
- Criterion 6: Demonstrating the ability to solicit, examine, and respond to supervision and feedback from others through a critical lens.
- Criterion 7: Demonstrating the ability to reflect upon and examine their own strengths, weaknesses, and professional and personal obligations.
- Criterion 8: Demonstrating competence and self-direction in a simulated or live working legal environment requiring a range of practical legal skills.

Learning Outcome 8: Graduates will recognize the value of community and public service. Graduates will demonstrate achievement of this learning outcome by:

- Criterion 1: Contributing to the profession's fulfillment of its responsibility to ensure that adequate legal services are provided to those who cannot afford to pay for them.
- Criterion 2: Participating in school and outreach activities designed to improve the profession, the legal system, public policy, or society, especially in programs involving community and public service.[32]

As these examples from Washburn, Indiana—McKinney, McGeorge, and Memphis demonstrate, law schools vary widely in the number and types of institutional learning outcomes they articulate. Thus, the adoption of learning outcomes is particular to each school, based on its unique mission and the knowledge, skills, and values that it deems essential for its specific graduates.

Once institutional outcomes have been written and adopted, the ABA requires that law schools "conduct ongoing evaluation of [their] program of legal education, learning outcomes, and assessment methods" and "use the results of this evaluation to determine the degree of student attainment of competency in the learning outcomes and to make appropriate changes to improve the curriculum."[33] The ABA Standards, however, do not mandate the use of any particular method to conduct this evaluation.[34] Rather, the ABA recognizes that the "methods used to measure the degree of student achievement of learning outcomes are likely to differ from school to school," so it offers suggestions for schools to consider.[35] In light of the wide variety of institutional outcomes that law schools may adopt, it is helpful to use an example set of outcomes to explain the steps that law schools should follow to conduct this ongoing assessment and evaluation. Accordingly, the rest of this chapter uses the Washburn learning outcomes listed in Table 3.1 to illustrate the process for assessing graduates' achievement of institutional learning outcomes.

2. Ensuring Alignment Between Institutional Learning Outcomes and the Curriculum

If a school were to adopt outcomes like those chosen by Washburn, the next step in assessment would be to map the curriculum to ensure alignment between the outcomes and the required curriculum. As explained above, institutional learning outcomes generally are quite broad, so it is necessary to break them down into specific performance criteria to make them clear and measurable. Specifying the performance criteria also allows assessment leaders to identify the courses in which the criteria are addressed and in which evidence of student learning can be found. Washburn has identified the specific performance criteria that make up each of its six outcomes. For example, it has separated its outcome for communication skills into the following performance criteria:

- Students will write in a clear, concise, well-organized, professional manner that is appropriate to the audience and the circumstances.
- Students will speak in a clear, concise, well-organized, professional manner that is appropriate to the audience and the circumstances.
- Students will demonstrate active listening in communications with others, including legal professionals and laypersons.

Once assessment leaders have identified the performance criteria, they should complete a curriculum map that identifies the required courses in which each criterion is addressed, and the level of depth at which the courses address that criterion (*i.e.*, Introduced (I), Practiced (P), or Competency Expected (C)). Thus, the portion of a curriculum map for Washburn's communications skills outcome might look like this:

Table 3.7: Portion of Sample Curriculum Map

	Res. & Writ.	Civ. Pro.	Prop.	Crim. Law	Con tracts	Torts	Trial Adv.	Crim. Pro.	Prof. Resp.	Evid.	Con. Law	Clinic
Write in clear, concise, well-organized, professional manner appropriate to audience and circumstances.	I						I,P					C
Speak in clear, concise, well-organized, professional manner that is appropriate to audience and circumstances.	I						I,P					C
Demonstrate active listening in communications with others, including legal professionals and laypersons.							I,P					C

While this single learning outcome is highlighted here for purposes of illustration, all of the performance criteria for all of the outcomes should be combined in a single curriculum map. Having all of the information in one chart makes it easier to work with and provides a unified picture of all of the performance criteria and their treatment in the curriculum. If a school does not identify the underlying performance criteria when it first writes and adopts its learning outcomes, it will need to do so when it undertakes the curriculum-mapping process.

Once a school completes its mapping process,[36] it should have an accurate inventory of its curriculum that will allow it to make thoughtful decisions about the alignment between its outcomes and its course offerings and content. For example, if the mapping process for the communication outcome discussed above reveals that students are not introduced to the skill of speaking in a professional manner, then the curriculum or courses should be changed to introduce that skill. Similarly, if the mapping process were to indicate that students do not receive sufficient opportunities to practice and achieve competency in professional speaking skills, then those opportunities must be enhanced or increased. It is unrealistic to expect graduates to achieve competency in outcomes that are not sufficiently presented and addressed in the curriculum.

3. Developing an Assessment Plan for Institutional Learning Outcomes

a. Creating an Assessment Schedule

As explained in Chapter 1, it is not feasible or advisable to assess each institutional outcome every year. Assessment should be a sustainable process, and assessment leaders need time to engage in a meaningful review of the information that their process produces. Accordingly, the number of performance criteria that comprise an outcome and must be evaluated will affect how frequently each outcome can be assessed. Each of the six Washburn outcomes, for example, has three or four performance criteria that need to be assessed. Another factor to consider is the number and complexity of the assessments that will be reviewed in conjunction with each outcome and performance criterion. For example, the outcome regarding knowledge of the law and the legal system might be measured by using bar exam results, student work products like exams or papers, or some combination of both. If the outcome is measured primarily with bar exam results compiled and provided by state bar authorities, then it likely will take less time to assess.

Accordingly, it might be efficient to design a schedule in which multiple outcomes involving data that require less time to review (such as bar results or survey results) are scheduled for assessment during the same year. Other years might be scheduled for assessing a single outcome that involves data that are more time-consuming to review, such as student exams, papers, or skills performances. In this way, the assessment workload from year to year remains somewhat consistent. The table below provides a sample schedule for assessing the six Washburn outcomes:

Table 3.8: Sample Assessment Schedule

Learning Outcomes	2021–2022	2022–2023	2023–2024	2024–2025	2025–2026	2026–2027	2027–2028	2028–2029	2029–2030
Knowledge of the law and the legal system	X				X				X
Demonstrate analytical and problem-solving skills		X				X			
Communicate effectively		X				X			
Competency in legal practice skills			X				X		
Recognize and resolve dilemmas in an ethical and professional manner.				X				X	
Demonstrate knowledge of the importance of service to the profession and the community at large, both nationally and internationally.				X				X	

Under this schedule, each outcome is assessed every four years.

b. Deciding the Types and Number of Assessment Measures to Use

When assessment leaders are mapping the curriculum to determine the courses in which each performance criterion is addressed, they should use that review to also identify embedded assessments for measuring achievement of the criteria. The Washburn outcome for effective communication can be used to illustrate this principle. The outcome is divided into three performance criteria, which focus, respectively, on writing, speaking, and active listening. When mapping the curriculum to locate the courses in which these skills are addressed, assessment leaders should look for the assessments used in those courses that measure student achievement of these three skills. Once this information is gathered, it is helpful to put it into a grid, which then is incorporated into a school's written assessment plan. Depending on the courses that it offers and the assignments in those courses, the grid for Washburn's communication outcome and its performance criteria might look like this:

Table 3.9: Excerpt from Sample Assessment Plan[37]

Communication Outcome	Direct Assessment	Indirect Assessment
Write in clear, concise, well-organized, professional manner appropriate to audience and circumstances.	Seminar papers for upper-level writing requirement	Surveys or focus groups of employers rating graduates' writing skills
Speak in clear, concise, well-organized, professional manner appropriate to audience and circumstances.	Faculty evaluations of student performance in trial advocacy, clinical, or externship courses	Student self-evaluations of their speaking skills
Demonstrate active listening in communications with others, including legal professionals and laypersons.	Faculty evaluations of student performance in trial advocacy, clinical, or externship courses	Student self-evaluations of their active-listening skills

If the courses that address the performance criteria do not have any existing, embedded assessments that can be used to measure achievement of the criteria, then the faculty will need to create such assessments. They can choose to add assignments to the courses, or they can consider creating "add-on" assessments that are used solely for institutional assessment, such as surveys of students, alumni, or employers. Any assessments that are selected or created to measure students' learning regarding the performance criteria must meet the requirements of validity, reliability, and fairness explained in Chapter 1.

4. Collecting the Assessment Data for Institutional Outcomes

a. Determining the Amount of Data to Collect

After determining the number and types of assessment measures to use, assessment leaders will need to decide the number of students about whom they will collect evidence of learning. For institutional outcomes, this question is essentially whether to review assessments completed by every student in the cohort being assessed, or whether to review the work of a representative sample of students. There is no consensus among assessment experts about the number of students who should be included, and most experts agree that representative samples are acceptable. Some universities, however, may have policies requiring assessment of all students. Accordingly, law schools affiliated with universities should find out whether their parent universities have such a mandate.

Whether to collect data from all students or a representative sample likely will depend on class size. Some law schools have over 500 students in a graduating class,[38] while others have fewer than 100.[39] At schools with larger class sizes, it may not be feasible for assessment leaders to review assessments or rubrics for work completed by every student in the class. If it is not practicable to assess the performance of all students, then assessment of a representative sample of students is an acceptable alternative, so long as university policies permit the use of a sample. If assessment leaders decide to use a representative sample, they should use the largest sample size possible, since the error margin decreases as sample size increases.

b. Methods for Gathering the Assessment Data

As discussed in Chapter 1, assessment leaders should create a written process for collecting, storing, and protecting the assessment data. To assess institutional outcomes, leaders will gather data from many different courses across the entire curriculum. They also may collect results of surveys and focus groups that various administrative units of the law school conduct. A systematic process is crucial for managing this large amount of information.

To prevent assessment data from being lost or inadvertently destroyed, it is best to collect it as soon as it becomes available. Thus, assessment leaders need to determine when the embedded assessments they are relying on are administered, and they should work with the faculty administering those assessments to gather them, or the rubrics for them, as soon as they are completed. Likewise, assessment leaders should work with members of the school's administrative team to obtain any indirect assessments, such as LSSSE results or the results of other surveys, once they are provided to the school's administrative leaders.

The process for gathering assessment data also may be affected by university policies requiring law schools and other colleges within the university to submit annual assessment reports to the central administration. For example, the University of Arkansas at Little Rock William H. Bowen School of Law must submit an annual report to its university assessment office in mid-May of every year. Thus, the law school's assessment leaders must ensure that they collect all of the assessment data in time to analyze it and prepare the assessment report by the annual mid-May deadline.

5. Evaluating the Assessment Data for Institutional Learning Outcomes

To evaluate whether graduates are achieving institutional learning outcomes, assessment leaders must establish a definition of competence for each of the assessment instruments they use to measure the outcomes. Institutional assessment almost always uses local, criterion-referenced standards for measuring competency.[40]

As explained in Chapter 1, criterion-referenced standards are set forth in a rubric, which is simply a grid that breaks an assessment instrument down into its essential elements and then describes performance levels for each of those elements. Once assessment leaders have identified the assessments they will use to measure the performance criteria comprising each institutional outcome, they will need to create a rubric to evaluate the level of performance on those assessments. Rubrics usually are created to assess student work products like exams, presentations, seminar papers, reflection papers, or skills performances, but they should not be necessary for other types of instruments that do not need to be given a score, such as surveys or focus groups, or instruments that already have been scored, such as the bar exam.

The Washburn communication outcome described above can be used to illustrate the process for creating rubrics to assess the performance criteria for that outcome. The example assessment plan provided that two direct measures — seminar papers and faculty evaluations of student performance in trial advocacy, clinical, or externship courses — would be used to assess some of the performance criteria. In addition, the assessment plan provided that the following indirect measures would be used: surveys or focus groups of employers rating graduates' writing skills, student self-evaluations of their active-listening skills, and student self-evaluations of their speaking skills.

Based on these measures, assessment leaders would need to create a rubric to evaluate the seminar papers and additional rubrics to evaluate the student performances in the trial advocacy, clinical, or externship courses (depending on which performance the faculty decide upon as the measure). Rubrics should be created for any measure that is included in the assessment plan that needs to be scored.[41] In creating the rubrics, the assessment leaders also will need to set benchmark scores for each of them. As explained in Chapter 1, the benchmark score is the score that indicates minimum competence on the assessment that the rubric is used to evaluate. Thus, for the communication outcome, assessment leaders would need to set a benchmark score for the rubric used to evaluate the seminar papers, a benchmark score for the rubric used to evaluate students' speaking skills, and a benchmark score for the rubric used to evaluate students' active-listening skills.

The rubrics then should be provided to the professors who are teaching the courses in which the seminar papers are written and the courses in which the student performances occur. The professors teaching the courses should grade the seminar papers and the student performances according to their regular grading procedures. As the professors grade the seminar papers and student performances, they also should complete the rubrics for the institutional outcomes and then submit the completed rubrics to the assessment leaders as provided by the process for collecting assessment data. The assessment leaders then should review the completed rubrics to ascertain the information they provide for institutional assessment purposes.

Rubrics should not be needed for indirect assessments like survey results and student self-evaluations. Rather, assessment leaders should simply be able to tabulate the results of those assessments according to the scale set out in the instruments. For example, 30% of students might rate their active-listening skills as below average, 50% might rate their skills as average, and 20% might rate their skills as above average. While indirect assessments like student self-evaluations typically are not scored with a rubric, assessment leaders still should set benchmark scores for indirect assessments in order to make them meaningful. For example, if students are rating themselves in a self-evaluation using questions based on a five-point scale, assessment leaders might set an average of three as a minimum score to indicate that students are sufficiently confident in their skills. Assessment leaders should set a minimum benchmark score for each assessment instrument that they use.

As assessment leaders create rubrics and set benchmark scores for the assessment instruments, they also must establish the percentage of students who must meet the benchmark scores in order to state that the learning outcome has been achieved. As explained in Chapter 1, this percentage is known as the performance threshold. Using the example of the communication outcome, assessment leaders would identify the percentage of students who must achieve the minimum benchmark scores on the student self-evaluations and on the rubrics for the seminar papers, students' speaking skills, and students' active-listening skills. Assessment leaders should set a performance threshold for each assessment that they use in their assessment process.

6. Using Data to Improve Student Learning at the Institutional Level

Once a law school has applied its benchmark scores and performance thresholds to assess how well students currently are achieving the articulated outcomes, it then should "use that information to inform institutional efforts to increase the number of students attaining those results."[42] If the designated percentage of students is achieving the minimum competency scores on the assessment instruments, then a law school has good evidence that its program of legal education is effective. Assessment is a continuous process of improvement, though, so schools should not merely celebrate positive results and maintain the status quo. Rather, they should examine their positive results and try to determine why particular teaching methods, instructional designs, and assessments were effective and how they might be refined to produce even better learning in the future.

Conversely, if the designated percentage of students *does not* achieve the minimum competency scores on the assessment instruments, then assessment leaders should review the curriculum, pedagogy, and assessments to try to determine the reasons for the shortcomings. In particular, they should look for patterns of mistakes or common misunderstandings that reveal the areas of knowledge, skills, or values in which student learning fell short. Once the assessment leaders identify these areas, they should present these findings to the faculty as a whole, so the faculty can discuss possible corrective measures, such as refining the learning outcomes, revising the curriculum, or changing teaching methods or other instructional approaches.[43] Using some of the sample learning outcomes from Table 3.1, and possible assessment measures for those outcomes, the chart below provides examples of hypothetical assessment results and actions that could be taken to improve student learning:

Table 3.10: Example Learning Outcomes, Assessment Evidence, and Corrective Measures

Learning Outcomes	Evidence of Student Learning	Possible Corrective Measures
Graduates will demonstrate knowledge of the law and the legal system.	Assessment evidence: Most recent bar exam results show that graduates did not meet bar pass rate that school set for itself.	Add a required "mini" bar exam at the end of the first-year curriculum. Revise bar preparation program to increase focus on subjects in which graduates scored lower.
Graduates will demonstrate analytical and problem-solving skills.	Assessment evidence: Supervisor evaluations in clinic and externship courses reveal that requisite number of students did not meet minimum competency score when rated on problem-solving skills.	Assign in-class exercises in which students work in groups to devise a strategy to solve a client problem. Have a "rounds" discussion in which students share experiences of working to solve client problems and provide feedback and critiques to each other. Assign students to write a strategy for addressing a hypothetical client problem.
Graduates will communicate effectively.	Assessment evidence: Client letters written for a second-year trial advocacy simulation course reveal that the requisite number of students did not meet the minimum competency score for the letter-writing assignment.	Add a client-letter assignment in first-year research and writing course. Require students in the simulation course to submit a draft of the client letter, receive feedback on it from the instructor, and then submit the final draft.
Graduates will demonstrate competency in legal practice skills.	Assessment evidence: Supervisor evaluations from clinical and externship courses reveal that requisite number of students did not meet minimum competency score when rated on factual investigation skills.	Add a class on fact investigation to the trial advocacy simulation course that students take prior to clinic or externship. As part of the clinic or externship seminar, add an assignment requiring students to write a fact-investigation plan for a hypothetical client scenario.

Graduates will possess the requisite skills to recognize and resolve dilemmas in an ethical and professional manner.	Assessment evidence: Results of Multi-State Professional Responsibility Exam show that graduates did not meet MPRE pass rate that school set for itself.	Add a midterm examination to the required professional responsibility course. Assign more practice problems for students to complete in the required professional responsibility course.
Graduates will demonstrate knowledge of the importance of service to the profession and the community at large, both nationally and internationally.	Assessment evidence: Survey of graduates indicates that average scores are lower than minimum score school has set for its graduates.	Add a pro bono requirement as a condition of graduation. Implement an "across the curriculum" focus on the importance of service to the profession, with all professors addressing this topic in some way in their courses.

Thus, the institutional assessment process should reveal opportunities for making improvements in the curriculum, course design, or teaching methods that will enhance students' learning regarding the institutional outcomes.[44] Once faculty agree on the changes that should be made, assessment leaders should document them in the assessment plan, and those responsible for making the changes should implement them. The next time that a particular learning outcome is assessed, assessment leaders then will be able to compare the most recent results with prior results to determine if the changes have had a positive effect.

Endnotes

1. *See* ABA Section of Legal Educ. & Admissions to the Bar, Transition to and Implementation of the New Standards and Rules of Procedure for Approval of Law Schools at 2 (Aug. 2014), www.americanbar.org/content/dam/aba/administrative/legal_education_and_admissions_to_the_bar/governancedocuments/2014_august_transition_and_implementation_of_new_aba_standards_and_rules.pdf (last visited July 14, 2020).

2. ABA Standards and Rules of Procedure for Approval of Law Schools 2020–2021, Standard 301(a).

3. ABA Standards and Rules of Procedure for Approval of Law Schools 2020–2021, Standard 302.

4. As part of the accreditation process, ABA Standard 204 requires each law school to have a statement of its "mission and of its educational objectives in support of that mission[.]" ABA Standards and Rules of Procedure for Approval of Law Schools 2020–2021, Standard 204(b)(1).

5. Mary J. Allen, Assessing Academic Programs in Higher Education 29 (2004); *see also* Building on Best Practices: Transforming Legal Education in a Changing World 26 (Deborah Maranville et al., eds., 2015) (hereinafter "Building on Best Practices") (mission statements "can provide a sense of grounding principles and values, as well as institutional identity").

6. Building on Best Practices, *supra* note 5, at 26; Roy Stuckey et al., Best Practices for Legal Education: A Vision and a Road Map 49 (2007) (hereinafter "Best Practices for Legal Education") ("Outcomes should be consistent with and serve the school's mission") (*citing* Gregory S. Munro, Outcomes Assessment for Law Schools 94–95 (2000)); *see also, e.g.*, Mary E. Huba & Jann E. Freed, Learner-Centered Assessment on College Campuses: Shifting the Focus from Teaching to Learning 100 (2000) (schools' "missions reveal differences in educational values, and these differences are reflected in their learning outcomes.").

7. *Mission, Vision, and Values*, Gonzaga Univ. Sch. of Law, https://www.gonzaga.edu/school-of-law/about/mission-vision (last visited July 8, 2020).

8. *About Us*, Univ. of Ark. at Little Rock William H. Bowen Sch. of Law, http://www.ualr.edu/law/about-us/ (last visited July 8, 2020).

9. *Our Mission*, Washington Univ. in St. Louis Sch. of Law, https://law.wustl.edu/about/our-mission/ (last visited July 8, 2020).

10. ABA Section of Legal Education and Admissions to the Bar, Managing Director's Guidance Memo: Standards 301, 302, 314, and 315 at 4 (June 2015), www.americanbar.org/content/dam/aba/ administrative/legal_education_and_admissions_to_the_bar/governancedocuments/2015_learning_outcomes_guidance.pdf (last visited July 14, 2020).

11. Lori E. Shaw & Victoria L. VanZandt, Student Learning Outcomes and Law School Assessment: A Practical Guide to Measuring Institutional Effectiveness 62 (2015).

12. *Id.* Other terms for performance criteria include "assessment criteria," "performance elements," and "performance indicators." *Id.*

13. *Id.*; *see also, e.g.*, Anthony Niedwiecki, *Prepared for Practice? Developing a Comprehensive Assessment Plan for a Law School Professional Skills Program*, 50 U. San Fran. L. Rev. 245, 251 (2016) (recommending that schools "break down the learning outcomes for the law school into more narrow and specific outcomes that can more easily be placed into particular academic programs or specific courses.")

14. *Juris Doctor Degree*, Washburn Univ. Sch. of Law, https://washburnlaw.edu/academics/jurisdoctor/ (last visited July 8, 2020).

15. *See, e.g.*, Best Practices for Legal Education, *supra* note 6, at 49. ("A faculty should adopt an outcome only upon arriving at consensus after dialogue and deliberation. By this means, an outcome gains acceptance and permanence.").

16. Shaw & VanZandt, *supra* note 11, at 76.

17. William M. Sullivan et al., Educating Lawyers: Preparation for the Profession of Law (2007) (hereinafter "Educating Lawyers").

18. ABA Section of Legal Education and Admissions to the Bar, Legal Education and Professional Development—An Educational Continuum (Report of the Task Force on Law Schools and the Profession: Narrowing the Gap) (1992) (hereinafter "MacCrate Report").

19. Best Practices for Legal Education, *supra* note 6.

20. Marjorie M. Shultz & Sheldon Zedeck, *Predicting Lawyer Effectiveness: Broadening the Basis for Law School Admission Decisions*, 36 Law & Soc. Inquiry 620 (2011).

21. Alli Gerkman & Logan Cornett, Foundations for Practice: The Whole Lawyer and the Character Quotient (2016), iaals.du.edu/sites/default/files/documents/ publications/foundations_ for_ practice_whole_lawyer_quotient.pdf (last visited July 14, 2020) (hereinafter "Foundations for Practice").

22. EDUCATING LAWYERS, *supra* note 17, at 27–29.
23. MACCRATE REPORT, *supra* note 18, at 138–40.
24. *Id.* at 140–41.
25. BEST PRACTICES FOR LEGAL EDUCATION, *supra* note 6, at 65–91.
26. Shultz & Zedeck, *supra* note 20, at 630.
27. FOUNDATIONS FOR PRACTICE, *supra* note 21.
28. *Id.* at 30–34.
29. *Mission Statement*, INDIANA UNIV. ROBERT H. MCKINNEY SCH. OF LAW, https://mckinney-law.iu.edu/about/administration/mission-statement.html (last visited July 8, 2020).
30. *Learning Outcomes*, UNIV. OF THE PACIFIC MCGEORGE SCH. OF LAW, https://www.mcgeorge.edu/students/academics/jd-degree/learning-outcomes (last visited July 8, 2020).
31. *Learning Outcomes & Criteria*, THE UNIV. OF MEMPHIS CECIL C. HUMPHREYS SCH. OF LAW, https://www.memphis.edu/law/current-students/learningoutcomes.php (last visited July 8, 2020).
32. *Id.*
33. ABA STANDARDS AND RULES OF PROCEDURE FOR APPROVAL OF LAW SCHOOLS 2020–2021, STANDARD 315.
34. ABA STANDARDS AND RULES OF PROCEDURE FOR APPROVAL OF LAW SCHOOLS 2020–2021, STANDARD 315, INTERPRETATION 315-1.
35. *Id.*
36. For other examples of curriculum maps, see ANDREA SUSNIR FUNK, THE ART OF ASSESSMENT: MAKING OUTCOMES ASSESSMENT ACCESSIBLE, SUSTAINABLE, AND MEANINGFUL 124–31 (2017); Anthony Niedwiecki, *Law Schools and Learning Outcomes: Developing a Coherent, Cohesive, and Comprehensive Law School Curriculum*, 64 CLEV. ST. L. REV. 661, 699–702 (2016); Niedwiecki, *Prepared for Practice?*, *supra* note 13, at 281–85; SHAW & VAN ZANDT, *supra* note 11, at 205–12.
37. As an alternative to one direct measure and one indirect measure, assessment leaders might choose to review two direct measures.
38. 2019 Standard 509 Information Report, GEORGETOWN UNIV. SCH. OF LAW, https://www.law.georgetown.edu/wp-content/uploads/2019/12/2019_Standard_509_Report.pdf (last visited July 14, 2020).
39. 2019 Standard 509 Information Report, APPALACHIAN SCH. OF LAW, http://asl.edu/wp-content/uploads/2015/08/Std509InfoReport-2019.pdf (last visited July 14, 2020).
40. SHAW & VANZANDT, *supra* note 11, at 93; *see also* ALLEN, *supra* note 5, at 158 ("Faculty generally set their own standards when they do program assessment.").
41. *See* Andrea A. Curcio, *A Simple Low Cost Institutional Learning-Outcomes Assessment Process*, 67 J. LEGAL EDUC. 489, 493–501 (2018) (describing process for creating rubrics for assessing institutional learning outcomes); Melissa N. Henke, *When Your Plate Is Already Full: Efficient and Meaningful Outcomes Assessment for Busy Law Schools*, 71 MERCER L. REV. 529 (2020) (discussing how rubrics created for assignments in legal-writing courses were adapted for use in assessing institutional-learning outcomes related to writing).
42. Mary Crossley & Lu-in Wang, *Learning By Doing: An Experience With Outcomes Assessment*, 41 U. TOL. L. REV. 269, 271 (2010); *see also* Ruth Jones, *Assessment and Legal Education: What Is Assessment, and What the *# Does It Have to Do with the Challenges Facing Legal Education*, 45 MCGEORGE L. REV. 85, 102 (2013) ("The final stage of an on-going assessment process is analyzing and employing information in institutional decision-making.").
43. *See, e.g.*, SUSAN BRYANT ET AL., TRANSFORMING THE EDUCATION OF LAWYERS: THE THEORY AND PRACTICE OF CLINICAL PEDAGOGY 14 (2014) ("When the students fail to meet the goals, teachers can assess whether to refine or reject the goals or take a different approach to meeting them.").

44. Other actions that might be taken, depending on the shortcomings that the assessment evidence reveals, might include adding a course to the required curriculum, dividing first-year courses into smaller sections, adding a required third-year bar preparation course, revamping a Career Development Office, or increasing faculty development on teaching and assessment techniques. *See* FUNK, *supra* note 36, at 90. *See also, e.g.*, BUILDING ON BEST PRACTICES, *supra* note 5, at 30 (discussing potential curricular changes that can be made in response to assessment evidence).

CHAPTER FOUR

Individual Courses

Following the process explained in Chapter 1, this chapter discusses how to apply assessment principles within the context of individual courses.

1. Developing Course-Level Learning Outcomes

Course-level learning outcomes are the most narrowly tailored of all outcomes statements, as they focus specifically on "the important doctrine, theory, thinking skills, performance skills, and values that students should learn"[1] from completing an individual course within the J.D. curriculum. Teachers are responsible for establishing the learning outcomes for their individual courses, and their course outcomes should align with the school's broader institutional outcomes and any relevant program outcomes. In deciding on their course outcomes, teachers should focus on learning that endures and the knowledge, skills, and values that will be most important to graduates as they transition into and undertake the practice of law. To identify these attributes, teachers might consider what they hope students will retain from their courses.[2] Alternatively, a teacher might ask, "How do I want my students to be different at the end of the course?"[3] Course outcomes may target learning within one particular domain, such as the cognitive domain of content knowledge, or they may encompass learning that involves a combination of the cognitive, psychomotor, and affective domains.[4] Experts recommend establishing no more than three or four overarching learning outcomes per course.[5]

Course learning outcomes are most effective when they have the following three characteristics: (1) they "focus on the student — not the teacher"; (2) they "identify high-level intellectual activities or important values, not just knowledge"; and (3) they "are concrete and not abstract."[6] Outcomes are focused on students when they describe what students will be able to do or what values they will appreciate as a result of the course, rather than what a teacher will do or say in class.[7] While identifying specific topics to cover is a frequent concern in course design, "coverage" is not a student-centered learning outcome because "the attention is on the teacher and a march through topics without any unifying themes."[8] In a student-focused course, "the attention is on the students' learning."[9]

Course outcomes identify high-level intellectual activities or important values when they focus on "having students apply learning to new problems."[10] Some examples of higher-level skills in legal education include "drafting law-related documents, analyzing and solving legal problems, evaluating cases, [and] conducting client and witness interviews."[11] To complete these more-advanced tasks, students must apply foundational skills they have already learned, such as case reading, recall of legal doctrines, and knowledge of closed and open-ended questions.

Outcomes are concrete if they have sufficient clarity to allow a teacher to measure whether students have attained them.[12] Outcomes framed as students "appreciating" or "understanding" certain ideas or values typically lack such clarity because they do not include a way for students to demonstrate that appreciation or understanding.[13] Measuring attainment, however, "does not require statistical precision — good, better, and best are forms of measurement that, so long as the rater applies the same criteria consistently, can provide plenty of information about student learning and permit comparisons across time or classes."[14]

In drafting the actual language of their course outcomes, teachers should use the "stem-action verb-outcome" formula explained previously in Chapter 1.[15] Below are examples of learning outcomes from various types of courses that encompass learning in the cognitive, psychomotor, and affective domains:

Table 4.1: Examples of Learning Outcomes

Cognitive Domain: Knowledge/Content Outcomes
Civil Procedure Students will be able to identify the basic law and policy of civil procedure: jurisdiction, venue, pleading, discovery, motions, joinder, pretrial disposition, trial, appeal, preclusion, and choice of law.

Contracts[16]

Students will be able to articulate and apply, with accuracy, the law that governs:

1. Contract formation.
2. Defenses to lawsuits for breach of contract.
3. Remedies for breach of contract.
4. The parol evidence rule.
5. Contract interpretation.
6. Third party beneficiaries.
7. Assignment and delegation.

Criminal Law[17]

By the end of the course, students should be able to:

1. Explain and apply the theories of punishment.
2. Present and summarize cases in an effective and targeted manner.
3. Articulate basic principles of substantive criminal law as well as specific offenses
4. and defenses.
5. Spot issues and solve complex criminal law problems under New York law, the common law, and the Model Penal Code.
6. Craft arguments in support of and in opposition to criminal liability.

Employment Discrimination[18]

Students will be able to:

1. Demonstrate knowledge of the law and the legal system related to discrimination in the workplace.
2. Read, understand, and articulate the reach and limits of anti-discrimination statutes and regulations.
3. Differentiate between lawful employment practices and unlawful discriminatory employment practices.
4. Differentiate between intentional and unintentional discrimination and understand the procedural and remedial consequences of each.
5. Navigate the administrative process for bringing and responding to workplace discrimination claims.
6. Demonstrate an understanding of the organization, hierarchy, and relationships between federal, state, and local laws governing the employer/employee relationship.

Environmental Law

Students will learn the overview and most important details of the following:

1. Environmental law perspectives (personal, ecological, economic, philosophical).
2. Administrative agency actions and judicial review.
3. National Environmental Policy Act.
4. Clean Water Act.
5. Endangered Species Act.
6. Clean Air Act.

Externship Seminar

After completing the course, all students should be able to explain the concept of "equal access to justice" and the lawyer's professional duty to promote access to justice for all.

continued on next page

Table 4.1: Examples of Learning Outcomes *continued*

Real Estate Transactions

By the end of this course, students will have developed an approach to solve a real estate problem:

1. Substantively:
   a. Skills:
      i. Legal Problem Solving:
         1. Identify legal issues in simple and complex facts situations and real estate deals.
         2. Identify the relevant legal authority and policy.
         3. Identify potential alternatives to achieve the client's goals.
      ii. Legal Argument:
         1. Identify legal issues.
         2. Identify the relevant facts, authority, and policy.
         3. Distinguish unfavorable or unnecessary facts, authority, and policy.
      iii. Critical Thinking:
         1. Evaluate cases, statutes, arguments, documents, and attorneys' actions on their effects on the clients, the real estate system, and society.
         2. Evaluate the strategy and ethics of applying different approaches to solving the real estate problem.
         3. Challenge assumptions made by judges, legislatures, attorneys, students, professors, themselves.
   b. Content:
      i. Basics of broker contracts, broker duties, conditions of the property of sale, closing documents, remedies, allocating title risks, land descriptions, public records, title products, mortgages and junior mortgages, and foreclosures.

Trusts and Estates

Students will be able to read and analyze state and uniform statutes concerning intestacy, wills, and trusts.

Psychomotor Domain: Lawyering Skills Outcomes

Civil Procedure

Students will be able to effectively:

1. Draft a complaint that complies with the Federal Rules of Civil Procedure and applicable case law.
2. Draft discovery documents that comply with the Federal Rules of Civil Procedure and applicable case law.
3. Make an oral argument on a pretrial motion.

Contracts

Students will be able to draft effective versions of the following common contract terms: liquidated damages clause, merger clause, express condition, force majeure clause, clause making timely performance an express condition.

Criminal Law

By the end of the course, students should be able to interview police officers, witnesses, and clients to determine appropriate criminal charges.

Employment Discrimination

Students will be able to:

1. Understand how workplace dynamics and human dimensions impact the commencement and resolution of workplace discrimination allegations.
2. Advocate on behalf of employees and employers.
3. Identify and apply the controlling legal (and non-legal) principles in case-based scenarios to counsel clients and resolve workplace disputes.
4. Where controlling legal principles are indeterminate, use analogical reasoning, policy, and practical considerations to identify possible legal rules to predict and explain how case-based scenarios would likely be resolved.
5. Understand and apply basic skills associated with fact investigation necessary to advise clients in employment-related matters.
6. Speak in a clear, concise, well-organized, professional manner that is appropriate to the audience and the circumstances.
7. Develop team-based problem-solving techniques by, among other things, engaging in active listening and clear communication with other team members in the context of group research projects.

Environmental Law

Students will:

1. Refine statutory analysis skills by applying these elements of statutory analysis in the context of environmental disputes: standard of review, statutory language, statutory purpose and policy, overall statutory scheme, legislative history, regulations applying the statute, cases interpreting the statute.
2. Apply key elements of the Clean Water Act, Clean Air Act, Endangered Species Act, and National Environmental Policy Act to real-life problems.

Externship Seminar

After completing the course, all students should be able to engage effectively in the skill of reflection to learn from their experiences.

Trusts and Estates

Students will be able to:

1. Know and apply common-law rules to estate planning situations.
2. Offer advice to clients on how to accomplish estate planning goals.
3. Draft documents that future clients will need to implement their estate plan.

Affective Domain: Professional Values Outcomes

Civil Procedure

Students will:

1. Demonstrate respect for students, staff, and faculty.
2. Develop an attitude of cooperation with students, faculty, lawyers, judges.
3. Identify ethical issues involved in civil dispute resolution.
4. Begin to formulate his or her version of the moral lawyer.
5. Demonstrate honesty, reliability, responsibility, judgment, self-motivation, hard work, and critical self-reflection.

continued on next page

Table 4.1: Examples of Learning Outcomes *continued*

Employment Discrimination

Students will be able to identify and resolve some common ethical and professionalism issues arising in the practice of employment discrimination law.

Externship Seminar

After completing the course, all students should be able to:

1. Identify fundamental values of the legal profession and recognize the presence or absence of those values in practice situations.
2. Explain the concept of a "professional identity," facets of their own professional identity, and common challenges to a lawyer's professional identity.

Real Estate Transactions

Personal: Students will

a. Examine their own reliability, responsibility, judgment, self-motivation, hard work, and critical self-reflection.
b. Learn about themselves as learners.
c. Make strides toward being self-directed learners.
d. Really ponder the question: am I ready to put in the time this career demands.

Ethical: Students will

a. Demonstrate respect for students, staff, and faculty.
b. Develop an attitude of cooperation with students, faculty, lawyers, and judges.
c. Develop ongoing investment and monitoring of professional development.
d. Identify ethical issues involved in real-estate issues.

Once established, course learning outcomes should be communicated to students. Making students aware of the course outcomes has many benefits, including creating interest in the instruction, establishing the teacher's expectations for the students' learning, allowing students to monitor and direct their own learning, and allowing students to communicate what they have learned to others, such as employers.[19] To achieve these benefits, the ABA requires teachers to include their course learning outcomes in their syllabi.[20]

2. Ensuring Alignment and Developing a Plan for Course-Level Assessment

a. Aligning Course Content and Learning Activities with Course Outcomes

Once teachers have identified their course-level learning outcomes, they should create an assessment plan that includes all the outcomes, learning activities, and assessment measures for the course. "The primary factor teachers should consider when choosing teaching and learning methods is congruence—select methods appropriate to help students achieve learning objectives."[21] Selecting methods and activities typically will involve a process of reduction, as teachers should brainstorm a broad list of options and then examine the course content, teaching methods, and learning activities to ensure that they align with the learning outcomes and "do not devolve to cramming in as many topics and activities as possible."[22] Educational experts recognize that creating an assessment plan right after articulating learning outcomes ensures that syllabi, class sessions, and assessment instruments are congruent with the outcomes.[23]

Various types of teaching and learning methods are more effective or less effective for particular types of outcomes, and no single method is appropriate for every kind of learning outcome.[24] For example, the Socratic/case-dialogue method can be an effective way for students to learn legal doctrine and analytical skills. Class discussions can be an appropriate method for achieving learning outcomes relating to thinking, analysis, attitudes, and values. Simulations and role-plays can help students integrate doctrine, theory, and practice, making them useful methods for teaching practice skills like interviewing, counseling, negotiation, oral advocacy, teamwork, and trial skills. Writing exercises can help students learn substantive law, develop thinking skills, hone communication skills, and reflect on their values. Experiential-learning methods can help students learn substantive law and practice skills, as well as foster development of professional attitudes, values, and habits.[25] The key in selecting teaching and learning methods is to ensure that they align with the course learning outcomes and provide opportunities for students to develop the knowledge, skills, and values that the outcomes encompass.[26]

Once teachers have selected their learning outcomes and their learning activities, they should include them in a written assessment plan. The assessment plan might take the form of a chart, such as the one below:

Table 4.2: Template for Assessment Plan

Course Learning Outcomes	Learning Activities for Each Outcome	Assessment Measure(s) for Each Outcome
Course Outcome 1		
Course Outcome 2		
Course Outcome 3		
Course Outcome 4		

The selection of assessment measures to include in the plan is discussed below.

b. Decide the Type and Number of Assessment Measures to Use: Direct, Indirect, or Both

Teachers also must decide whether they will use direct measures, indirect measures, or some combination of both to evaluate student achievement of their course learning outcomes. Examples of direct assessments that teachers might use include quizzes, mid-term exams, drafting assignments, essays, skills performances, presentations, final exams, and final papers. Forms of indirect assessment include students' self-evaluations of their development of identified knowledge, skills, and values, as well as students' peer assessments of one another's learning. In selecting the types of assessments, teachers should always keep in mind that the assessments should align with the course's stated learning outcomes and actually measure the knowledge, skills, and values that teachers intend for the students to learn. Just as at the institutional level, assessments at the course level must be valid, reliable, and fair.

To obtain the most comprehensive and accurate picture of student ability, teachers should use more than one assessment instrument and also different types of instruments to measure student learning.[27] Multiple measures are recommended because no single assessment instrument, even if it is very well-designed and executed, "can provide the comprehensive view needed to determine whether a criterion is being achieved."[28] Students may perform better on one type of assessment than another, so using multiple assessments of different types provides students with more opportunities to demonstrate their learning and produces a more accurate picture of whether they are achieving learning outcomes.[29] Using multiple measures also enhances credibility in the assessment process by allowing faculty to compare results from multiple methods.[30] When multiple methods of assessment produce similar findings, greater confidence may be placed in the results.[31]

In deciding how many assessments are necessary to obtain an accurate picture of students' learning, teachers should consider the time demands of their students' other courses. For example, should a teacher give a mid-term in her course the same week that students must submit the first draft of their appellate brief in their required legal-writing course? Coordination with other faculty members will be necessary to make determinations like this. In addition, teachers should consider their own capacity to evaluate multiple assessments over the course of the semester and provide timely feedback on them. No useful purpose is accomplished by administering assessments that the teacher does not have sufficient time to review and critique.

c. Decide Whether Assessments Will Be Formative, Summative, or Both

In selecting the direct and indirect measures to use in their courses, teachers also should consider whether the purpose of the assessment instrument is formative or summative.[32] An assessment is formative if its primary purpose is to provide feedback to students and faculty on student performance. This feedback is important because it provides students opportunities to identify weaknesses in their performance and make improvements before a final evaluation is made. Formative assessments can include in-class activities like clicker questions, multiple-choice questions, or polls that give teachers "real-time" information on student learning and do not require time outside of class to grade.

Summative assessments, on the other hand, are used for assigning a grade or otherwise indicating a student's level of achievement at the end of a course or unit of study. "In contrast to formative evaluation, which looks forward to ways in which students might continue to learn, *summative* evaluation looks back and judges how much students have learned."[33] The table below summarizes the primary differences between formative and summative assessments:[34]

Table 4.3: Formative and Summative Assessment

What	When	Where	Why	How
Formative Assessment	Ongoing throughout the course → Looks forward	In class or outside of class	Provides feedback to students (to improve learning) and faculty (to improve teaching) regarding student progress in meeting course outcomes	Graded or ungraded assignments, exercises, or other assessment tools
Summative Assessment	At the end of the course or unit ← Looks back	In class or outside of class	Measures what students have learned and whether they have met course outcomes	Generally, graded final assignments, projects, or exams

Teachers should use both formative and summative assessment methods.[35] Indeed, a single assessment instrument can serve both formative and summative purposes. A mid-term examination is an example of an assessment that is both formative and summative. The mid-term is summative because it evaluates students' learning of the knowledge, skills, and values that the course has addressed up until the time of the examination. The mid-term also is formative because the teacher's feedback on the exam should identify students' weaknesses in the areas that were tested and ways that students can improve in those areas during the remainder of the semester.

d. Examples of Assessment Plans for Various Types of Courses

Once faculty have decided the types and number of assessments that they will administer, and whether those assessments will be summative, formative, or both, they can add them to their written assessment plan. Examples of sample assessment plans for various types of courses are set out below:

Table 4.4: Sample Assessment Plan for Civil Procedure Course

Civil Procedure

Course Learning Outcomes	Learning Activities For Each Outcome	Assessment Measure(s) For Each Outcome
Content Students will be able to identify the basic law and policy of civil procedure: jurisdiction, venue, pleading, discovery, motions, joinder, pretrial disposition, trial, preclusion, and choice of law.	Reading and problem assignments. Large- and small-group class discussion. Class exercises and problem solving. Individual and group flow chart construction.	• Feedback in class on problems • Ungraded quizzes and practice exams • Graded mid-term exam • Graded final exam
Skills 1. Case Analysis. Students will master the following skills: • Identification of the elements of a reported opinion: procedural facts, issue, holding, rationale, legal rules, policy. • Synthesis of a line of related opinions. 2. Statutory Analysis. Students will master the elements of statutory analysis: • Close reading of the words of the statute. • Identifying the purpose of the statute. • Fitting the statute into the broader statutory scheme. • Using legislative history. • Using cases interpreting the statute. 3. Legal Problem Solving. Students will master these problem-solving skills: • Identifying legal issues in simple and complex fact situations. • Identifying the relevant legal authority and policy. • Identifying potential alternatives to achieve the client's goals. 4. Legal Argument. Students will be able to make effective legal arguments: • Identifying the legal issues. • Identifying the relevant facts, authority, and policy. • Supporting the client's position with facts, authority, and policy. • Distinguishing unfavorable facts, authority, and policy.	For case analysis, statutory analysis, legal problem solving, legal argument, and critical thinking: Reading and problem assignments. Large- and small-group class discussion. Class exercises and problem solving. Individual and group flow chart construction.	For case analysis, statutory analysis, legal problem solving, legal argument, and critical thinking: • Feedback in class on problems and flow charts • Ungraded quizzes and practice exams • Graded mid-term exam • Graded final exam

continued on next page

Table 4.4: Sample Assessment Plan for Civil Procedure Course
continued

Skills		
5. Legal Drafting. Students will draft legal documents that communicate clearly, are persuasive, and comply with applicable rules. 6. Critical Thinking. Students will: • Evaluate cases, statutes, arguments, documents, and attorneys' actions and their effects on (1) clients, (2) the civil litigation system, and (3) society. • Challenge assumptions made by judges, legislators, attorneys, students, professors, and themselves.	For legal drafting: Review sample litigation documents. Individual and small group drafting assignments of pleading and discovery documents.	For legal drafting: • In class feedback on draft documents • Graded final documents with written feedback
7. Lawyering Skills. Students will demonstrate basic lawyering skills, such as complaint drafting and oral argument.	For oral argument skills: Reading assignment and class discussion. In-class demonstration of oral arguments. Video of sample oral arguments. Individual oral arguments.	For oral argument skills: • Oral feedback on in-class demonstrations • For individual oral arguments outside of class—video feedback, oral feedback, written feedback from peers
Values Students will: • Demonstrate respect for students, staff, and faculty. • Develop an attitude of cooperation with students, faculty, lawyers, judges. • Understand the multiple roles of a lawyer in civil dispute resolution. • Identify ethical issues involved in civil dispute resolution. • Begin to formulate his or her version of the moral lawyer. • Demonstrate honesty, reliability, responsibility, judgment, self-motivation, hard work, and critical self-reflection.	Reading assignments. Large- and small-group class discussion. Court field trip. Lawyer interview. Reflection papers.	• Oral feedback on class discussions • Written feedback on reflection papers

Table 4.5: Sample Assessment Plan for Environmental Law Course

Environmental Law

Course Learning Outcomes	Learning Activities For Each Outcome	Assessment Measure(s) For Each Outcome
Content Students will learn the overview and most important details of the following: • Environmental Law Perspectives (personal, ecological, economic, philosophical). • Administrative agency actions and judicial review. • National Environmental Policy Act (NEPA). • Clean Water Act (CWA). • Endangered Species Act (ESA). • Clean Air Act (CAA).	Reading and problem assignments. Large- and small-group class discussion. Class exercises and problem solving. CALI exercises. Reviewing sample documents related to administrative practice, NEPA, CWA, ESA, CAA.	• Feedback in class on problems • Feedback via CALI exercises • Ungraded quizzes and practice exams • Graded final exam
Skills Students will: • Refine statutory analysis skills through standard of review, statutory language, statutory purpose and policy, overall statutory scheme, legislative history, regulations applying the statute, cases interpreting the statute. • Analyze problems involving environmental law in real life.	For statutory analysis skills: Identify statutory analysis elements in cases. Large and small group discussion. Practice statutory analysis via problems and exercises. For environmental law in real life: Research paper analyzing real-life environmental law problem. Field trip. Lawyer interview. Reviewing sample documents. Reflection papers.	For statutory analysis skills: • Feedback on class discussions, exercises, and problems • Statutory analysis component of ungraded practice exam • Statutory analysis component of graded final exam For environmental law in real life: • Written feedback on draft research paper • Written feedback on reflection papers • Graded final research paper

Table 4.6: Sample Assessment Plan for Externship Course

Externship Course

Course Learning Outcomes	Learning Activities For Each Outcome	Assessment Measure(s) For Each Outcome
Engage effectively in the skill of reflection to learn from their experiences.	Reading assignments and class discussion on reflection Weekly journal assignments In-class exercise applying journal rubric to sample journal	Weekly journals Mid-semester self-evaluation Final reflective essay
Identify fundamental values of the legal profession and recognize the presence or absence of those values in practice situations.	Reading assignments and class discussions on professional values In-class rounds discussion and student presentations on professional values	Weekly journals In-class rounds discussion and student presentations on professional values Final reflective essay Supervisor evaluation
Explain the concept of a "professional identity," facets of their own professional identity, and common challenges to a lawyer's professional identity.	Reading assignments and class discussions on professional identity In-class "core values" exercise presenting a professional-identity challenge	Final reflective essay Supervisor evaluation
Explain the concept of "equal access to justice" and the lawyer's professional duty to promote access to justice for all.	Reading assignments and class discussions on equal access to justice In-class exercise designing a pro bono program for a hypothetical law firm	Guided journal entry on the topic of pro bono Final reflective essay

Table 4.7: Sample Assessment Plan for Real Estate Transactions Course

Real Estate Transactions

Course Learning Outcomes	Learning Activities for Each Outcome	Assessment Measure(s) for Each Outcome
Legal Problem Solving • Identify legal issues in simple and complex facts situations and real estate deals. • Identify the relevant legal authority and policy. • Identify potential alternatives to achieve the client's goals.	Group discussions and presentations on cases assigned. For example, if the students read cases on broker liability, they would work in groups to answer these questions, and then the groups would present their answers.	Weekly TWEN quizzes and feedback on presentations.

Legal Argument • Identify legal issues. • Identify the relevant facts, authority, and policy. • Distinguish unfavorable or unnecessary facts, authority, and policy.	Group discussions and presentations on cases assigned. For example, if the students read cases on broker liability, they would work in groups to answer these questions, and then the groups would present their answers.	Weekly TWEN quizzes and feedback on presentations.
Critical Thinking • Evaluate cases, statutes, arguments, documents, and attorney's actions and their effects on the clients, the real estate system, and society. • Evaluate the strategy and ethics of applying different approaches to solving the real estate problem. • Challenge assumptions made by judges, legislatures, attorneys, students, professors, themselves.	Students take time in class and out of class to respond to questions/prompts regarding ethics, different solutions, and court assumptions. Students write reflective journals on these subjects.	Feedback provided on journals and formal responses.
Content Knowledge • Basics of broker contracts, broker duties, conditions of the property of sale, closing documents, remedies, allocating title risks, land descriptions, public records, title products, mortgages and junior mortgages, and foreclosures.	Daily classroom activities focus on content. These activities include outline creation, flow chart creation, test question creation, practice quizzes, and presentations.	Weekly TWEN quizzes
Personal and Ethical Students will: • Examine their own reliability, responsibility, judgment, self-motivation, hard work, and critical self-reflection. • Learn about themselves as learners. • Make strides to being self-directed learners. • Really ponder the question: am I ready to put in the time this career demands. Students will: • Demonstrate respect for students, staff, and faculty. • Develop an attitude of cooperation with students, faculty, lawyers, and judges. • Develop ongoing investment and monitoring of professional development. • Identify ethical issues involved in real-estate issues.	Students respond to prompts in their journals which deal with how they might deal with ethical issues, directing their own career, handling workplace situations, etc.	Teacher feedback on journals

Table 4.8: Sample Assessment Plan for Trusts and Estates Course

Trusts and Estates

Course Learning Outcomes	Learning Activities For Each Outcome	Assessment Measure(s) For Each Outcome
Read and analyze state and uniform statutes concerning intestacy, wills, and trusts.	Readings and class discussion. Charts to complete re: statutory provisions. Multiple-choice questions and weekly writing assignments.	Self-check of answers in chart by comparing to answer key. Teacher feedback on writing assignments. Multiple-choice feedback from learning management system.
Know and apply common-law rules to estate planning situations.	Readings and class discussions about common-law rules.	Socratic class discussions. Weekly quizzes on substantive common law. Sample exam essay questions with feedback from teacher.
Offer advice to clients on how to accomplish estate-planning goals.	Reading assignments and class discussion on working with clients.	Assignments to write client letters in various estate-planning situations—avoiding will contests, creating a charitable trust.
Draft documents that future clients will need to implement their estate plan.	Readings and class discussions on relevant documents.	Writing assignments to create a probate inventory form, a will, and a provision in a discretionary trust.

3. Collecting the Assessment Data

Collecting the assessment data at the course level should not be difficult. The data will consist of all the assessment instruments that the teacher has administered during the course, and the data should all be within the teacher's possession and control. The teacher should simply create a process for organizing and maintaining all of the assessments, whether using paper files, an Excel spreadsheet, or an electronic course-management system such as Canvas, Blackboard, or TWEN. In addition, it should be feasible to assess the learning of all the students in an individual course, so there should be no need to use representative samples for course-level assessment.

4. Evaluating the Assessment Data

a. Deciding the Standard for Measuring Student Performance

As explained in Chapter 1, various standards exist for measuring student performance, including norm-referenced standards and criterion-referenced standards.[36] A norm-referenced standard evaluates student performance in relation to the performance of all the students in a course and ranks students based on how they perform in comparison to each other, usually for the purposes of satisfying a grade curve. It does not require students to meet an absolute standard of achievement, such as the course learning outcomes. Thus, an "A" on a norm-referenced assessment does not indicate that a student achieved mastery of a course's learning outcomes; rather, it "means the student's performance ranked at the top of the class, without regard to whether this student or the class as a whole performed at an excellent, mediocre, or poor level."[37]

A criterion-referenced standard, in contrast, measures student competency in relation to established levels of performance derived from the course's learning outcomes and evaluates how well students achieved those outcomes. Scores are based on students' individual performance in relation to these specific standards, and there is no curve or pre-set distribution of scores. Thus, an "A" on a criterion-referenced assessment "means the student demonstrated excellent mastery of the course concepts and skills, without regard to how other students did."[38]

Teachers should use criterion-referenced standards for course-level assessment because these standards measure whether students have achieved the course learning outcomes, which is the fundamental purpose of assessment. Since norm-referenced standards do not measure student performance in this manner, they are inappropriate for an assessment process. Thus, teachers will need to develop criterion-referenced standards for measuring attainment of their course learning outcomes. This assessment process will be separate and apart from any procedure that teachers must follow to comply with a school-mandated curve for determining the final grades in a course.

As explained in Chapter 1, criterion-referenced standards generally are measured using rubrics, which are detailed written criteria that describe what students should learn and how they will be evaluated. Professor Sophie Sparrow has explained the benefits that rubrics provide to both teachers and students:

> To develop explicit criteria that will be distributed to students in writing, we must necessarily be clear about what we expect students to learn; we must identify the core skills and knowledge that are necessary to be competent or proficient in the particular area of law. These are fundamental questions focusing not on what we will "cover" in class and how we will fill up the time, but on what we want students to take away with them, hold on to, and return to in the future.[39]

Rubrics also increase fairness in assessment because they cause teachers to evaluate each assignment according to the same criteria, thus creating consistency in scoring.[40]

A rubric can be created for any direct assessment that a teacher uses in a doctrinal, skills, or experiential course. Below are examples, respectively, of rubrics for evaluating a complaint drafted for a civil procedure course,[41] an essay exam in a property course,[42] and a journal in an externship course. Other rubric examples are available on the website of the Institute for Law Teaching and Learning at www.lawteaching.org.

Rubric for Complaint in Civil Procedure

Exemplary: Advanced Work for 1L at this Time in the Course—On a Job the Work Would Need Very Little Revision for a Supervising Attorney to Use	Competent: Proficient Work for a 1L at this Time in the Course—On a Job the Work Would Need to Be Revised with Input from a Supervising Attorney	Developing: Work Needs Additional Content or Skills to be Competent—On a Job the Work Would Not Be Helpful and the Supervising Attorney Would Need to Start Over
Correctly joined and named all appropriate parties	Missed one appropriate party (or did not correctly name a party)	Missed more than one appropriate party and/or did not correctly name an appropriate party
Correctly identified the proper court and signed complaint per Rule 11	Correctly identified the proper court and signed complaint per Rule 11	Did not correctly name the appropriate court or failed to sign per Rule 11
Correctly pled the necessary facts to establish jurisdiction and identified the jurisdictional basis	Correctly pled the necessary facts to establish jurisdiction and identified the jurisdictional basis	Did not plead the necessary facts to establish jurisdiction and/or correctly identify jurisdictional basis
Identified all potentially viable claims against each party and did not have any claims that were not viable (per Rule 11)	Identified all but one potentially viable claim against each party; no claims that were not potentially viable (per Rule 11)	Did not identify two or more potentially viable claims and/or had claims that were not potentially viable (per Rule 11)
Pled all necessary facts to support each element of each claim and did not plead immaterial facts	Pled most necessary facts to support each element of each claim and pled few, if any, immaterial facts	Did not plead many facts necessary to support each element of each claim and/or pled many immaterial or unnecessary facts
Pled all necessary elements of each potential claim	Missed one or two necessary elements in pleading claims	Did not plead a number of elements necessary for each claim
Had sound/logical/tactical reasons why excluded parties/claims	Had sound/logical/tactical reasons why excluded parties/claims	Failed to identify valid reasons for excluding parties/claims, or reasons weren't based upon sound legal/tactical grounds
Clearly and logically organized and easy to follow; allegations were concise—whenever possible, allegations contained only one fact per allegation	Generally clearly and logically organized; allegations were generally concise	Claims and facts organized in a way that made it difficult to follow the story of what happened; allegations often contained multiple facts per allegation
No grammatical, typographical, or spelling errors—presentation professional	One or two grammatical, typographical, or spelling errors	Numerous grammatical, spelling, or other typographical errors

Figure 4.1: Rubric for Civil Complaint

Figure 4.2: Rubric for Essay Exam

Rubric for Essay Exam in Property

Substance:

	Ideal	Generally Earns All Available Points	Generally Earns 50% of Available Points	Earns 0 Points
Issue	Issue as set forth is **dispositive** for overall question being asked. Issue is **clearly stated** in a way that appropriately **links it to the specific facts** of the question.	Issue as set forth is **relevant** to overall question being asked. Issue is **clearly stated**.	Issue as set forth is **relevant** to overall question being asked, but not **clearly stated**.	Issue as set forth is **not relevant** to overall question being asked, OR **No issue set forth at all**.
Rule	**Dispositive portions of relevant rule** are stated fully as given in outline (or are phrased in a **legally equivalent** way). **Non-dispositive portions** of rule (or relevant but non-dispositive rules) stated as **succinctly** as possible. **Irrelevant rules are not mentioned at all.** **Rules** relied upon are **stated in a way that specifically applies to the facts** of the exam question.	**Relevant rule** for stated issue is **set forth fully** as given in outline (or rephrased in a **legally equivalent** way).	**Relevant rule** for stated issue is set forth, **but** is either **not stated fully** as given in outline, **or is partially incorrect**, or is rephrased in a way that is not legally equivalent.	**Wrong rule** set forth for stated issue, **OR** **Correct rule** set forth for stated issue but is stated **with such significant errors or omissions** that it functionally amounts to the wrong rule, **OR** **No rule** stated at all.

Application/ Analysis	**All relevant facts** in fact pattern are utilized. **No irrelevant facts** are mentioned. Facts used are **clearly linked to the applicable elements** or sub-rules of the stated rule. Thorough demonstration of **how each stated fact tends to prove or disprove the associated element** or sub-rule of the applicable rule.	**Many** of the relevant available facts are utilized. **Few** irrelevant facts are mentioned. Facts are **linked to applicable elements** or sub-rules of stated rule, but either not done with great clarity **OR** done inconsistently. Significant demonstration of **how each stated fact tends to prove or disprove the associated element** or sub-rule, **OR** thorough showing but for only some facts.	At least **some** relevant available facts are utilized for at least some elements and/ or **significant number** of irrelevant facts included. At least some demonstration of how at least some of the relevant available facts tend to prove or disprove at least some of the associated elements or sub-rules of the applicable rule.	**No** facts stated, **OR** Facts set forth in l**aundry-list style**, with **no linkage** to the applicable elements or sub-rules of the stated rule, **OR** **Some efforts** to use facts to prove or disprove elements or sub-rules of applicable rule, **but so poorly or wrongly done as to amount to no real analysis**.
Conclusion	Conclusion is **clearly stated** in a way that appropriately **links it to the stated rule and the ensuing analysis**.	Conclusion is **clearly stated**.	Conclusion is **stated**.	**No conclusion**.

continued on next spread

Figure 4.2: Rubric for Essay Exam *continued*

Organization and Writing:	Earns 80–100% of Available Points	Earns 50–80% of Available Points	Earns 25–50% of Available Points	Earns 0–25% of Available Points
Organization	Coherent essay structure for entire answer. Good flow from paragraph to paragraph (or from issue to issue), causing no significant reader confusion. Individual sections or paragraphs also well-organized and coherent. Little or no need to re-read earlier portions of answer to understand argument and award all substantive points earned.	Every paragraph, issue, or other portion of an answer is coherent, but overall answer either somewhat lacking in flow or flow is somewhat confused or causes some reader confusion. Some need to re-read earlier portions to understand argument and award all substantive points earned.	Some portions very well-organized while others are not, OR All portions moderately well-organized but overall answer includes some fractured discussion or some digression and/or causes substantial reader confusion. More than a little need to re-read earlier portions to understand argument and award all substantive points earned.	Overall organization is fractured. Overall answer difficult to read without significant reader confusion. Individual sections and/or paragraphs may also be fractured. Significant re-reading of earlier portions required to make any sense of argument; substantive points earned difficult to identify.

Quality of Writing	Consistently follows format requested in the call of the question. Overall essay shows a sense of proportion and balance that signifies a substantial understanding of the relative importance of the various issues discussed. Dispositive issues are treated thoroughly; relevant issues are given some attention; irrelevant issues are not discussed. Sentences are consistently well-crafted in a highly readable style. Traditional, moderately formal rules of English grammar are consistently followed. Appropriate legal diction employed. Jargon eschewed.	Generally follows format requested in the call of the question. Overall essay shows some sense of proportion and balance that signifies some understanding of the relative importance of the various issues discussed. Dispositive issues are treated thoroughly, most relevant issues are given some (but not too much) attention, and very few irrelevant issues are discussed at all (and none extensively), **OR** some effort made to distinguish relevant importance of issues, but with some misidentification of dispositive issues. Consistent use of complete sentences with very few (or no) incomplete sentences (fragments) or run-ons. Traditional, moderately formal rules of English grammar generally followed.	Significantly departs from format requested in the call of the question. All issues treated with the same degree of detail, **OR** significant errors made in identifying dispositive issues. Moderately consistent use of complete sentences. More than a few incomplete sentences (fragments) or run-ons. Informal English grammar utilized (but generally correctly) **OR** appropriate grammar attempted but with significant or frequent errors in application.	Ignores the format requested in the call of the question. Treatment of most or all issues does not correlate to their relative importance. Repeated use of incomplete sentences (fragments) or run-ons. Other significant errors appear with sufficient frequency to produce an essay that is, overall, of unacceptable grammatical quality.

Rubric for Journal in Externship Course

Task Description:	Students shall write a two-page journal entry for each work week reflecting on their learning from their externship experiences.		
	Needs Work	**Competent**	**Excellent**
Professionalism: Punctuality _______4	□ Submitted late. ***(0 pts)***	□ Submitted by deadline or requested extension for good cause prior to deadline. ***(4 pts)***	
Professionalism: Compliance w/ Instructions _______6	□ Less than two full pages. ***(0 pts)*** □ Doesn't list week for which written. ***(0 pts)***	□ Two full pages in length. ***(3 pts)*** □ Lists week for which written. ***(3 pts)***	
Introspection _______10	□ Journal does not include self-examination of writer's own thoughts and feelings in response to an externship experience or reading; for example, it merely describes an experience or reading in narrative form, summarizes work performed, or summarizes case law or legal analysis from an externship work product.***(0–5 pts)***	□ Journal explores an externship experience or reading with some self-examination of writer's own thoughts and feelings in response to the experience or reading. It has sufficient depth to allow teacher to respond with comments or questions that prompt additional insight or thought.***(6–8 pts)***	□ Journal explores an externship experience or reading with meaningful self-examination of writer's own thoughts and feelings in response to the experience or reading. Writer thinks deeply about issues raised, insights gained, or changes in writer's knowledge, values, or beliefs in response to the experience or reading.***(9–10 pts)***

Figure 4.3: Rubric for Externship Journal

Quality of Reflection ________**15**	□ Journal lacks "reflection on action"; writer makes no connections between prior knowledge and new knowledge gained from externship experience, reading assignment, or class discussion. □ Journal lacks complexity; it considers experiences from only the writer's perspective. □ Journal lacks self-assessment; it does not consider writer's own strengths and weaknesses. ***(0–8 pts)***	□ Journal shows some "reflection on action"; writer makes some connections between prior knowledge and new knowledge gained from externship experience, reading assignment, or class discussion. □ Journal shows some complexity; writer shows awareness of others' perspectives but does not consider experiences from their perspectives. □ Journal shows some self-assessment; writer identifies own strengths and weaknesses, but only in a general way and does not identify steps to take for improvement. ***(9–13 pts)***	□ Journal shows meaningful "reflection on action"; writer explains how he or she applied new knowledge gained from externship experience, reading assignment, or class discussion to a new situation, or writer explores how such new knowledge could be applied to a new situation. □ Journal shows significant complexity; writer considers the perspectives of others and evaluates experiences from their perspectives. □ Journal shows significant self-assessment; writer evaluates own strengths and weaknesses and identifies concrete steps to take for improvement.***(14–15 pts)***

b. Setting Minimum Scores for Competence on Assessment Instruments

For course-level assessment, teachers also should set a benchmark score for each assessment instrument that indicates minimum competence in the learning outcome or outcomes that the instrument is being used to assess. As explained in Chapter 1, setting these scores for minimum competence is a subjective process that requires teachers to use their informed judgment, and the scores should reflect the basic skills needed by an entry-level attorney. Using their rubrics, teachers have a couple of different options for setting their benchmark scores: they can base them on either a student's overall performance on the relevant parts of the assignment, or they can base them on the student's performance in specific categories of the assignment.

The rubric for an externship journal in Figure 4.3 above can be used to illustrate these options. One of the learning outcomes for the externship course in which this rubric is used states that students will be able to "engage effectively in the skill of reflection to learn from their experiences." Two categories of the journal rubric measure this outcome—the categories of Introspection and Quality of Reflection. Together, these two categories account for 25 points of the 35 points available for each journal assignment. To set a minimum benchmark score for this assessment in the skill of reflection, a teacher might state that students must receive a total of at least 18 points from these two categories combined, regardless of their scores in each individual category. If a teacher followed this method, a student could receive a score of five in the category of Introspection, which is below competence as defined by the rubric, and a score of thirteen in the category of Quality of Reflection, and still achieve the overall benchmark score for minimum competence in the skill of reflection. With this method, the higher score in one category of the rubric offsets the lower score in the other category. Alternatively, a teacher might state that a student must receive at least the lowest available score indicating competence in each of the two rubric categories, which is six points for Introspection and nine points for Quality of Reflection, to achieve the benchmark score for minimum competence in the skill of reflection. There is no right or wrong method, and the choice essentially depends on the relative degree of importance that the teacher places on each of the two categories.

c. Setting Performance Thresholds

Once teachers have established their benchmark scores for minimum competence, they should decide the percentage of students in the course who must achieve those scores in order to declare that students have successfully met the course learning outcomes. As with setting benchmark scores for minimum competence, setting performance thresholds requires teachers to use their discretion and professional judgment. To establish performance thresholds, it can be helpful for teachers to look to past student performance on assessment instruments.

For example, assume that a civil procedure teacher assigns students to write a civil complaint in order to assess a course learning outcome relating to the ability to draft pleadings. Assume further that the teacher uses the rubric in Figure 4.1 above to evaluate the students' complaints, and the benchmark score for minimum competence on this assessment is set at 70 points (out of a possible 100 points). Assume further that the teacher has used the rubric for two years. In the first year of using the rubric, 70% of the students in the course achieved the benchmark score. In the second year of using the rubric, 80% of the students achieved the benchmark. In setting a performance threshold for this assessment, the teacher has several options. First, the threshold could simply be set at 70%, since evidence exists that students can meet that threshold. Second, the threshold could be set at 75%, since that is the average percentage for the two years that the rubric has been used. Third, the threshold could be set at 80% or even higher, since that percentage seems attainable in light of past performance, and the teacher wants to have high standards for students. The ability to draft pleadings for a lawsuit is an important skill for lawyers, which is a factor that weighs in favor of setting a high threshold. However, there is no "perfect" threshold, so this question must be decided by the teacher's informed judgment and expectations regarding the percentage of students who should demonstrate minimum competence in the course learning outcome for drafting pleadings.

Teachers also should keep in mind that setting performance thresholds for their course learning outcomes is a separate and distinct process from awarding course grades or satisfying a mandatory curve. In setting performance thresholds, teachers are identifying the percentage of students in the course who must achieve minimum competence with respect to a learning outcome in order to conclude that the students as a whole have achieved that outcome. In awarding grades, however, teachers are determining whether students have performed sufficiently to receive credit for a course and are ranking students in comparison to one another. For example, a student who receives a grade of "D" in a course typically passes and receives credit for the course, even though most teachers likely would view a "D" as indicating performance below minimum competence. Thus, performance thresholds should not be conflated with grades and mandatory curves.

5. Using Data to Improve Student Learning

As the final step in their course-level assessment process, teachers must analyze the information produced by applying the benchmarks and performance thresholds, evaluate their students' learning, and determine if changes in teaching methods or course design should be made in order to improve student learning. Using the sample assessment plan for a trusts and estates course in Table 4.8, below are examples of hypothetical assessment results and actions that could be taken to improve student learning:

Table 4.9: Possible Corrective Measures Based on Assessment Evidence

Course Learning Outcomes	Assessment Results	Possible Corrective Measures
Read and analyze state and uniform statutes concerning intestacy, wills, and trusts.	Requisite number of students did not achieve minimum competency score on writing assignment.	Add an initial ungraded writing assignment on which teacher provides feedback, followed by a second writing assignment that is graded.
Know and apply common-law rules to estate planning situations.	Requisite number of students did not achieve minimum competency score on quiz on substantive common law.	Identify the areas of common law that students are struggling with, then add problems involving those areas for students to work on.
Offer advice to clients on how to accomplish estate planning goals.	Requisite number of students did not achieve minimum competency score on assignment to write client letter.	Have students prepare a draft letter. In class, the teacher walks students through a rubric or score sheet for the letter. Students then trade drafts and give one another feedback based on the rubric or score sheet.
Draft documents that future clients will need to implement their estate plan.	Requisite number of students did not achieve minimum competency score on writing assignment to create a provision in a discretionary trust.	Add an in-class assignment in which students work in pairs to draft a provision in a discretionary trust and provide feedback to each other.

Endnotes

1. Gerald F. Hess, *Value of Variety: An Organizing Principle to Enhance Teaching and Learning*, 3 Elon L. Rev. 65, 71 (2011).

2. Michael Hunter Schwartz, Sophie M. Sparrow, & Gerald F. Hess, Teaching Law by Design: Engaging Students From the Syllabus to the Final Exam 35 (2d ed. 2017) (hereinafter "Teaching Law by Design").

3. Carwina Weng, Danielle R. Cover, Margaret E. Reuter, & Chris Roberts, Learning Law Through Experience and by Design 33 (2019) (hereinafter "Learning Law Through Experience").

4. Chapter 1, *supra*, at pp. 5–6; *see also* Learning Law Through Experience, *supra* note 3, at 46–49 (discussing examples of learning outcomes that focus on a single domain and outcomes that combine multiple domains of learning).

5. Teaching Law by Design, *supra* note 2, at 35.

6. *Id.*

7. *Id.*

8. Building on Best Practices: Transforming Legal Education in a Changing World 95 (Deborah Maranville et al., eds., 2015) (hereinafter "Building on Best Practices").

9. *Id.*

10. Teaching Law by Design, *supra* note 2, at 35.

11. *Id.*

12. *Id.*

13. *Id.*

14. Building on Best Practices, *supra* note 8, at 96–97.

15. Chapter 1, *supra*, at pp. 5–8 (discussing "stem-action verb-outcome" formula).

16. The authors thank Dean Michael Hunter Schwartz of the University of the Pacific McGeorge School of Law for sharing the learning outcomes from his contracts course.

17. Larry Cunningham, *Syllabus Examples*, Law School Assessment (Aug. 18, 2016), https://lawschoolassessment.org/2016/08/18/syllabus-examples/ (last visited July 14, 2020).

18. The authors thank Professor Aïda Alaka of the Washburn University School of Law for sharing the learning outcomes from her employment discrimination course.

19. *See* Mary J. Allen, Assessing Academic Programs in Higher Education 44 (2004); Susan Bryant et al., Transforming the Education of Lawyers: The Theory and Practice of Clinical Pedagogy 14 (2014) ("If we set clear expectations, students will be motivated to meet them."); Michael Hunter Schwartz, *Teaching Law by Design: How Learning Theory and Instructional Design Can Inform and Reform Law Teaching*, 38 San Diego L. Rev. 347, 403–04 (2001) ("[I]f communicated to the learners, objectives can arouse interest in the instruction and enable the learners to engage in metacognitive self-assessment; students can ask themselves whether they have learned to do what they were supposed to learn to do.").

20. ABA Section of Legal Educ. & Admissions to the Bar, Managing Director's Guidance Memo: Standards 301, 302, 314, and 315, at 4 (June 2015), https://www.aals.org/wp-content/uploads/2015/06/ABA-Guidance-Stds-301-302-314-315-June-2015.pdf (last visited July 14, 2020).

21. Hess, *supra* note 1, at 79.

22. Learning Law Through Experience, *supra* note 3, at 75.

23. Teaching Law by Design, *supra* note 2, at 39.

24. Hess, *supra* note 1, at 79.

25. This discussion of various teaching and learning methods is adapted, with permission, from Hess, *supra* note 1, at 79–81.

26. Selecting teaching methods and learning activities is a key component of one's overall course design. An exhaustive treatment of course design principles is beyond the scope of this book. For excellent resources on course design, see TEACHING LAW BY DESIGN, *supra* note 2, and LEARNING LAW THROUGH EXPERIENCE, *supra* note 3.

27. *See* Kelly S. Terry, *Embedding Assessment Principles in Externships*, 20 CLIN. L. REV. 467, 482 (2014).

28. LORI E. SHAW & VICTORIA L. VANZANDT, STUDENT LEARNING OUTCOMES AND LAW SCHOOL ASSESSMENT: A PRACTICAL GUIDE TO MEASURING INSTITUTIONAL EFFECTIVENESS 112 (2015).

29. *See* PEGGY L. MAKI, ASSESSING FOR LEARNING: BUILDING A SUSTAINABLE COMMITMENT ACROSS THE INSTITUTION 156–57 (2d ed. 2010).

30. *E.g.*, TRUDY W. BANTA & CATHERINE A. PALOMBA, ASSESSMENT ESSENTIALS: PLANNING, IMPLEMENTING, AND IMPROVING ASSESSMENT IN HIGHER EDUCATION 31 (2d ed. 2015).

31. Susan Hanley Duncan, *They're Back! The New Accreditation Standards Coming to a Law School Near You—A 2018 Update, Guide to Compliance, and Dean's Role in Implementing*, 67 J. LEGAL EDUC. 462, 477 (2018) ("Greater accuracy and authority are achieved when several methods of assessment produce similar findings."); ANDREA SUSNIR FUNK, THE ART OF ASSESSMENT: MAKING OUTCOMES ASSESSMENT ACCESSIBLE, SUSTAINABLE, AND MEANINGFUL 74 n.3 (2017) ("Taken together, information gleaned from multiple sources will strengthen your confidence in your observations and conclusions.").

32. This discussion of formative and summative assessment is adapted from Terry, *supra* note 27, at 476–78.

33. Lynn M. Daggett, *All of the Above: Computerized Exam Scoring of Multiple Choice Items Helps to: (A) Show How Exam Items Worked Technically, (B) Maximize Exam Fairness, (C) Justly Assign Letter Grades, and (D) Provide Feedback on Student Learning*, 57 J. LEGAL EDUC. 391, 397 (2007) (emphasis in original).

34. The authors thank Professor Kendall Kerew of the Georgia State University College of Law for permission to reprint this table that she created.

35. *E.g.*, BUILDING ON BEST PRACTICES, *supra* note 8, at 230.

36. This discussion of norm-referenced and criterion-referenced assessments is adapted from Terry, *supra* note 27, at 478–80.

37. Daggett, *supra* note 33, at 399.

38. *Id.*

39. Sophie Sparrow, *Describing the Ball: Improve Teaching by Using Rubrics—Explicit Grading Criteria*, 2004 MICH. ST. L. REV. 1, 18 (2004).

40. *See, e.g.*, TEACHING LAW BY DESIGN, *supra* note 2, at 179 (Explaining that when teachers have explicit criteria like rubrics, "we know what we are looking for, and we are much more consistent.").

41. The authors thank Professor Andrea Curcio of the Georgia State University College of Law for sharing this rubric with the Institute for Law Teaching and Learning.

42. The authors thank Professor Julia Belian of the University of Detroit-Mercy School of Law for sharing this rubric with the Institute for Law Teaching and Learning.

CHAPTER FIVE

Other Academic and Non-Academic Programs

Program-level assessment "focuses on the effectiveness of a particular program within the law school, such as a legal writing program, intellectual property track or concentration, etc., where program learning outcomes are created; evidence on attainment of the outcomes is gathered and analyzed; and the data is used to improve the program's offerings."[1] In addition to academic programs, schools may assess the efficacy of co-curricular activities (moot court, law journal), various departments in the building (library, subject matter-focused centers) and non-academic offices (careers services office and the admissions office). This book will provide guidance for tackling these challenges; to that end, this chapter sets out general principles for assessing these varied units of the law school. Subsequent chapters then explain how to apply these principles in the assessment of experiential-learning programs, legal research and writing programs, centers and concentrations, co-curricular activities, and non-academic units.

While the ABA does not require the assessment of student learning outcomes for particular programs within law schools, it is a beneficial practice because, as explained in Chapter 1, it promotes the design of a cohesive, building-wide educational approach that is intentionally structured to foster students' professional development as they progress from novice to entry-level attorney.[2] By examining the effectiveness of programs as a whole, assessment from this perspective is "more likely to identify needs to improve connections between courses," rather than just improvements in an individual course.[3]

In addition to this integrative effect, creating and assessing program-level outcomes helps students become intentional and take responsibility for their own learning. "When students know the goals of an institution, an academic program, or a course, they are able to make more informed decisions about whether the institution, program, or course will meet their needs. They are also in a better position to profit from the experiences they have in the settings they choose."[4] Program or departmental outcomes also communicate faculty expectations to students, so students have clear targets on which to focus their efforts and know the type of learning that faculty expect them to be able to demonstrate.[5] Assessing students as they complete distinct academic programs, participate in co-curricular activities, or engage with non-academic departments also provides a law school with information about whether its students "are at the competency level the school expects of its students at different stages in the curriculum."[6]

While assessment beyond course-level or institutional-level review may be a new endeavor for many law schools,[7] it need not be overwhelming. It likely will entail reviewing the same student work products that faculty and administrators review for course-level assessment and other purposes, simply from a different and broader perspective.

1. Developing Learning Outcomes

Program-level outcomes are statements of the knowledge, skills, and values in which students should achieve competency as a result of participating in a distinct component within the overall curriculum.[8] These outcomes should follow from the law school's mission and institutional learning outcomes and be consistent with them.[9] The program outcomes "will not be identical to the institutional outcomes, but will be more specific and tailored to the program's subject area."[10]

Because student learning outcomes for a program or department may be integrated across multiple courses or activities, "they should be developed not in isolation but as the result of research, reflection, and informed collaborative discussion"[11] among those involved with the program or department. The outcomes should "target only the most important goals" because addressing "a small number of well-focused outcomes enhances the cost effectiveness of the assessment program."[12] Assessment expert Linda Suskie recommends that institutions should focus on just three to six key learning outcomes for a program.[13] When drafting the actual language of the outcome statements, the program faculty or administrators can use the stem-action verb-outcome formula explained in Chapter 1.

The sections that follow discuss how to develop an assessment plan for program learning outcomes, collect and evaluate evidence of student achievement of the outcomes, and use information gathered from that evaluation to improve student learning.

2. Ensuring Alignment Between Program Outcomes and Program Content

After articulating the program outcomes, relevant faculty and administrators should work together to inventory the content of all of the courses or activities in the program to ensure that they are providing students sufficient opportunities to develop competency in the program learning outcomes.[14] In reviewing courses and activities, program faculty and staff should look for gaps and patterns in the treatment of the program outcomes.[15] This inventory process should reveal a great deal of information about the content of the relevant courses or activities and how that content aligns with the broader program outcomes.

3. Developing a Plan for Program Assessment

a. Designate a Leader for Program Assessment

To ensure that a program-assessment process is meaningful and well implemented, it should have a designated leader. Depending on how a program or department is structured, the leader could be an associate dean, an assistant dean, or a faculty member or director who oversees the program or office. The leader will be responsible for implementing the program-assessment process, documenting the steps of the process and the information that it produces, and working with faculty or staff to make program improvements based on the assessment data.

b. Create a Written Assessment Plan

The designated leader for program assessment should start by working with the relevant faculty or staff to create an assessment plan, which is simply a written document setting out the process to be followed in determining whether students are achieving the stated program learning outcomes.[16] The plan should include the program learning outcomes, the inventory of the courses or activities in which the outcomes are addressed, a schedule specifying when and how often each outcome will be assessed, the types of evidence of student learning that will be used to evaluate student attainment of each outcome, and the number of measures of student learning that will be considered. These components of an assessment plan are discussed individually in the sections that follow.

1) Create an Assessment Schedule

There is no established rule mandating how often law school program outcomes should be assessed. Most experts recommend creating a cycle for assessing each outcome every few years on a repeating basis.[17] The schedule likely will be determined primarily by the number of program outcomes, the amount and complexity of the evidence that must be gathered and reviewed, and the number of program faculty or staff who are available to participate in this process. For example, if a program has only two outcomes, the faculty or staff should be able to assess both of them every year, or at least assess each outcome every other year. A larger number of outcomes likely will need to be spread out over a series of multiple years.

The diagram below illustrates a possible timeline for assessing five program outcomes three times over the course of nine years:

Table 5.1: Sample Timeline for Assessing Program Outcomes

Program Learning Outcomes	2021–2022	2022–2023	2023–2024	2024–2025	2025–2026	2026–2027	2027–2028	2028–2029	2029–2030
1	X			X			X		
2			X			X			X
3		X			X			X	
4		X			X			X	
5	X			X			X		

2) Decide the Types of Assessment Measures to Use

Program assessment generally relies on embedded assessments, which are assignments or learning tasks that students complete as part of a regular course or co-curricular activity.[18] In addition to being reviewed for specific courses, these same assignments are reviewed for evidence of student learning with respect to the learning outcomes of the particular academic program or activity. Experts recommend using embedded assessments whenever possible because they allow the gathering of assessment information through the use of assignments that already have been created for other purposes, which saves faculty time and energy.[19] Students also should be motivated to perform their best on assignments that determine their course grades, so these assessments should produce a more accurate picture of their learning than instruments that they are asked to complete solely for assessment purposes, such as surveys and interviews.[20]

The embedded assessments available for program review likely will include both direct and indirect measures. As explained in Chapter 1, direct measures are based on actual student work or performance and require students to display their knowledge and skills to a trained evaluator.[21] Indirect measures, on the other hand, "are based upon opinion, either the student's opinion or any other observer's opinion."[22] Indirect assessments could include students' self-evaluations of their own learning, as well as surveys and focus groups of employers asking for their perceptions about students' abilities.[23]

For each program outcome, the assessment leader, working in conjunction with the program faculty or staff, will need to identify the assessments from each course or departmental activity that can be used for program assessment. This identification usually can be made when the program or department is inventoried to determine how it addresses its particular outcomes. If there are no embedded assessments available to use for program evaluation, faculty or staff should decide whether they want to incorporate such assessments into the programs and activities, or whether they want to ask students to complete "add-on" assessments or gather data elsewhere. Once the assessment leader and the faculty have decided which assessments will be used for program evaluation, the assessment leader should record that information in the assessment plan.

3) Decide the Number of Assessment Measures to Use

The assessment leader and relevant faculty or staff also must decide how many assessments to consider in evaluating whether students are achieving competency in the program outcomes. A minimum of two measures should be used for each outcome. The measures might consist of only direct measures, or they might include a combination of direct and indirect measures. Program faculty and leaders are advised to start with just two measures and then decide whether to include more measures later, if they determine that more information is desirable and they have sufficient time to review additional information.

4. Collecting the Assessment Data

a. Determine the Amount of Data to Collect

Once assessment leaders decide the type and number of assessment instruments to review, they will need to determine how many students will be asked to complete them. How many students need to be assessed in order to draw reliable conclusions about whether students are achieving the program or departmental outcomes? There is no established answer to this question. Since confidence in assessment results increases as larger numbers of students are assessed and more data are collected,[24] schools should try to assess as many students as is reasonable at the program level. Additionally, university policies may require assessment of all students, so program leaders should find out whether their parent university has such a mandate.

In the absence of a university mandate, assessment leaders will need to decide whether it is feasible for them to review and evaluate assessments completed by every student who has interacted with a particular program or department, or whether they will need to use a representative sample of student work instead, if their university policy permits. Methods for choosing representative samples and determining appropriate sample sizes are discussed in Chapter 1. University assessment offices also may be able to provide guidance on sampling methods and sizes. As with institutional assessment, program or department assessment should use the largest sample size that is feasible in order to reduce the error margin and enhance the reliability of the assessment results.

b. Methods for Gathering the Assessment Data

Once the amount of data to collect has been decided, the assessment leader should design a system for gathering, protecting, and storing that data. The nature of the assessment instruments likely will determine the method for collecting them. If the assessment data are embedded assessments created as part of a program or activity, the assessment leader will need to set up a process to work with the faculty or staff administering the assessments to collect copies of them, a representative sample of them, or the rubrics used to evaluate them. The assessment leader and the program faculty or staff could simply agree on a designated deadline by which the faculty or staff will provide this information directly to the leader. Assessment data that originate outside of the law school may need to be obtained from the dean or another law school administrator. For example, if assessment of a program involves review of data from focus groups or surveys of employers or alumni, the assessment leader should identify the law school administrator who receives that information and set up a process for obtaining the data from that person. Assessment leaders at the program level also will need to decide how long they will retain assessment data after they have reviewed it and the measures that will be taken to maintain the confidentiality of the data.

5. Evaluating the Assessment Data

Once the evidence of student learning has been gathered, it must be evaluated to determine what it demonstrates regarding student learning of the program's outcomes. Depending on how the program-assessment process is structured, this evaluation might be performed by the program director, a committee of faculty members, or others who work directly with the relevant office or department. As Chapter 1 explained, the fundamental question that must be answered in evaluating the evidence at any level of assessment — whether institutional, program, or course — is "[o]n what basis do we decide that a sufficiently high percentage of our students have been shown to have learned a sufficient amount for us to say, 'This is good enough'?"[25] To answer this question, assessment leaders should set benchmark scores for minimum competence on the instruments designated for program assessment, and they should set performance thresholds stating the percentages of students in the program who should achieve those benchmark scores in order to conclude that the program outcomes have been successfully achieved.

6. Using Data to Improve Student Learning

To close the assessment loop, the program or department leaders should use the information produced by the assessment process to improve student learning and program effectiveness. If the designated percentage of students is not achieving the minimum competency scores on the assessment instruments, then the faculty should review the program design, pedagogy, and assessments to try to determine the reasons for the shortcomings. Faculty should look for patterns of mistakes or common misunderstandings that reveal the areas of knowledge, skills, or values in which student learning fell short. Once faculty identify these areas, they can decide whether to refine the learning outcomes or change teaching methods or other instructional approaches.[26]

Thus, the program- and department- assessment process should reveal opportunities for making improvements in program design, pedagogy, or co-curricular opportunities that will enhance students' learning or departmental effectiveness regarding the chosen outcomes. After these changes are documented in the assessment plan and then implemented, faculty can compare subsequent assessment results to prior results to determine if the changes have led to improvements.

Endnotes

1. Lori E. Shaw & Victoria L. VanZandt, Student Learning Outcomes and Law School Assessment: A Practical Guide to Measuring Institutional Effectiveness 188 (2015) (hereinafter "Shaw & VanZandt"); *see also, e.g.*, David Thomson, *When the ABA Comes Calling, Let's Speak the Same Language of Assessment*, 23 Perspectives: Teaching Legal Res. & Writing, 68, 71 (2014) ("The idea of program-level assessment is to look at all similar courses, or the legal writing program as a whole, or the clinic as a whole, or courses in a certificate program as a whole.").

2. Regional accreditors that regulate a law school's parent university may require program-level assessment. *See, e.g.*, ABA Section of Legal Educ. & Admissions to the Bar, Report of the Outcome Measures Committee 47 (2008), https://www.americanbar.org/content/dam/aba/administrative/legal_education_and_admissions_to_the_bar/reports/2008_outcome_measures_committee_final_report.pdf ("As the regional accreditors have begun holding accredited schools accountable for demonstrating educational effectiveness at all levels, law schools are no longer able to fly beneath the regional radar screen") (last visited July 14, 2020); Shaw & VanZandt, *supra* note 1, at 23 ("The current push for law schools to up their assessment game is, at least in part, the result of the tightening of the regional accreditors' standards over the past decade.").

3. Mary J. Allen, Assessing General Education Programs 131 (2006); *see also, e.g.*, Docia L. Rudley, *Bridging the Divide Between Assessment and Accreditation*, 62 N.Y.L. Sch. L. Rev. 35, 37 (2017/2018) (Program-level assessment allows law faculty "to systematically collect information about our educational programs to discover the strengths and weaknesses of students as a group.").

4. Mary E. Huba & Jann E. Freed, Learner-Centered Assessment on College Campuses: Shifting the Focus from Teaching to Learning 97 (2000).

5. Peggy L. Maki, Assessing for Learning: Building a Sustainable Commitment Across the Institution 103 (2d ed. 2010).

6. Anthony Niedwiecki, *Prepared for Practice? Developing a Comprehensive Assessment Plan for a Law School Professional Skills Program*, 50 U. San. Fran. L. Rev. 245, 255 (2016).

7. *See* Thomson, *supra* note 1, at 71 ("Program-level assessment is something that is in its infancy in law schools, but will likely be a part of most assessment plans going forward.").

8. *E.g.*, Andrea Susnir Funk, The Art of Assessment: Making Outcomes Assessment Accessible, Sustainable, and Meaningful 43 (2017); *see also* Maki, *supra* note 5, at 90 ("Outcome statements become more specific at the program or department level, reflecting the kinds of writing within a discipline, profession, or field of study.").

9. *E.g.*, Niedwiecki, *supra* note 6, at 257.

10. Funk, *supra* note 8, at 43.

11. Linda Suskie, Assessing Student Learning: A Common Sense Guide 51 (3d ed. 2018); *see also* Huba & Freed, *supra* note 4, at 93 (Developing program outcomes is a task for faculty "to complete collectively, and it is a task that takes time and deliberation.").

12. Huba & Freed, *supra* note 4, at 73; *see also id.* ("Assessments at the program level should be as focused as possible on important aspects of learning in order to yield useful information without wasted effort.").

13. Suskie, *supra* note 11, at 50.

14. This process is similar to the curriculum mapping that occurs in institutional assessment. *See* Chapter 1, *supra*.

15. *See, e.g.*, Maki, *supra* note 5, at 61 (Curriculum maps "identify gaps in student learning opportunities or identify concentrations of learning experiences without further opportunity for students to transfer, build on, or apply learning.").

16. *See, e.g.*, TRUDY W. BANTA & CATHERINE A. PALOMBA, ASSESSMENT ESSENTIALS: PLANNING, IMPLEMENTING, AND IMPROVING ASSESSMENT IN HIGHER EDUCATION 20 (2d ed. 2015) ("An assessment plan captures agreement about what matters, gives direction for actions, and provides a means to determine if progress is being made."); FUNK, *supra* note 8, at 30 (describing assessment plan); SHAW & VANZANDT, *supra* note 1, at 54–57 (same).

17. SHAW & VANZANDT, *supra* note 1, at 83. *Cf.*, *e.g.*, SUSKIE, *supra* note 11, at 99 (suggesting that key learning outcomes should be assessed at least every three years and preferably every two years.)

18. For some law school departments or offices, for which students do not complete course work, assessment will likely involve other metrics of success, as discussed *infra*.

19. FUNK, *supra* note 8, at 29; *see also* BANTA & PALOMBA, *supra* note 16, at 25; SUSKIE, *supra* note 11, at 156.

20. *See* SHAW & VANZANDT, *supra* note 1, at 100 ("Using embedded tools is preferable because students tend to take assignments more seriously (and hence perform better) in the context of a class. Therefore, embedded tools may provide better evidence of student learning."); *see also, e.g.*, Rudley, *supra* note 3, at 45 ("When possible, use assessment that is already embedded in the curriculum to ensure that students are invested in their performance and that the results are genuinely of interest to them and to faculty members."); SUSKIE, *supra* note 11, at 279 ("Grades are a powerful incentive for students to participate in an assessment and to give it serious thought and effort.").

21. BANTA & PALOMBA, *supra* note 16, at 23; SHAW & VANZANDT, *supra* note 1, at 104.

22. SHAW & VAN ZANDT, *supra* note 1, at 104.

23. BANTA & PALOMBA, *supra* note 16, at 23; HUBA & FREED, *supra* note 4, at 11; SHAW & VANZANDT, *supra* note 1, at 105–07.

24. *E.g.*, FUNK, *supra* note 8, at 37.

25. Cecilia L. López, *A Decade of Assessing Student Learning: What We Have Learned, and What Is Next*, *in* OUTCOMES ASSESSMENT IN HIGHER EDUCATION: VIEWS AND PERSPECTIVES 67–68 (Peter Hernon & Robert E. Dugan eds. 2004); *see also* SUSKIE, *supra* note 11, at 288 ("Defining successful outcomes means having a clear sense of what is good enough.").

26. *See, e.g.*, SUSAN BRYANT ET AL., TRANSFORMING THE EDUCATION OF LAWYERS: THE THEORY AND PRACTICE OF CLINICAL PEDAGOGY 14 (2014) ("When the students fail to meet the goals, teachers can assess whether to refine or reject the goals or take a different approach to meeting them.").

CHAPTER SIX

Experiential-Learning Programs

1. Developing Learning Outcomes for an Experiential-Learning Program

As explained in Chapter 5, learning outcomes for a particular academic program within the law school should flow from the school's mission and institutional outcomes. For example, a law school's broad institutional outcomes might state that its graduates should be able to communicate effectively orally and in writing. The school's experiential-learning program then might have a subsidiary and more specific outcome stating that students completing that program should be able to demonstrate effective verbal communication skills when speaking with a supervising attorney.

Program-level outcomes span across all of the courses in the program. Accordingly, to create outcomes for an experiential-learning program, assessment leaders first must determine which courses constitute the "program." The ABA Standards define "experiential courses" to include simulation courses, law clinics, and field placements (more commonly known as "externships").[1] Thus, for program-assessment purposes, a law school should first decide whether its experiential-learning program includes all three of these types of courses, or whether it includes only courses in which students are placed in actual practice situations and work with real clients, such as clinics and externships. Since simulation courses do not involve live clients, the work that students perform in those courses differs significantly from the work that students perform in clinics and externships. The nature of the work will have an impact on establishing learning outcomes for the program. For example, if an experiential-learning program were to include only clinics and externships, it might identify the ability to communicate effectively with a supervisor in a work setting as a program outcome. However, if simulation courses also were included in the program, this outcome likely would not be feasible, since students in simulation courses do not have the opportunity to communicate with supervisors in actual work settings.

Since program-level assessment has not yet become common in law schools, few examples of outcomes statements for experiential-learning programs have been published. ABA Standard 304, however, provides some guidance in identifying possible outcomes for experiential-learning programs. The Standard states that, for a simulation, clinical, or field-placement course to qualify as an experiential course, it must be "primarily experiential in nature" and:

(1) integrate doctrine, theory, skills, and legal ethics, and engage students in performance of one or more of the professional skills identified in Standard 302;

(2) develop the concepts underlying the professional skills being taught;

(3) provide multiple opportunities for performance;

(4) provide opportunities for student performance, self-evaluation, and feedback from a faculty member, or, for a field placement, a site supervisor;

(5) provide a classroom instructional component; or, for a field placement, a classroom instructional component, regularly scheduled tutorials, or other means of ongoing, contemporaneous, faculty-guided reflection; and

(6) provide direct supervision of the student's performance by the faculty member; or, for a field placement, provide direct supervision of the student's performance by a faculty member or a site supervisor.[2]

Thus, depending on the nature of the courses in an experiential-learning program, the program leaders might establish learning outcomes such as:

- the ability to apply substantive law and rules of procedure;
- the capacity to engage in problem solving;
- the ability to engage in effective written and oral communication in professional settings;
- the ability to properly exercise an attorney's professional and ethical responsibilities in real or simulated practice situations;[3]
- the ability to receive and implement feedback from a supervisor;
- the ability to engage in a reflective process to learn from one's experiences; or

- the ability to effectively perform other practice skills, such as interviewing, counseling, negotiation, fact development and analysis, trial practice, document drafting, conflict resolution, organization and management of legal work, collaboration, cultural competency, and self-evaluation.[4]

Similarly, in her book *The Art of Assessment: Making Outcomes Assessment Accessible, Sustainable, and Meaningful*, Professor Andrea Susnir Funk provides the following examples of program outcomes for a lawyering-skills program:

1. Students will demonstrate the ability to solve a problem or accomplish an objective.
2. Students will demonstrate analytical and reasoning skills.
3. Students will demonstrate the ability to conduct legal research.
4. Students will demonstrate the ability to conduct a factual investigation.
5. Students will communicate effectively.
6. Students will demonstrate the ability to counsel a client.
7. Students will demonstrate the ability to negotiate on behalf of a client.
8. Students will demonstrate competency in legal practice skills, including drafting documents used in legal practice and knowledge of alternative dispute resolution procedures.
9. Students will demonstrate the ability to organize and manage a legal task.
10. Students will possess the requisite skills to recognize and resolve ethical dilemmas.[5]

The leader of the experiential-learning program, such as an associate dean or a program director, and the professors who teach in the program, should participate in the discussion to identify and determine the program's learning outcomes. If an experiential-learning program also employs adjunct professors, it could be helpful to include them in the discussion to have their perspective on the competencies that students need to develop for practice. If it is not practicable to include all of the adjuncts in the discussion, a school could survey them to get their input on the program learning outcomes. Additionally, the experiential-learning faculty also must decide the appropriate number of learning outcomes for their program.

Since little scholarship exists on the topic of program-level outcomes assessment in legal education, the remaining steps of the assessment process are best illustrated through the use of a hypothetical set of outcomes for an experiential-learning program. Accordingly, the remainder of this chapter will assume that a law school has defined its experiential-learning program to include all of its clinical and externship courses. The clinical courses include a family law clinic that handles primarily divorce, custody, and guardianship cases; a consumer protection clinic that handles primarily landlord-tenant disputes and debt-collection cases; a low-income taxpayer clinic that handles tax disputes involving the Internal Revenue Service; and an immigration clinic that represents clients seeking asylum or citizenship. The externship course includes placements with trial and appellate courts, nonprofit organizations, and state and federal government agencies. The chapter will assume further that the faculty who teach the clinic and externship courses have established the following learning outcomes for the experiential-learning program as a whole:

Table 6.1: Hypothetical Learning Outcomes for an Experiential-Learning Program

After completing a course in the experiential-learning program, students will be able to:
1. draft a well-written practice-related document,
2. demonstrate effective verbal communication skills in a professional environment,
3. use problem-solving skills effectively on behalf of a client,
4. recognize ethical issues and effectively apply ethical rules in practice situations, and
5. explain the concept of a professional identity and articulate the elements of their own professional identity.

The sections that follow discuss how to develop an assessment plan for these program learning outcomes, collect and evaluate evidence of student achievement of the outcomes, and use information gathered from that evaluation to improve student learning.

2. Ensuring Alignment Between the Program Outcomes and Courses in the Program

Using the hypothetical outcomes in Table 6.1, the faculty members teaching the externship course and the four clinics would review their courses to determine if all of their students have the opportunity to draft practice-related documents, demonstrate verbal communication skills, engage in problem solving, recognize ethical issues and apply ethical rules, and formulate a professional identity. Evaluating this alignment will allow the program faculty to look for gaps and patterns in the treatment of the program outcomes.[6] For example, are all of the students in each of the experiential-learning courses receiving the opportunity to develop the knowledge, skills, and values associated with each of the five program learning outcomes? If the students are not being exposed to the program outcomes in their work with their clinic clients or in the work at the externship placement sites, are the outcomes being addressed in the seminar classes that accompany the courses? Is there a program outcome that is addressed in some of the experiential-learning courses, but not all of them?[7] Do the courses address the program outcomes with sufficient depth to allow students to achieve competency in them?

This inventory process should reveal a great deal of information about the content of the experiential-learning courses and how that content aligns with the broader program outcomes. For example, if the process reveals that the skill of problem solving is not addressed in all of the experiential-learning courses, then the faculty should ask if that skill is a necessary outcome for the program. If problem solving is sufficiently addressed in another part of the required law-school curriculum, then it may not be. If the faculty determine that problem solving is *not* an essential skill for all students who complete an experiential-learning course, then it should be discarded as a program outcome. However, if the faculty determine that problem solving *is* an essential program outcome, then they should change the content of the courses to ensure that all incorporate that skill. Those changes could include working with site supervisors to ensure that students receive opportunities to engage in problem solving at their externship sites, asking students in the clinical courses to draft a written plan addressing and proposing an action plan for a client issue, or restructuring the externship or clinic seminars to include the skill of problem solving. Similarly, changes to course content should be made if an outcome that is deemed essential is merely introduced in the experiential-learning courses, but students do not receive adequate opportunities to practice and achieve competency in it. This change could involve creating more assignments or in-class exercises relating to the outcome to broaden students' exposure to it.

3. Developing a Plan for Program Assessment

An experiential-learning program should have a designated leader for its assessment process. Depending on how a school structures its experiential-learning offerings, the leader could be an associate dean for experiential learning, a director of the experiential-learning program, a faculty member who teaches in the program, or a group of faculty members who form a program-assessment committee. The designated leader for program assessment should start by working with the experiential-learning faculty to create a written assessment plan, as detailed in Chapter 5, including a timeline for reviewing each outcome. Using the five hypothetical program outcomes described in Table 6.1, the diagram below illustrates a possible timeline for assessing each outcome three times over the course of nine years:

Table 6.2: Timeline for Assessing Experiential-Learning Program Outcomes

Learning Outcomes	2021–2022	2022–2023	2023–2024	2024–2025	2025–2026	2026–2027	2027–2028	2028–2029	2029–2030
Drafting Practice-Related Documents	X			X			X		
Verbal Communication Skills			X			X			X
Problem-Solving Skills		X			X			X	
Recognizing Ethical Issues and Applying Ethics Rules		X			X			X	
Professional Identity	X			X			X		

Program assessment generally relies on assessments, either direct or indirect, that are embedded into the courses themselves. Examples of direct assessments available in experiential-learning courses might include journals, timesheets, quizzes, essays, reflection papers, drafting assignments, documents drafted for clients, case files, class presentations, skills performances in court or in seminar classes, and evaluations by externship and clinical supervisors. Indirect assessments could include students' evaluations of their own learning as well as surveys and focus groups of employers asking for their perceptions about students' abilities.[8]

Using the five hypothetical program outcomes discussed above, the leaders of the program-assessment process would review the clinical and externship courses to determine if any of the existing course assignments provide evidence of student learning with respect to the program outcomes. For example, for the outcome relating to drafting a well-written practice document, the assessment leaders could review documents that the clinic students prepare for their clients and written work that externship students produce at their placement sites. If materials such as these are selected, measures must be put in place to preserve client and workplace confidentiality, since these documents are prepared for actual practice situations.[9] Alternatively, simulated practice documents that students draft for a class assignment might be considered. For the outcome relating to professional identity, student journals or a final reflective essay might be reviewed. Assignments in which students have been asked to evaluate their progress in developing a professional identity also might be considered. If there are no embedded assessments available to use for program evaluation, the experiential faculty should decide whether they want to incorporate such assessments into their courses, or whether they want to ask students to complete "add-on" assessments. The assessments ultimately selected for review should be documented in the program's assessment plan.

4. Collecting the Assessment Data

After determining the assessments to review, the assessment leaders should next decide how many students will be assessed—whether all students enrolled in the experiential-learning program, or a representative sample, as discussed in Chapter 5. For example, using the hypothetical program outcomes in Table 6.1, assume that the program leaders have decided to use a pleading or a research memo completed by the students in the clinical and externship courses to assess their ability to draft a well-written practice-related document. Assume further that the externship course has 50 students, while each of the four clinics has ten students. It may not be practicable for a small group of experiential-learning faculty to review 90 student-written documents for program-assessment purposes. Accordingly, they might decide to use a representative sample of student work instead, if their university policy permits.

5. Evaluating the Assessment Data

After establishing benchmark scores for minimum competence on each of the assessments selected for program review, as discussed in Chapters 1 and 5, program faculty can evaluate the data collected. If the program benchmark scores are consistent with the benchmarks that program faculty have set for their individual courses, then the course results may be generalizable to the program as a whole, thus making it unnecessary to review the assessment evidence a second time solely for program review.[10] The hypothetical program outcomes in Table 6.1 can illustrate this concept. One of the outcomes states that students completing the experiential-learning program will be able to "draft a well-written practice-related document." Assume further that the five courses in the hypothetical experiential-learning program—the family law clinic, the consumer protection clinic, the low-income taxpayer clinic, the immigration clinic, and the externship course—have the following course learning outcomes:

- Family Law Clinic: students will be able to draft an effective complaint for a divorce;
- Consumer Protection Clinic: students will be able to draft an effective answer to a complaint;
- Low-Income Taxpayer Clinic: students will be able to draft an effective written protest to an IRS demand;
- Immigration Clinic: students will be able to write an effective petition for asylum;
- Externship Course: students will be able to write an effective written document of the type typically prepared at their placement site.

Each of these assignments, which is a regular part of the clinics or the externship course, is an example of an "embedded assessment." The faculty teaching the respective clinics and the externship course would evaluate these written work products according to the criteria and benchmark scores they have established for their individual courses. If the course-level criteria and benchmark scores for these assessments are similar to the criteria and benchmark score for the program-level outcome of a "well-drafted practice-related document," then the course-level results should be generalizable to the program level, making a second review of the students' assignments for program assessment unnecessary. However, if the course-level criteria do not align with the program-level criteria, then the experiential-learning faculty will need to create a rubric for assessing the students' written work products for program-level assessment and then review the assignments using that rubric. The process for creating rubrics is discussed in Chapter 1.

Finally, the experiential-learning faculty also will need to determine the performance thresholds that must be satisfied in order for the faculty to declare that the program-level learning outcomes have been successfully achieved. While these percentages may be the same for the course and program levels, variation is likely to occur. For example, at the course level, the professor teaching the course sets the percentage at which he or she will declare that a sufficient number of students have successfully achieved the course learning outcomes, according to the professor's individual standards. At the program level, however, that percentage should be determined by the experiential-learning faculty as a whole as a performance threshold for all of the students in the program. Thus, it is possible that a group of experiential-learning faculty might set a performance threshold for program assessment that is lower or higher than the percentage set by individual professors for their own courses.

6. Using Data to Improve Student Learning

To close the assessment loop, the experiential-learning faculty should use the information produced by the program-assessment process to improve student learning. Using the hypothetical program outcomes in Table 6.1, the chart below provides examples of the evidence that program assessment might produce and actions that could be taken to improve student learning:

Table 6.3: Outcomes Evidence and Possible Corrective Measures

Program Outcome	Evidence of Student Learning	Possible Corrective Measure
Draft a well-written practice-related document.	Evaluations by supervising attorneys reveal requisite number of students did not achieve minimum competency score when rated on writing practice documents.	Add a class on drafting practice documents to seminar, or make changes to existing class on that topic. Add a document-drafting assignment to seminar. Provide more opportunities for clinic and externship students to draft practice documents.
Demonstrate effective verbal communication skills in a professional environment.	Evaluations by supervising attorneys reveal requisite number of students did not meet minimum competency score when rated on verbal communication skills.	Add a class on professional communication skills to seminar, and then require students to role-play a telephone call with an opposing counsel.
Use problem-solving skills effectively on behalf of a client.	Evaluations by supervising attorneys reveal requisite number of students did not meet minimum competency score when rated on problem-solving skills.	Add a class on problem-solving skills to seminar, or change existing class. Use in-class exercise in which students work in teams to devise a litigation strategy for a hypothetical client.
Recognize ethical issues and effectively apply ethical rules in practice situations.	Evaluations by supervising attorneys reveal requisite number of students did not meet minimum competency score when rated on recognizing ethical issues and applying ethical rules.	Increase emphasis in seminar on ethical issues and application of ethical rules. Assign students to complete problems on ethics issues. Ask supervisors to highlight ethical issues and discuss them with students.
Explain the concept of a professional identity and articulate the elements of their own professional identity.	Review of students' final reflective essays on this topic reveals that the requisite number of students did achieve the minimum competency score.	No corrective measure needed. Celebrate!

After these corrective measures are documented in the assessment plan and then implemented, program faculty can compare subsequent assessment results to prior results to determine if the changes have led to improvements in student learning.

Endnotes

1. ABA Standards and Rules of Procedure for Approval of Law Schools 2020–2021, Standard 304(a).

2. *Id.*

3. These first four bullet points are some of the enumerated "professional skills identified in Standard 302." ABA Standards and Rules of Procedure for Approval of Law Schools 2020–2021, Standard 304(a)(1).

4. *See* ABA Standards and Rules of Procedure for Approval of Law Schools 2020–2021, Standard 302, Interpretation 302-1 (listing examples of other professional skills appropriate for learning outcomes).

5. Andrea Susnir Funk, The Art of Assessment: Making Outcomes Assessment Accessible, Sustainable, and Meaningful 117–18 (2017).

6. *See, e.g.*, Peggy L. Maki, Assessing for Learning: Building a Sustainable Commitment Across the Institution 61 (2010) (noting that curriculum maps "identify gaps in student learning opportunities or identify concentrations of learning experiences without further opportunity for students to transfer, build on, or apply learning").

7. *See, e.g.*, Trudy W. Banta & Catherine A. Palomba, Assessment Essentials: Planning, Implementing, and Improving Assessment in Higher Education 72 (2d ed. 2015) ("If a particular outcome is getting too much coverage or too little, the curriculum map will reveal the imbalance.").

8. *Id.* at 23; Mary E. Huba & Jann E. Freed, Learner-Centered Assessment on College Campuses: Shifting the Focus From Teaching to Learning 11 (2000); Lori E. Shaw & Victoria L. VanZandt, Student Learning Outcomes and Law School Assessment: A Practical Guide to Measuring Institutional Effectiveness 105–07 (2015).

9. *See* Model Rules of Prof'l Conduct r. 1.6 (2019) (duty of attorney-client confidentiality); U.S. Code of Conduct for Judicial Employees, Canon 3.D(3) (2019) ("A judicial employee should never disclose any confidential information received in the course of official duties except as required in the performance of such duties.").

10. *See* Mary J. Allen, Assessing General Education Programs 125 (2006) ("Assuming course outcomes are well aligned with program outcomes, results can be generalized to the program, as a whole.").

CHAPTER SEVEN

Legal Research and Writing Programs

Assessing a legal writing program requires following the same steps set forth in Chapter 5: developing programmatic learning outcomes, developing a plan for program assessment, collecting the data, evaluating the data, and using the data to improve student learning. As pointed out in Chapters 1 and 5, assessing programs, such as the legal research and writing ("LRW") program, is a process that will provide professors with data that can be used to build a cohesive curriculum (within the program and throughout the building) to help students progress to mastering these skills while at the law school. While going through the programmatic assessment of the legal writing program, members of the department will learn what the professors are teaching and what the students are learning. The professors will also learn if LRW skills are being taught and assessed elsewhere in the curriculum, and, if they are, what are the results of the assessments. For example, when collecting data to assess the LRW department at Gonzaga University School of Law, the LRW professors learned that Gonzaga's externship and clinic programs' end-of-the-year questionnaires contain questions asking the supervisors to rank the students' legal research and writing skills. That information was helpful to the LRW professors. Lastly, programmatic assessment allows professors to take a hard look at student learning across courses taught by both full-time faculty and adjunct professors. This information helps with establishing curricular consistency for students.

1. Develop Learning Outcomes

Each LRW program should develop learning outcomes that are related to the institutional outcomes but are more detailed as to the knowledge, skills, and values the program expects the students to learn, practice, and master. To do this, the program should review its school's institutional outcomes, choosing the ones that are covered in the LRW program. After choosing which institutional outcomes are covered by the LRW program, the department should come up with just three to six programmatic outcomes for each institutional outcome.[1] Once those programmatic outcomes are determined, the program can do a mini-curriculum map to determine in what courses these skills, knowledge, and value outcomes are taught and assessed. Then the program can move on to developing a plan to assess the program's outcomes. Subsequently, the program can determine the assessment devices, assess the programmatic outcomes, and review the data. Lastly, the program will close the loop on assessment and work to fill gaps.

a. Developing Program Outcomes from the Institutional Outcomes

By way of example, the following are the outcomes and accompanying competencies from Gonzaga University School of Law that deal with the knowledge, skills, and values taught and assessed by Gonzaga's LRW program:

Table 7.1: Learning Outcomes and Competencies for Gonzaga LRW Program

1. Graduates will demonstrate the ability to communicate effectively as professionals.

   Competency 1: Students will write in a clear, concise, well-organized, professional manner that is appropriate to the audience and the circumstances.

* * *

2. Graduates will demonstrate analytical and problem-solving skills.

   Competency 1: When there is controlling legal principle, students will be able to identify and apply to case-based or hypothetical fact scenarios the controlling legal principles that apply.

   Competency 2: When the controlling legal principle is indeterminate, students will be able to:

   A. Use analogical reasoning to identify and determine possible legal rules to predict and explain how case-based or hypothetical fact scenarios will likely be resolved.

   B. Identify policy and practical considerations to predict and explain how case-based or hypothetical fact scenarios will likely be resolved.

When developing programmatic outcomes from institutional outcomes such as these, the LRW professors may have to write more granular, department-specific outcomes, but they may not. For example, Competency 1 of Outcome 1 above states that "[s]tudents will write in a clear, concise, well-organized, professional manner that is appropriate to the audience and the circumstances." The LRW program at Gonzaga assesses that outcome directly in every one of its four LRW courses. Therefore, the LRW program did not create a separate programmatic outcome for that competency.

On the other hand, Outcome 2 regarding analytical and problem-solving skills does need more granular, program-specific outcomes. To come up with these programmatic outcomes, the LRW professors should agree on what skills, knowledge, and values a student must learn and possess to meet the standard. Some examples of programmatic outcomes that can be assessed to show graduates can analyze and solve legal problems are as follows:

- Students learn the organization and hierarchy of the legal system well enough to determine jurisdictional questions about the legal problem.
- Students understand the need for and how to use secondary sources to familiarize themselves with an unknown area of law.
- Students can research and find relevant case law, and/or statutes, and/or regulations in the online and print versions of legal sources.
- Students understand how to determine and can determine if the problem is covered by statutes, constitutions, case law, or all three.
- Students can identify and synthesize legal rules from cases.
- Students can read and interpret a statute, including definitions, and the purpose for the statute.
- Students can show how the rule has been applied in the past by the courts in similar cases, including appropriate definitions, reasoning, and policy.
- Students can apply controlling principles to the problem needing to be solved and produce a supported conclusion.
- Students can cite to sources correctly and can use citations to improve their writing.
- Students write in a clear, concise, well-organized, and professional manner appropriate to the circumstances.
- Students communicate professionally during conferences about their writing.

- Students engage in active listening during conferences about the writing project.

These are a sampling of the types of programmatic outcomes an LRW program may have. The number may vary, depending on the goals of the program.

b. Mapping the Curriculum

After the LRW professors determine their programmatic outcomes, it is necessary to map the LRW curriculum to see where the various programmatic outcomes are introduced, practiced, and mastered. The LRW curriculum at Gonzaga consists of four two-credit courses that are all required. The courses are: LRW I, which covers case law research and writing for objective analysis; LRW II, which covers enacted law research and writing for objective analysis; LRW III, which covers complex persuasive analysis through litigation documents and appellate briefs; and, lastly, LRW IV, which gives the students a choice to take advanced litigation, advanced appellate advocacy, or transactional drafting.[2] The following is an example of a curriculum map for the outcomes for Gonzaga's LRW program:[3]

Table 7.2: Curriculum Map for Learning Outcomes for Gonzaga's LRW Program

Programmatic Outcome	Introduced	Practiced	Mastered
Students understand the organization and hierarchy of the legal system well enough to determine jurisdictional questions about the legal problem.	LRW I LRW II	LRW I LRW II	LRWIII LRW IV (Advocacy and Litigation)
Students understand the need for and how to use secondary sources to familiarize themselves with an unknown area of law.	LRW I LRW II	LRW I LRW II	LRWIII LRW IV (Advocacy and Litigation)
Students can research and find relevant case law, and/or statutes, and/or regulations in the online and print versions of legal sources.	LRW I LRW II	LRW I LRW II	LRW III LRW IV (Advocacy and Litigation)

Completing the curriculum map helps LRW professors see where the program may not be providing enough practice and coverage of an outcome as well as if an outcome is being covered too much. As a general matter, it is unlikely the students ever get too much practice at legal research or writing, but mapping is a good exercise that allows the LRW program to identify gaps in the curriculum.[4] This process can also illuminate outcomes that are being over- or under-assessed. As stated in Chapter 5, this inventory process reveals a great deal of information about the content of the relevant courses and how that content aligns with the broader program outcomes.

2. Create an Assessment Plan

Creating an assessment plan is the next step in the process of assessing an LRW program. Depending on the size of the LRW program, it may be necessary to appoint a leader to ensure the assessment process is completed in a timely manner.[5] The first task in developing an assessment plan is to create a timeline of when the LRW program will assess each programmatic outcome, as outlined in Chapter 5. The next task is to decide what assessments, either direct or indirect, the program feels are the best to produce the needed data for each outcome. Examples of direct data available to LRW professors in LRW courses include: legal memoranda, client letters, research exams, TWEN quizzes, clicker questions, live-grading sessions, student presentations, research pathfinders, motions, complaints, and briefs. These direct assessment methods are embedded in the LRW courses. Indirect methods of assessing LRW programmatic outcomes include students' reflections on how and what they are learning, surveys to employers and externship supervisors, and surveys of in-house clinic supervisors. For most LRW programs, the direct assessment materials are already being assigned and will just need to be mined for the information. Indirect assessment methods, however, may or may not exist.[6] Before creating them from scratch, check with your externship and clinics as they may already be asking some questions about LRW in their supervisors' student assessment information. Also, check with your alumni coordinator and your center for career services. They also may already be asking LRW questions of employers of the graduates.

The following is a chart exemplifying the schedule for programmatic assessment, the type of method, and the instrument.

Table 7.3: Schedule for Programmatic Assessment

Programmatic Outcome	Schedule	Method	Instrument
Students understand the organization and hierarchy of the legal system well enough to determine jurisdictional questions about the legal problem.	2020–2021	Direct	Embedded assessment using TWEN, clicker question, or in-class writings.
Students understand the need for and how to use secondary sources to familiarize themselves with an unknown area of law.	2020–2021	Direct	Embedded pathfinder which tests students' ability to use and find secondary sources.
Students can research and find relevant case law, and/or statutes, and/or regulations in the online and print versions of legal sources.	2021–2022	Direct and indirect	Professors can add a section to a rubric assessing this (direct). As for an indirect method, clinics and career services offices might be asking employers and supervisors for this information. LRW can access that data.

3. Collecting the Assessment Data

In collecting data to assess the LRW program's outcomes, if every professor is assigning a memorandum or brief that can assess a particular outcome, this embedded assessment can do double duty. It can serve to grade the students for an individual course and also serve to assess how many students are meeting the benchmark score for minimum competence for the program outcome.[7] If the benchmark score set for the LRW course assignment is the same as the benchmark score established for the program outcome, then the course-level results should be generalizable to the program level, making a second review of the students' assignment at the program level unnecessary.

If, however, the course-level benchmark score differs from the program-level benchmark score for minimum competence, then the LRW faculty must create a rubric for assessing the students' work product for the program-level assessment and use that rubric to assess the students' work. To do this, the LRW faculty must decide on the sample size to use. Deciding how many students should be assessed is discussed in Chapter 5, and the method for choosing a sample size is discussed in Chapter 1. That being said, this is an individual program question with no right answer — unless the university policy requires a certain sample size. As discussed in Chapter 5, the larger the number of students assessed, the more reliable the results are. Since, however, every student is required to take LRW, this could amount to collecting data from hundreds of students. This is likely not practical for a small LRW faculty. Therefore, a representative sample is a good option.[8] One way to do this is have the registrar randomly select three memoranda or briefs from each class: one from the top 25% of the class, one from the middle 50% of the class, and one from the bottom 25% of the class. [9]

Once the sample pool is collected, all of the LRW faculty can be involved in assessing the selected direct evidence. In this way, the reviewers can check on each other to ensure one reviewer is not biased. To accomplish this, once a reviewer is done reviewing a memorandum or brief, another reviewer can review the same document to ensure accuracy. The two reviews do not have to match, but the assessments should be similar. If this exercise is performed at least once for each reviewer, it will help avoid bias on the part of the reviewer and ensure consistency, but it does not have to be done more than that.[10] If the reviewers disagree with each other about the assessments, another assessor can be brought in for a third opinion. If the group of assessors cannot come up with a consensus, the LRW department can use this as a signal that something may need to change in the curriculum or the professors can agree to disagree. That disagreement can and should be noted in the assessment report to the faculty.

The LRW faculty should then create the rubric, as discussed in Chapter 1. A type of rubric which works well and is easy to use for LRW courses is one which states the programmatic goals being assessed on a form with a scale. For example:

Table 7.4: Sample Rubric

Programmatic Outcome	Not Meeting Standards	Meeting Standards	Exceeding Standards
Students understand the organization and hierarchy of the legal system well enough to determine jurisdictional questions about the legal problem.			
Students understand the need for and how to use secondary sources to familiarize themselves with an unknown area of law.			
Students can research and find relevant case law, and/or statutes, and/or regulations in the online and print versions of legal sources.			

The LRW faculty must decide the benchmark score for minimum competence on program-level rubrics and the performance thresholds that must be satisfied in order for the faculty to state that the programmatic outcomes were successfully achieved. Since this is determined by the LRW faculty as a whole, there may be variation from the course-level benchmark scores and performance thresholds.

4. Using Data to Improve Student Learning

Below is a chart with the programmatic outcomes used in this chapter, the evidence of student learning, and some suggestions for possible corrective measures:

Table 7.5: Evaluation of Assessment Data

Programmatic Outcome	Evidence of Student Learning	Possible Corrective Measures
Students understand the organization and hierarchy of the legal system well enough to determine jurisdictional questions about the legal problem.	Embedded assessment in the research exam showed students are not meeting standards in understanding jurisdictional questions.	Assigning additional reading on jurisdictional questions; dedicating a class period to using different jurisdictional hypotheticals; finding other areas in the curriculum to touch on this subject
Students understand the need for and how to use secondary sources to familiarize themselves with an unknown area of law.	Embedded assessment in the research exam showed the requisite number of students do not recognize the importance of using secondary sources and are not willing to access them.	Bringing in lawyers who are practicing to discuss the importance of this step in the legal research process; giving additional secondary source assignments; designing assignments where secondary sources are necessary (*i.e.*, not in an area of law in which students are familiar)
Students can research and find relevant case law, and/or statutes, and/or regulations in the online and print versions of legal sources.	Embedded assessment pathfinders showed the requisite number of students are not proficient in using computer aided legal research to solve legal issues.	Dedicating numerous classes to CALR throughout the semester to give many touch points and practice for the students; having CALR reps visit the LRW classrooms to do tutorials; giving additional pathfinder assignments to those who are not meeting standards

After the faculty make some or all of the suggested changes, it is important to perform subsequent assessments and compare the results. This subsequent data will determine if the changes have improved student learning. If they have not, the LRW faculty should look for additional practice methods aimed at filling in the gaps.

Endnotes

1. Linda Suskie, Assessing Student Learning: A Common Sense Guide 50 (3d ed. 2018).
2. *Gonzaga University School of Law Course Content Descriptions*, Gonzaga Univ. (updated Jan. 23, 2020), https://www.gonzaga.edu/-/media/Website/Documents/Academics/School-of-Law/Academics/Curriculum/Course-Descriptions-1-23-20.ashx?la=en&hash=D8EF5B1F75753C-0CF4400F6586AC2CD0A182C621 (last visited July 8, 2020). Beginning in the fall of 2020, Gonzaga changed its LRW and course curriculum. As of the publishing of this book, the author of this chapter is in the first semester of the new curriculum and has yet to assess it with the new course structure.
3. The chart includes only a few of Gonzaga's outcomes for brevity purposes. This chart, however, is complete enough help a program create its own map.
4. See, e.g., Peggy L. Maki, Assessing for Learning: Building a Sustainable Commitment Across the Institution 61 (2010).
5. At Gonzaga, the LRW department is small enough that the professors worked on the assessment as a team, assigning different parts to each professor. One professor acted as the leader, but the work was done collectively as a team.
6. At Gonzaga, the assessment used in the clinic and externship program asked supervisors several questions that dealt directly with how well the students researched and wrote. The LRW professors were able to use that data to assess how students were doing after they left classes.
7. Determining benchmark scoring for minimum competence is discussed in Chapter 5.
8. *See* Suskie, supra note 1, at 158–160 (discussing sample size needed for accuracy). At Gonzaga, assessing all or most of the students was not a workable sample size. Instead the LRW professors used the "purposeful sample" that involves choosing students who should be representative of what is being assessed.
9. The additional benefit to looking at data from each section of Gonzaga's LRW program was that the professors were able to assess how adjunct-taught courses compared to full-time-professor-taught courses. This information will also help Gonzaga when it moves to more online courses. It is vitally important to have a mechanism to ensure the online curriculum is providing similar educational experiences to the in-residence courses.
10. *See* Suskie, supra note 1, at 155 (discussing how double scoring increases the accuracy but also the burden and the time for assessors). This is a judgment call for each program: how much time and effort can the program sustain?

CHAPTER EIGHT

Centers and Concentrations, Co-Curricular Activities

Using Chapter 5 as a guide for the assessment process, this chapter will focus on assessing centers and concentrations at a law school and will offer some ideas and suggestions for assessing various law school co-curricular activities. Included in this category are law journal, moot court, and other competition events (client counseling, negotiation, etc.).

1. Developing Learning Outcomes

Learning outcomes for centers and concentrations will reflect what knowledge, skills, and values students should gain through participation in the center activities or by obtaining a particular certificate. Learning outcomes will flow from the institutional learning outcomes and will likely include more subject-matter specific goals. They should span across all activities sponsored or required by the center. In this way, center faculty can evaluate the program as a whole and not just the individual components.

As with the broad experiential learning assessment discussed in Chapter 6, centers will need to determine which activities or courses fall under the umbrella of the center or concentration. The assessment team will need to inventory that programming to ensure sufficient opportunity for students to practice and achieve the specified learning outcomes.

Below are some examples targeting a variety of subject matter certificates or concentrations.

Table 8.1: Learning Outcomes for Washburn University School of Law J.D. Business and Transactional Law Certificate[1]

Students will demonstrate competent knowledge and understanding of the terms, rules, and principles of business and transactional law subjects.
Students will demonstrate an understanding of the authorities and sources of business and transactional law.
Students will demonstrate analytical and problem-solving skills when presented with issues of business and transactional law, including the ability to apply controlling legal principles to legal problems.
Students will be exposed to issues related to the practice of business and transactional law and some of the questions confronting practitioners in the area.
Students will demonstrate the ability to write in a clear, concise, well-organized, professional manner that is appropriate for business and transactional legal practice.
Students will demonstrate competency in business and transactional practice skills expected of attorneys in the area.

Table 8.2: Learning Outcomes for Washburn University School of Law J.D. Certificate in Workplace Law[2]

Students will demonstrate competent knowledge and understanding of the substantive law related to labor and employment practice.
Students will demonstrate the ability to understand clients' objectives and recommend practical strategies to achieve those objectives in the labor and employment field.
Students will demonstrate the ability to efficiently employ strategies for identifying, analyzing, researching, and solving specific legal problems within the field of labor and employment law in the manner expected of a competent lawyer.
Students will demonstrate the ability to communicate with clients, decision makers, and the range of other stakeholders in the manner expected of a new lawyer through thorough and efficient research and writing in the area of labor and employment law.
Students will demonstrate the ability to employ strategies for organizing and managing professional time, working cooperatively with others, and meeting professional deadlines in a manner expected of a new lawyer.

Table 8.3: Learning Outcomes for Boston University School of Law Estate Planning Certificate[3]

Students will demonstrate detailed knowledge of the substantive case law, statutory rules, and regulatory guidance with respect to the tax aspects of estate planning.
Students will demonstrate a fundamental understanding of the relevant considerations involved in drafting an estate plan.

Table 8.4: Learning Outcomes for Boston University School of Law Concentration in Intellectual Property and Information[4]

Students will demonstrate an understanding of the several federal and state legal domains for regulating intangibles and encouraging or rewarding creative/inventive effort. One or more of these domains will be federal copyright, federal trademark, or federal patent law. Students who pursue cyber issues will also demonstrate an understanding of the various empirical, normative, and legal issues posed by digital technologies, such as cybersecurity, database regulation, or cyberlaw.
Students will show competence in modes of statutory interpretation and an understanding of how to assess and deploy legislative history.
Students will demonstrate an ability to perform legal analysis and reasoning, including the ability to formulate arguments based in legislative history, economics, normative ethics, or caselaw, and demonstrate an ability to engage in problem-solving and strategic planning for litigation.
Students in the IP branch of the concentration will demonstrate an ability to draw across more than one subject-matter area to assess how best a client's IP issues should be framed for purposes of litigation or transactions.
Students will demonstrate an understanding of the challenges posed by differences between the many kinds of information products, both in comparing the intangible products and their different legal domains among themselves, and/or in comparing information products or the computer environment with the ordinary physical environment and tangible products such as land or chattels.
Students will demonstrate a basic understanding of what analogies from common-law physical property and torts might be illuminating in IP and information law, and the nature of the analogies' various shortcomings.
Students will demonstrate the ability to effectively prepare and deliver written and oral communication in the legal context, whether in negotiation, drafting or commenting on statutory proposals, client counseling, or in litigation.
Students will demonstrate an understanding of the many ways in which rapidly changing technology can affect, and be affected by, the law, in a way that can assist clients with their planning or legislators with their proposals.

For co-curricular activity outcomes, many law schools have learning outcomes related to skills that are prevalent in co-curricular activities—writing and oral advocacy, counseling or negotiating, listening and communication. Learning outcomes for the co-curricular programs thus can track institutional outcomes and perhaps even provide more detail about how those outcomes can be accomplished.

The institutional learning outcomes adopted by a law school could be tailored to the precise nature of the activity. The outcomes below, which are modified versions of the learning outcomes adopted by Washburn University School of Law,[5] could be used for moot court, journal, or other competitions as appropriate:

Table 8.5: Example Learning Outcomes for Moot Court, Journal, or Student Competitions

Students will write in a clear, concise, well-organized, professional manner that is appropriate to the audience and the circumstances.
Students will conduct legal research necessary for a scholarly written work.
Students will conduct legal research necessary for writing an effective appellate brief.
Students will demonstrate professionalism in their interactions with each other and with outside constituents.
Students will develop and strengthen their editing and cite-checking skills.
Students will use analogical reasoning to solve legal problems.
Students will use policy-based reasoning to solve legal problems.
Students will demonstrate active listening in communications with others, including legal professionals and laypersons.
Students will speak in a clear, concise, well-organized, professional manner that is appropriate to the audience and the circumstances.
Students will demonstrate the ability to conduct a factual investigation.
Students will demonstrate the ability to interview and counsel a client.
Students will demonstrate the ability to negotiate and advocate on behalf of a client in appropriate circumstances.
Students will consistently exercise professional and ethical responsibilities.
Students will recognize the existence and value of diversity both within the legal profession and among the clients it serves.

2. Developing a Plan for Program Assessment

As discussed in Chapter 5, when creating the written plan for assessing centers or concentrations, the assessment team will need to decide what kind of measures to use to assess each learning outcome, which will depend on the nature of the programming offered by the center. If these specialty units include certain courses (if, for example, the business law center requires each student to take the business associations course), then work done in those courses could be used as embedded assessments. Depending on the number of faculty members involved in the center, the assessment team may have a wide variety of sources to consider—written assignments in certain courses, final capstone projects, or quizzes and exams administered by center faculty. Assessment could also include surveys of current students, recent graduates, or employers about the students' abilities in the substantive area.

For co-curricular activities, most learning outcomes will likely be assessed through embedded assessments—those assignments or tasks that students will complete as part of participation in the activity. Recall that assessment methods can be either direct or indirect. Direct assessment would include things like the student note produced for a law journal or the brief written for a moot court competition. Additionally, scores or evaluations received from competitions would count as direct measures of performance. Indirect assessments could include students' evaluations of their own performance or surveys from other stakeholders about the students' abilities and performance.

3. Collecting the Assessment Data

Data collection will include conversations about how much data to collect—something from every student or a sampling of students participating in center activities. For co-curricular activities, it seems plausible that, given the limited number of students who participate in various co-curricular activities, the assessment plan could include review of all students involved.

The assessment leader will also need to identify when and how to collect the relevant data—getting copies of the student work, creating a rubric to evaluate the work, and deciding who will do the evaluating. Perhaps the faculty sponsor or coach for the various activities could evaluate the student work product. Or perhaps the work could be sent to outside reviewers—other faculty members, alumni or attorneys in the community, scholars at other institutions.

It may help to create rubrics or checklists specific to the activity and the student work, again tracking the wording of the learning outcomes specific to an activity. For example, the following checklist might be used to evaluate writing for a moot court brief or law journal:

Table 8.6: Scoresheet for Upper Level Writing Project

Evaluation Criteria	Unsatisfactory 1	2	Meets Expectations 3	4	Exceptional 5	N/A
Student's understanding of the terms, rules, and principles of law						
Student's ability to identify legal rules and to synthesize those rules into a logical framework for analysis						
Student's understanding of organization, hierarchy, and relationships within the legal system						
Student's understanding of primary and secondary sources of law and how they relate to each other						
Student's ability to apply controlling legal principles						
Student's ability to use analogical reasoning						
Student's ability to use policy-based reasoning						
Student's ability to write in a clear, concise, well-organized, and professional manner appropriate to the circumstances						
Student's ability to communicate professionally during conferences about the writing project						
Student's ability to engage in active listening during conferences about the writing project						
Student's ability to conduct legal research						

A similar checklist could be used to evaluate a student's oral presentation, either in a competition or for some other scholarly work:

Table 8.7: Scoresheet for Oral Presentation

	Unsatisfactory		Meets Expectations		Exceptional	
Evaluation Criteria	1	2	3	4	5	N/A
Student's understanding of the terms, rules, and principles of law						
Student's ability to identify legal rules and to synthesize those rules into a logical framework for analysis						
Student's understanding of organization, hierarchy, and relationships within the legal system						
Student's understanding of primary and secondary sources of law and how they relate to each other						
Student's ability to apply controlling legal principles						
Student's ability to use analogical reasoning						
Student's ability to use policy-based reasoning						
Student's ability to speak in a clear, concise, well-organized, and professional manner appropriate to audience and the circumstances						
Student's ability to engage in active listening in communications with others, including classmates and the professor						
Student's ability to conduct legal research						

4. Evaluating the Assessment Data

As with assessment of other sub-divisions of the law school, the assessment committee will need to decide what counts as satisfactory performance by the students. What scores on the rubric or the competition or on surveys mean that the students have achieved competency in the particular outcome at issue and that the center or activity is accomplishing its objectives?

5. Using Data to Improve Student Learning

To evaluate the data, the assessment team will need to identify the standard for performance on each of the learning outcomes. After evaluating the data, the assessment team can coordinate conversations with all faculty members involved in the center or activity to decide how to close the loop. If students are falling short of the standard for performance, the team could decide to require more or different courses, or offer additional instruction independently during outside events or guest speakers. Or the team could decide that a particular learning outcome is not a good fit for this particular center or concentration.

In the co-curricular activities, for example, if the scores for "accurate citation" are substandard, perhaps the law journal can increase its Bluebook training for students. If moot court students are continually falling below the threshold for success in oral argument, the moot court coach can identify additional oral argument practice opportunities or recruit more faculty members to help judge and offer advice.

This last step, as always, is the key. How can the information gathered be used to improve student learning in the future?

Endnotes

1. *Certificate in Business and Transactional Law* Washburn Univ. Sch. of Law, http://washburnlaw.edu/practicalexperience/transactional/certificate.html (last visited July 8, 2020).
2. *Certificate in Workplace Law*, Washburn Univ. Sch. of Law, http://washburnlaw.edu/practicalexperience/transactional/workplacecertificate.html (last visited July 8, 2020).
3. *Learning Outcomes for Degree Programs and Concentrations* Boston Univ. Sch. of Law, https://www.bu.edu/law/academics/learning-outcomes/ (last visited July 8, 2020).
4. *Id.*
5. *Juris Doctor Degree*, Washburn Univ. Sch. of Law, http://washburnlaw.edu/academics/jurisdoctor/ (last visited July 8, 2020).

CHAPTER NINE

Non-Academic Units

As part of a building-wide assessment effort, law schools can include departments and offices that serve non- or quasi-academic functions. The admissions office, the career services office, the alumni office, the library — all of these units perform vital roles within the law school and contribute to student success. Working through the assessment process as described in Chapter 5 can ensure these departments are aligned with the overall student learning outcomes of the institution.

The "non- or quasi-academic" label is not intended to suggest that these offices fail to perform any of the school's academic work. Professionals in these offices may be involved in teaching (a research class offered by librarians, for example) or other academic programs. And those activities should be assessed along with other courses or experiential offerings. This chapter focuses instead on the other operations of these departments — the programming and functions that are not part of the law school's official academic curriculum.

To the extent the mission of any particular office in the law school connects to or includes student learning, that department's contribution to student learning should be assessed according to the institutional student learning outcomes. If instead an office primarily serves administrative functions, it should be monitored and evaluated in conjunction with administrative outcomes.[1]

1. Developing Learning Outcomes

Identifying learning outcomes for other departments may be more difficult than for other assessment ventures because these offices interact with law students in ways different from academic programs or courses. For purposes of this assessment process, the outcomes should focus, as discussed in Chapter 1, on student learning: "After engaging with this office or this department, students should be able to. . . ."

Each of the offices in the law school will regularly and systematically be evaluating its own effectiveness based on its administrative goals and service outcomes. For example, the admission office reviews statistics on applications received, students admitted, and students matriculated to evaluate the reach and success of its recruitment efforts. Similarly, the career services office notes successes and trends in student interviews, job placement, and alumni connections. Libraries keep track of how many students and members of the public use their facilities and services. That process is valuable and necessary for efficient functioning of these law school units. But it is separate and distinct from the institutional assessment process of student learning that this book discusses.[2]

To that end, departments should identify the programming that they offer that is directly related to student learning—mock interviews, alumni mentorship programs, professionalism lectures, small group research sessions, pro bono opportunities—and describe the learning outcomes they wish students to obtain through participation in those programs. The learning outcomes should flow from and be consistent with the institutional learning outcomes but tailored to the particular focus of each office.

For example, these are some of the institutional learning outcomes adopted by Washburn University School of Law[3] that might lend themselves to more specific learning outcomes for non-academic departments:

Table 9.1: Institutional Learning Outcomes to Adapt for Non-Academic Unit Outcomes

Students will write in a clear, concise, well-organized, professional manner that is appropriate to the audience and the circumstances.
Students will speak in a clear, concise, well-organized, professional manner that is appropriate to the audience and the circumstances.
Students will demonstrate active listening in communications with others, including legal professionals and laypersons.
Students will demonstrate an awareness of and a willingness to contribute to the profession's responsibility to ensure access to justice.
Students will demonstrate a willingness to contribute to serving the underserved and traditionally marginalized communities.

The career services office in a law school may have connections to student learning in terms of presentations or trainings to help students navigate the job market. Thus, some possible student learning outcomes for that office that align with the broader institutional outcomes might include:

Table 9.2: Example Learning Outcomes for a Career Services Office

Students will know how to assess their skills, interests, and values, and make informed career choices based on their self-assessment.
Students will be able to write an effective cover letter and resume, appropriate for the particular job opportunity being sought.
Students will know how to conduct an effective internship and job search.

Table 9.3: Learning Outcomes for Ave Maria School of Law Office of Professional Development[4]

Recognize the professional competencies required of first-year attorneys and develop a plan to reach an acceptable proficiency level in these competencies by graduation.
Define mentorship in a legal context, recognize the importance of mentorship as a law student and legal professional, understand how to find and develop mentorship relationship.
Recognize the importance of time management in the profession, develop proper time-management strategies, and utilize the time-management strategies to allow for internship application and participation at some point throughout law school.
Recognize the importance of networking in law school and throughout the legal profession, seeking opportunities to network and developing a comfort level with networking.
Display knowledge of legal application documents, including resume and writing sample, and ability to draft and update legal documents in such a manner that it increases visibility and marketability.
Define professionalism, display knowledge of the importance of professionalism in the legal profession and development of professional reputation throughout law school.
Define professional development, increase awareness of role in professional development and creation of personal professional development plan before graduation.
Demonstrate knowledge of the importance of service to the community, including the legally underserved.
Identify the verbal and written communication skills necessary in a professional setting and grow personal communication style expected of a legal professional. Maintain consistent communication skill level necessary to build and maintain professional relationships.

Law libraries may offer programming (outside of involvement in teaching courses) to help students learn about their services or resources. Provided the library offers specific trainings or lessons, student learning outcomes may be appropriate. Depending on programming offered by the library, law schools may create student learning outcomes for the library such as these:[5]

Table 9.4: Sample Learning Outcomes for Law Library

Students will identify library services and availability of resources in order to develop a realistic overall plan for research.
Students will use information across multiple formats (print, visual, multimedia, data, etc.) and genres in order to seek and evaluate relevant or appropriate evidence.
Students will identify the features and content of different research tools (such as databases, catalogs, and websites) in order to search those most appropriate to the information needed.
Students will identify and use search language, controlled vocabulary, or search features appropriate to the research tool in order to retrieve relevant results.
Students will select appropriate means for recording or saving relevant sources in order to retrieve them when needed.
Students will identify library and information services, facilities, and collections, articulating how they are organized both digitally and physically.
Students will demonstrate awareness of discourses across academic disciplines, communities, and professions, including how each produces, contextualizes, and disseminates information.

To the extent the admissions office participates in new student orientation, it may have operational goals related directly to student learning — preparing for class, reading a case, briefing a case. Similarly, if the alumni office hosts events for students to learn more about networking or mentoring relationships with alumni, those might lend themselves to specific student learning outcomes.

2. Developing a Plan for Program Assessment

The assessment process will follow the same basic outline as discussed in Chapter 5. An assessment team leader will facilitate the process of creating an assessment plan, which should include a timeline and schedule for reviewing each learning outcome, as well as the methods for collecting data related to each learning outcome.

Given that students probably do not complete academic work as part of their interactions with these departments, likely methods for assessing the learning outcomes will be indirect — surveys of students or alumni about what they have learned from the department programming or surveys of employers about how well the institution's graduates perform in certain areas. Surveys[6] could very easily track the exact language of the learning outcome, asking students, alums, or employers how well the law school prepared students to perform that task — research, communication, professional letter writing, time management, etc. Additionally, departments could include focus group discussions or interviews of students, alums, or employers.

Something to keep in mind when using surveys is the risk of survey fatigue, the feeling survey respondents get when faced with too many questions or too many surveys. Survey fatigue can affect response rates and skew the accuracy of the information collected. If the institution is reaching out to area employers with a survey about learning outcomes this semester, employers may not be very enthusiastic about completing another survey next year. Instead, surveys could be sent to a subset of the employers or alumni, and future surveys to a different subgroup, on a rotating basis.

In addition to surveys or focus groups, assessment could include some direct measures. For example, if students create a cover letter and resume for someone in the career services office to review, it would be possible to create a rubric for evaluating resumes and cover letters. The example on the following spread is from The Language Flagship Technology Innovation Center at the University of Hawaii,[7] an online educational resource not specific to legal education, but law schools could easily create their own similar rubrics:

Table 9.5: Rubric for Resume and Cover Letter

Résumé	Excellent–4 pts	Good–3 pts	Fair–2 pts	Poor–1 pt
Content _______ **pts**	Lists **all the required components**: personal information, experience, education, skills, honors. Descriptions of work experience and education background **highlight applicant's strengths** while **matching the job qualifications**.	Lists most of the required components. Descriptions of work experience and education background are somewhat vague and insufficient, and not clearly targeted to the position.	Some of the required components missing. Descriptions of work experience and education background are vague and insufficient. Résumé is generic and not tailored to the position.	Most of the required components missing. Descriptions of work experience and education background are minimal and irrelevant to the position.
Organization _______ **pts**	The most important items listed on the top half of résumé. Items listed in **reverse chronological order**. Very easy to identify key ideas and skills.	Listing important items in reverse chronological order is inconsistent. Relatively easy to identify key ideas and skills.	Several sections or items are not in reverse chronological order. Difficult to identify key ideas and skills.	Sections and items are not well-organized (in random order). Key skills and ideas are very difficult to find.
Vocabulary & Grammar _______ **pts**	Uses **formal (academic, specialized) vocabulary** to describe work experience and education background precisely and concisely. **Strong action verbs** are used.	Uses mostly formal (academic, specialized) vocabulary to describe work experience and education background. Occasional use of colloquial vocabulary remains. Some strong action verbs are used, but some are generic.	Frequent use of informal and generic vocabulary. Some word usages correspond to applicant's first language.	Frequent inaccuracy in word use or selection. Word usages mostly correspond to applicant's first language. Only informal vocabulary is used.
Grammar _______ **pts**	Minimal (1–3) grammatical errors, punctuation errors, and typos.	4–6 grammatical errors, punctuation errors, and typos.	7–10 grammatical errors, punctuation errors, and typos. Some sentence structures correspond to applicant's first language.	Sentence structures mostly correspond to applicant's first language. Over 10 grammatical errors, punctuation errors, and typos.

Visual Appearance _______ **pts**	Consistent in choice of **layout** and **font style/size**. Fills **only one page**, but not overcrowding. Overall visually appealing and very professional.	Shows appropriate appearance. Some inconsistencies in choice of layout and font style/size remain. Does not exceed one page.	Page appears crowded but does not exceed one page. Many consistencies in choice of layout and font style/size.	Exceeds one page or does not fill the majority of the page. Font style/size is unreadable.

Cover Letter	Excellent–4 pts	Good–3 pts	Fair–2 pts	Poor–1 pt
Content _______ **pts**	Includes **all the required components**: appropriate salutation and closing statement, personal information, position sought, and purpose of the letter. Mentions attached résumé. Highlights **strengths/qualifications related to the job**. Elaborates on **reasons for applying for this position**.	Includes most of the required components. Mentions attached résumé. Highlighted strengths/qualifications are not convincing or clearly targeted to the position. Mentions reasons for applying for this job, but not in detail.	Includes some of the required components. Does not mention attached résumé. Strengths/ qualifications are not tailored to the position. Listed reasons for applying for this job are generic and not targeted to the position.	Most of the required components are missing. Does not mention attached résumé, strengths/ qualifications, or reasons for applying for this position.
Vocabulary _______ **pts**	Uses **formal (academic, specialized) vocabulary** and expressions.	Uses some formal (academic, specialized) vocabulary and expressions. Occasional use of informal vocabulary remains.	Frequent use of generic vocabulary and colloquial expressions.	Uses mostly informal vocabulary and colloquial expressions.
Grammar _______ **pts**	Minimal (1–3) grammatical errors, punctuation errors, and typos that do not impair comprehension.	4–6 grammatical errors, punctuation errors, and typos that do not impair comprehension.	7–10 grammatical errors, punctuation errors, and typos that may impair comprehension.	Over 10 grammatical errors, punctuation errors, and typos that may impair comprehension.
Format & Style _______ **pts**	Uses appropriate **font style and size**. Format is consistent. **Layout (e.g., margin, line spacing)** is visually appealing.	Some inconsistencies in choice of font style/size remain. Layout is clear.	Many inconsistencies in choice of font style/size. Choices in layout may affect readability.	Very inconsistent in choice of font style/size. Some font size/style does not appear professional. Unclear layout affects readability.

One caveat to consider: it may be more challenging to obtain a representative sample of direct evidence from non-academic offices like career services, since students typically are not required to engage with these offices. Students who use the career services offices for resume and cover letter review may self-select into the more motivated and self-directed students, which might skew the samples of their resumes and cover letters.

3. Collecting the Assessment Data

Logistics of data collection, particularly involving surveys of students or outside stakeholders, may include choosing the online platform for sending out the surveys, the type of program for storing the data, timelines, email lists to contact, etc. For focus groups or other discussion-based assessment methods, the data collected will likely be qualitative instead of quantitative, and the assessment team will need to decide how to gather and evaluate that information. If the focus group session is recorded, transcribe the conversation. Otherwise, review notes taken during the discussion. "In some cases, you can devise and use a coding system to 'score' the data and count the number of times a particular theme is expressed."[8]

4. Evaluating the Assessment Data

As part of reviewing and evaluating data gathered in the assessment process, the assessment team will need to establish thresholds for success for each of the student learning outcomes. If relying on surveys, those thresholds might look something like this:

Table 9.6: Threshold for Success for Survey Results

Career Services Student Learning Outcome	Threshold for Success
Recognize the importance of time management in the profession, develop proper time management strategies, and utilize the time management strategies to allow for internship application and participation at some point throughout law school.	The average answer for survey questions 1–3 will be 4 (out of 5).

Conversely, if the outcome is to be assessed based on work product, the threshold might be related to review of student work compared to a rubric:

Table 9.7: Threshold for Success for Work Evaluated on a Rubric

Career Services Student Learning Outcome	Threshold for Success
Students will be able to write an effective cover letter and resume, appropriate for the particular job opportunity being sought.	Of the cover letters and resumes reviewed by this office, the average score on the rubric will be 3.5 (out of 4).

5. Using Data to Improve Student Learning

As discussed in Chapter 5, once information is collected, it can be used to adjust programming to target areas that fall below the identified threshold for success. For example, if students are not successfully creating cover letters that are effective and efficient, the career services office may decide to provide additional sessions or resources for how to create those documents. Alternatively, the assessment team may decide that the learning outcome is not appropriate or necessary for that particular department to achieve as part of its mission within the law school. Either way, the conversations about student performance and student learning are important.

Endnotes

1. The administrative assessment process is beyond the scope of this book. Some resources addressing this process include: KAREN W. NICHOLS & JAMES O. NICHOLS, THE DEPARTMENT HEAD'S GUIDE TO ASSESSMENT IMPLEMENTATION IN ADMINISTRATIVE AND EDUCATIONAL SUPPORT UNITS (2001); JAMES O. NICHOLS, THE ADMINISTRATIVE UNIT ASSESSMENT HANDBOOK, https://oeas.ucf.edu/doc/adm_assess_handbook.pdf (last visited July 8, 2020); ASSESSMENT COMMONS: ASSESSING ADMINISTRATIVE AND SUPPORT UNITS, http://assessmentcommons.org/assessing-administrative-support-units/ (last visited July 8, 2020).

2. *Id.*

3. *Juris Doctor Degree*, WASHBURN UNIV. SCH. OF LAW, http://washburnlaw.edu/academics/jurisdoctor/ (last visited July 8, 2020).

4. *Professional Development*, AVE MARIA SCH. OF LAW, https://www.avemarialaw.edu/law-school-job-placement/ (last visited July 8, 2020).

5. These samples are taken from various undergraduate library websites: *Library Learning Outcomes*, PORTLAND STATE UNIV. LIBRARY, https://library.pdx.edu/services/library-instruction-services/library-learning-outcomes/ (last visited July 8, 2020); *Student Learning Outcomes*, TEX. A&M UNIV. LIBRARIES, https://library.tamu.edu/libraryInstruction/student-learning-outcomes.html (last visited July 8, 2020); *Student Learning Goals and Outcomes*, UNIV. OF WASH. (UW) LIBRARIES, https://www.lib.washington.edu/teaching/learning-goals (last visited July 8, 2020).

6. Scientific research suggests ways to create effective and valid surveys. Law schools may want to consider using professionally developed surveys rather than ones the assessment team creates itself.

7. *CHN 486 Virtual Work Experience: Résumé and Cover Letter Rubric*, The Language Flagship Technology Innovation Center, https://lftic.lll.hawaii.edu/wp-content/uploads/2016/05/Resume-Cover-Letter-Rubric.pdf

8. *Conducting Focus Groups*, Community Tool Box, https://ctb.ku.edu/en/table-of-contents/assessment/assessing-community-needs-and-resources/conduct-focus-groups/main (last visited July 8, 2020).

Section Three: Assessment of Teaching

CHAPTER TEN

Foundations of Assessment of Teaching

This chapter addresses three foundational aspects of the assessment of teaching: (1) the purposes and characteristics of formative and summative assessments of teaching; (2) the components of effective teaching; and (3) the strengths and weaknesses of self, peer, student, and administrator assessment of teaching.

1. Summative and Formative Assessments of Teaching

A comprehensive system for assessment of teaching includes both summative and formative components.[1] The purpose of summative assessment of teaching is to produce evidence of teaching effectiveness as part of personnel decisions such as retention, tenure, promotion, and salary determinations. The purpose of formative assessment of teaching is to provide feedback to help faculty members improve their teaching effectiveness.

The characteristics of summative and formative assessments of teaching differ considerably. Because personnel decisions are high stakes events, summative assessments should have formal, uniform processes and criteria established by the institution. Formative assessments are not high-stakes events and should be flexible, tailored to the needs of the individual teacher. The primary audience for summative assessments is the faculty members and administrators who are making the personnel decisions. The primary audience for formative assessment is the teacher. The focus of summative assessment is retrospective, looking to evaluate the past teaching effectiveness of a faculty member. The focus of formative assessment is prospective, aiming to improve future teaching effectiveness. Summative assessment of teaching occurs at intervals, such as annual or tenure reviews. Formative assessment of teaching is ongoing, throughout a faculty member's career.

Because the purposes and characteristics of summative and formative assessments of teaching differ substantially, an institution should have separate summative and formative assessment systems. The summative assessment system should be designed to produce an accurate and fair evaluation of a faculty member's teaching effectiveness. The formative assessment system should be designed to help faculty members improve their teaching in order to succeed in personnel decisions and to enhance students' learning.

Institutions that have both summative and formative systems for assessment of teaching face issues related to the use of data and information generated in the assessment systems. These issues arise because several sources of assessment information are the same in both systems — the teacher being assessed (self-assessment, teaching dossier or portfolio), peers (classroom observations, review of teaching materials), and students (student evaluations, student learning outcomes).

Although information generated in the summative assessment system is designed to inform personnel decisions, there is nothing to prevent a faculty member from using that information to improve future teaching performance. For example, it is perfectly appropriate for a teacher to use student course evaluations to identify teaching strengths to build upon and weaknesses to address in future teaching. Likewise, peer classroom observations and reviews of teaching material done as part of summative assessment may contain a wealth of information a faculty member can use to grow as a teacher.

A more difficult issue is whether information originally generated in formative assessment should be used in personnel decisions. On the one hand, a common recommendation is that information from formative assessment should never be used in summative assessments. For example, information from peers who observe classes and review materials as part of a teaching development program would not be used in personnel decisions. Nevertheless, many institutions allow information from formative peer review to be used in summative assessments, in part because it is very resource-intensive to operate completely separate assessment systems. In addition, candidates for tenure or promotion may wish to rely on material generated in formative assessment, such as peer observations and student learning outcomes, to demonstrate teaching effectiveness and growth as a teacher. Consequently, it is important for an institution to develop clear guidelines concerning the use of information from formative assessment in personnel decisions.

2. What Is Effective Teaching?

Given that the primary purpose of summative assessment is to evaluate a faculty member's teaching effectiveness as part of a personnel decision and that the primary purpose of formative assessment is ongoing improvement of a teacher's effectiveness, it is critical to define effective teaching. There is no single, established definition of effective teaching. That is not surprising because teaching is a multi-faceted, complex activity. Individual faculty members and institutions could articulate a wide variety of conceptions of what constitutes effective teaching. The vast literature on teaching and learning in higher education and legal education identifies many components of effective teaching, which faculty members and schools can draw upon when defining effective teaching. Eight of those components follow:

- Student Learning Outcomes,
- Learning Theory Principles,
- Subject Matter Expertise,
- Teaching and Learning Environment,
- Instructional Design,
- Instructional Delivery,
- Assessment of Students, and
- Ongoing Teaching Development.

a. Student Learning Outcomes

Teaching is effective only if it produces substantial student learning.[2] "Exceptional teachers produce exceptional learning."[3] Teaching is not effective if students fail to learn, even if the teacher designed a challenging course and worked diligently to engage students in and out of the classroom. Consequently, student learning outcomes are an important measure of effective teaching in a course. Much of this book describes the process of articulating and assessing student learning outcomes at the institutional, programmatic, and course levels.

On the other hand, student learning outcomes are not the *sole* measure of effective teaching. A course could result in substantial student learning in spite of, rather than because of, the teacher's performance.[4] As an extreme example, a teacher could assign out-of-date, inappropriate reading materials for

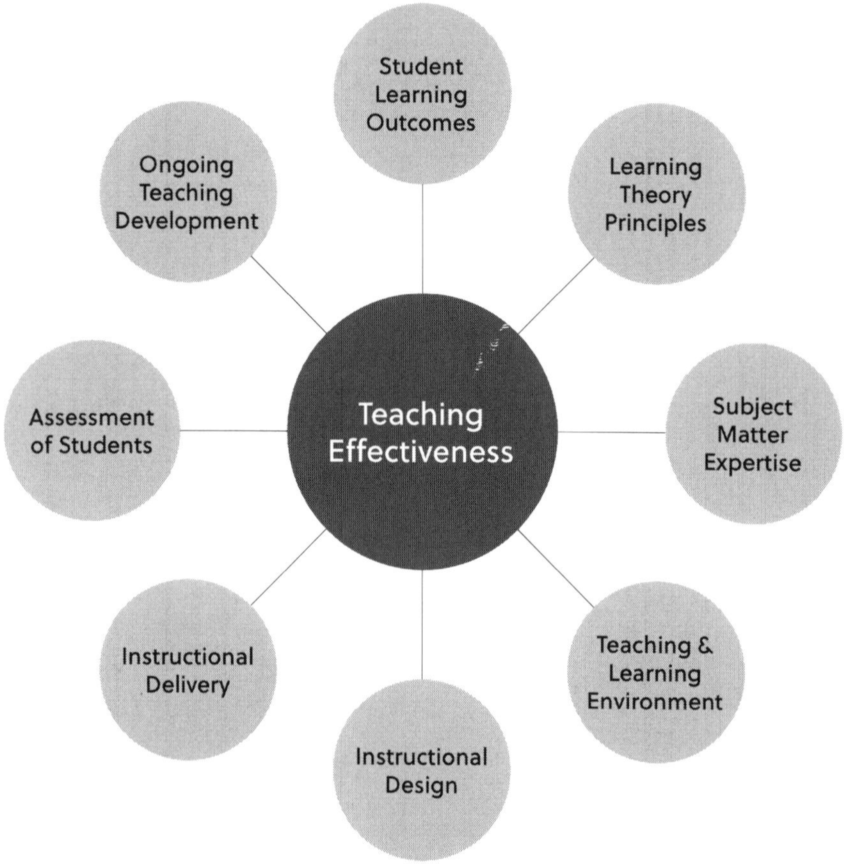

Figure 10.1: Components of Effective Teaching

a course and then fail to appear for any class sessions, yet the students learn significant content and skills by finding their own materials and teaching one another the course. Although that course may be successful because of the student learning outcomes, the teaching was not effective. The remainder of this section explores other potential components and measures of teaching effectiveness.

b. Learning Theory Principles

Another aspect of effective teaching is the extent to which a teacher's course design and delivery are consistent with principles of how people learn. Instructional designers define learning as lasting changes in students' knowledge, behavior, and attitudes. Learning theories attempt to describe and explain how people learn.[5] Three learning theories that have significant implications for assessing teaching effectiveness are summarized below: behaviorism, cognitivism, and constructivism.

Behaviorism.[6] Behaviorists believe that learning takes place when a student gives a correct response to an environmental stimulus and that the link between stimulus and response can be strengthened through reinforcement. Principles and implications of behaviorism include the following:

- Instruction should be sequenced so students master basic content and skills before encountering more complex material and problems.
- Learning is enhanced when students practice and get feedback on their performance.
- Learning can be facilitated by students' interaction with a teacher and by students' interaction with written material, electronic media, and computer programming without the presence of a teacher.

Cognitivism.[7] Cognitivists focus on how the brain processes and retains learning. For learning to last, it must become part of students' long-term memory. In the long-term memory, concepts, skills, and values are categorized and stored in cognitive structures that can be retrieved and applied in the future. The following factors make it more likely for learning to end up in students' long-term memory:

- Learning activities should help students connect new concepts and skills to what students already know.
- Instruction should present new concepts and skills through graphics and multiple examples.
- Students should actively process the new learning by organizing it, writing about it, discussing it, and applying it to problems.

Constructivism.[8] Constructivists focus on the process through which students acquire new learning. The core precept of constructivism is that students actively construct, rather than passively receive, learning. Three principles of learning emerge from constructivism:

- Students construct new learning from experience by actively engaging with new ideas and reflecting on their learning.

- Real-world experience is critical in developing new learning; students learn best in realistic contexts, such as practical problems, simulations, clinics, and externships.
- Learning is collaborative; students create learning through discussion and negotiation from various perspectives.

c. Subject-Matter Expertise

An essential component of teaching effectiveness is subject-matter expertise. Effective teachers understand at a deep level the subject's organizational scheme, legal doctrine, theory, policy, practical application, thinking skills, performance skills, ethical issues, and professionalism.[9]

d. Teaching and Learning Environment

Effective teachers create a positive teaching and learning environment in their courses.[10] A healthy teaching and learning environment is important in all forms of instruction, whether in a classroom, online, or in a clinic. Elements of a positive teaching and learning environment include the following:

- Respect,
- Expectations,
- Support,
- Passion,
- Inclusion,
- Engagement, and
- Collaboration.

Respect. Mutual respect among teachers and students is an essential element of a positive teaching and learning environment. Mutual respect goes from teachers to students, students to teachers, and students to students. In respectful environments, students are willing to engage in dialogue, explore ideas, share diverse perspectives, and solve problems creatively. Conversely, educational environments that feature humiliation, intimidation, or denigration hinder learning for many students. Teachers model respect by how they treat students, staff, and colleagues on a daily basis. Several of the other elements of positive educational environments also demonstrate respect, including high expectations for all students, inclusion of a variety of perspectives, and collaboration with students.

Expectations. Teachers' expectations greatly affect students' motivation and learning. High, realistic expectations lead to more student achievement; low expectations result in less student learning. Expectations that motivate students are clear, achievable, uniform, and reciprocal. Effective teachers clearly define their expectations for both themselves and their students. Their expectations are realistic and challenge students to stretch themselves to do their best work. They communicate their belief that every student can attain a high level of achievement. Finally, effective teachers impose high expectations on themselves and demonstrate every day that they are working diligently to make the course successful.

Support. A supportive teaching and learning environment should accompany high expectations. Effective teachers demonstrate their commitment to helping each student succeed in the course. A supportive environment is built upon teachers' attitudes and availability. One set of common descriptors of exemplary teachers focuses on their attitudes toward students — "helpful," "caring," "concerned," and "encouraging." Another set of attributes of excellent teachers is "available," "accessible," and "approachable." Teachers' attitudes and availability have strong positive effects on student motivation and active engagement in their own education. Teachers support students by serving as professional role models and mentors.

Passion. Students regularly identify teachers' passion or enthusiasm as the most important ingredient of effective instruction. Teachers' passion can inspire, energize, and motivate students. Effective teachers communicate to students their delight in teaching, working with students, and the subject matter of the course. They celebrate success in the classroom by providing positive reinforcement when students produce insight, solid analysis, or creative thinking.

Inclusion. Student motivation is an important ingredient in the quality of student learning. Motivation is enhanced when students feel welcome and included in a course. An inclusive teaching and learning environment values diverse student goals, experiences, interests, perspectives, and ways of learning.

Engagement. An effective teaching and learning environment actively engages teachers and students. Teachers demonstrate engagement by asking questions, encouraging students to respond, seeking a variety of viewpoints from students, answering students' questions, and listening carefully to students' responses. Students actively engage in learning by listening, reading, taking notes, asking questions, responding to questions, discussing, writing, and performing. Active student engagement helps achieve core goals of legal education, including thinking skills, deep understanding of doctrine and theory, lawyering skills, and professional values.

Collaboration. Two types of collaboration contribute to a positive teaching and learning environment. The first is collaborative learning in which students work in pairs or small groups in class discussion and projects out of class. Extensive research in university and legal education documents the effectiveness of cooperative learning in fostering student learning of complex concepts, problem-solving skills, reasoning, critical thinking, and students' ability to work collaboratively in a team. The second type of collaboration occurs when teachers treat students like collaborators and colleagues. For example, teachers can involve students in significant course design decisions, such as course goals, learning activities, and assessment methods.

e. Instructional Design

Another component of effective teaching is adherence to the principles of instructional design, which is the process of thoughtfully planning teaching and learning.[11] Instructional design principles apply to the development of an entire course and individual class sessions. Elements of instructional design include articulating learning objectives, choosing teaching and learning activities, identifying instructional materials, developing an assessment scheme, preparing a syllabus, and reviewing and revising the design.

Articulate Learning Objectives. The starting point in instructional design is for the teacher to clearly articulate what the students should learn. Effective teachers write learning objectives for their courses and for each class session. Learning objectives should define the legal doctrine, theory, thinking skills, performance skills, and professional values that students should learn in a course or class session. Learning objectives should drive the teacher's decisions about teaching and learning activities, materials, and assessment.

Choose Teaching and Learning Activities. Many teaching and learning methods are appropriate in legal education including Socratic dialog, lecture, large group discussion, small group work, problem solving, writing, reading, student presentations, and experiential learning. Several principles guide the choice of teaching and learning activities for a course and for each class session. The primary principle is to choose methods to maximize student learning and class objectives. Second, to enhance student interest and motivation, effective teachers plan to use more than one method for each class session and incorporate many methods throughout the course. Third, in every course, some content and skills are more important than others, so teachers should design instruc-

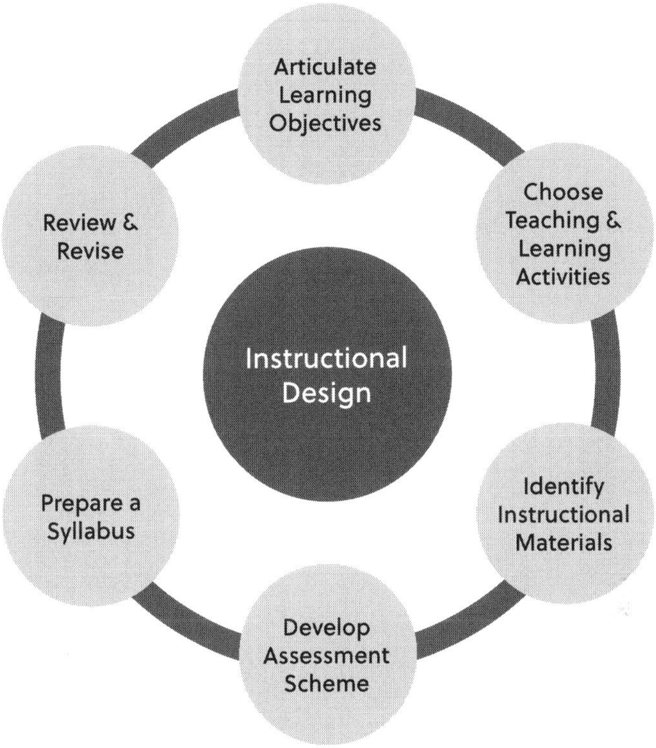

Figure 10.2: Instructional Design Cycle

tional activities that involve multiple methods for the most important aspects of the course. Fourth, effective teachers design teaching and learning activities that take place both in class and outside of class.

Identify Instructional Materials. Course materials include both print and electronic resources that students will use outside of class or that students and teachers will use during class. Print materials include textbooks (statutes, cases, problems), legal documents (pleadings, memoranda, contracts, wills), news stories, articles, and handouts (problems, charts, diagrams, hypotheticals). Electronic resources include a course web page, pictures, videos, slides, podcasts, CALI exercises, and websites. Two criteria guide teachers' selection of print and electronic resources. First, there should be congruence between learning objectives, teaching and learning methods, and instructional materials. The primary consideration is whether the material will help students achieve the learning objectives, aid student preparation for class, and support the accompanying teaching and learning methods. Second, variety in instructional materials can grab students' attention and maintain their interest and motivation.

Develop an Assessment Scheme. Every course should include both formative and summative assessment of student learning. Formative assessment is feedback to students during the course to help them improve their learning and achieve the learning objectives. Summative assessment includes the methods used to evaluate student performance and grade students. Both types of assessment are discussed in more detail in the Assessment of Students section below.

Prepare the Syllabus. The course syllabus is a contract between teachers and students. A thoughtful syllabus can help set the tone for the course, engage and inspire students, communicate high expectations, and display the teacher's professionalism and skill in designing the course. A comprehensive syllabus can provide the basic information students need to navigate the course successfully:

- The teacher's name and contact information, office hours, and process for making appointments;
- The course name, required materials, course web page, course description, and learning objectives;
- The teacher's expectations for student attendance, classroom conduct, and preparation for class;
- The teacher's educational philosophy and teaching methods;
- A schedule of class meetings, readings, projects, and other assignments;
- The grading scheme and policies for late assignments and failure to complete assigned projects; and
- Rules relating to plagiarism and academic misconduct.

Review and Revise the Instructional Design. Effective teachers engage in systematic and continuous instructional design. Throughout the course, teachers can keep detailed notes about the strengths and weaknesses of the design of the course and individual class sessions. Which assignments, materials, teaching methods, and exercises were most and least engaging? Which learning objectives were most and least achieved? Which assessments were most and least effective? What parts of the syllabus were most and least clear to students? The next time they offer the course, effective teachers reflect on their notes and revise the instructional design accordingly.

f. Instructional Delivery

Effective teachers not only carefully design their courses and class sessions, they excel at instructional delivery as well. Their teaching practices help turn well-crafted instructional plans into significant student learning. Instructional delivery includes a myriad of teacher skills and practices, including the following:

- Preparation,
- Organization,
- Communication,
- Interaction,
- Methodology, and
- Visuals.

These teacher skills and practices apply in all types of settings in legal education — in the classroom, in a clinic, in an individual conference, and online. Throughout this discussion, the term "class" is intended to encompass all of those settings.

Preparation.[12] Three types of preparation are important elements of effective classes. First, teachers need to do the work to understand at a deep level the content, skills, and values that will be the focus of the class. Second, effective teachers do detailed preparation to execute the class design. For example, they articulate the two to four concepts or skills that the students should learn in the class, decide what students will do during the class (discuss, write, listen, argue, perform), and prepare the appropriate exercises, examples, handouts, slides, and questions. Third, teachers can help students prepare for class by being clear about what they expect students to do outside of class (*e.g.*, reading assignments, problems, exercises, videos) and by having reasonable expectations about the time necessary for students to be well prepared.

Organization.[13] Effective teachers are organized. They begin and end classes on time. Their classes are structured with an opening, body, and closing. At the beginning of class, effective teachers grab students' attention, convey the learning objectives for the class, provide a roadmap for the class, and tie the class to previous classes. During the body of the class, teachers facilitate learning activities aimed at helping students attain the learning objectives. They transition effectively from one activity to another. Teachers can use the last few minutes of class to review, summarize, and give students an opportunity to consolidate their learning.

Communication.[14] Effective teachers have excellent communication skills. Their written communication with students (*e.g.*, syllabus, assignments, handouts, slides, email, web page) is thoughtful and clear. They have strong presentation skills (in class and videos outside of class) including clear annunciation, varying tone and volume, eye contact, enthusiasm, gestures, and movement. They illustrate concepts, skills, and values with real-life examples. They use silence to gain attention, emphasize a point, or give students time to respond to a question, work on a problem, or formulate questions. They listen carefully to student questions and comments.

Interaction.[15] Interactions in class between students and effective teachers build rapport. Teachers develop rapport by calling students by name, welcoming students' questions and participation, and incorporating students' ideas into the class. Effective teachers use positive reinforcement, expressing delight in student contributions. Teacher-student interactions include humor and joy in working together in class.

Methodology. Effective teachers are comfortable using a variety of teaching and learning methods in their classes, including Socratic dialog, discussion, group work, lecture, writing, real-life experiences, computer exercises, simulations, and student presentations. Of course, no single class period would include all of these methods, and most teachers do not use all of the methods in a course. However, effective teachers are adept at using the methods they choose for a particular class. The legal education literature includes many descriptions of good practice and creative uses of many types of teaching methodologies.[16]

Visuals.[17] Teachers can enhance the effectiveness of classes though the appropriate use of visuals to support their teaching and learning methods. A variety of visuals in class can focus students' attention, make teachers' presentations more effective, and facilitate student interaction and active learning. The following examples are just a few of the potential uses of visuals in class:

- Slides to transmit information, project images, and pose questions, hypotheticals, and problems;
- Videos to illustrate doctrine, skills, and values or to raise issues;
- Boards and flip charts to capture student contributions during a discussion;
- Diagrams, flow charts, and mind maps to organize concepts and illustrate relationships; and
- Handouts in electronic or paper form, including pictures, questions, problems, rubrics, or charts.

g. Assessment of Students

Assessment plays an important role in fostering learning and measuring student achievement.[18] Formative assessment is designed to enhance student learning during the course. It provides students an opportunity to perform (*e.g.*, practice exam, paper draft, first attempt at an oral argument) and get feedback (such as a score sheet or comments). Summative assessment is designed to evaluate student achievement and assign grades. Papers, final exams, and student presentations are examples of summative assessment. Course-level outcomes assessment is discussed in detail in Chapter 4 above.

1) Characteristics of Effective Assessment

To be effective, assessments must be valid and reliable. An assessment is valid if it measures what it purports to measure. Valid assessments feature congruence and completeness. Congruence requires that the assessment measure student achievement of the learning objectives of the course. Completeness means that all of the applicable learning objectives are assessed in ways that measure a range of difficulty. Different types of assessment will likely be needed to validly assess legal doctrine, analytical skills, performance skills, and professionalism.

An assessment is reliable if it consistently measures what it claims to measure. A test is reliable if students' test scores reflect their level of understanding of the tested skills, theory, and doctrine. Reliability depends on scoring consistency so that similar student performances receive similar scores. Reliability also depends on sufficient content sampling so that students' performance reflects the extent to which they met the major course objectives, rather than a small slice of the course.

2) Formative Assessment of Students

Formative assessment is an essential part of the learning loop—students engage in learning activities, perform orally or in writing, and get feedback on their performance. Formative assessment should occur throughout the course.

Effective formative feedback to students has four features: (1) specific: teachers articulate specific criteria for students and give students feedback based on those criteria; (2) positive: identifies strengths upon which students can build; (3) corrective: identifies weaknesses in student performance and provides strategies for improvement; and (4) prompt: students receive feedback soon after their performance and before the next assessment.

Sources of formative feedback include the teacher, other students, a computer program, or self-assessment. Formative assessment can occur in and out of class. Formative assessment can take many forms, including large-group feedback in class on practice exams and quizzes, individual comments on paper drafts or on student performances, computer feedback on CALI lessons, conferences outside of class with small groups or individual students, and quizzes, problems, rubrics, and exercises posted on the course web page.

3) Summative Assessment of Students

Summative assessment has high stakes for students. Grades determine student retention, eligibility for law school programs (law review and moot court), and employment opportunities.

Effective summative assessment schemes have several characteristics — multiple, varied, and fair. Multiple and varied means that grades are based on several types of assessment throughout the course (*e.g.*, exam, paper, presentation) rather than solely on a final exam. Many types of assessment instruments are appropriate in legal education, including exams (midterm, final, essay questions, multiple-choice questions), quizzes, papers, document drafting (pleadings, contracts, wills), participation in class or on the course web page, presentations, and performances (interviewing, negotiating, conducting a trial). Fairness means teachers test what they teach (enhancing validity), provide students with grading criteria in advance of the assessment, give students an opportunity to practice and get feedback before the graded event (formative assessment), and use explicit criteria, score sheets, and rubrics to improve consistency in grading (improving reliability).

h. Ongoing Teaching Development

Effective teachers are committed to continued development as teachers throughout their careers.[19] They engage in a variety of teaching development activities. Those activities fall into five categories: (1) reflection, (2) scholarship, (3) feedback from students, (4) collaboration with colleagues, and (5) conferences and workshops.

Reflection. Teachers can provide their own teaching development through systematic reflection. Reflective teachers spend significant time articulating their teaching philosophies, identifying their assumptions about teaching and learning, and analyzing the effectiveness of their teaching methods and interactions with students. Teachers can engage in more structured reflection as well. For example, teachers can develop a teaching portfolio, review a video recording of a class they taught, or keep an ongoing teaching journal. These and other self-assessment ideas are discussed in detail in Chapter 12 below.

Scholarship. Extensive print and electronic resources address the scholarship of teaching and learning. Those resources help teachers increase their pedagogical knowledge, providing ideas on instructional design, teaching strategies, educational materials, and assessment of student learning. Teachers who produce articles, essays, book chapters, and blog postings on teaching and learning will deepen their pedagogical knowledge even further.

Feedback from Students. Effective teachers value feedback from students about teaching and learning. Teachers can gather feedback from students on teaching effectiveness through course evaluations at the end of the course, questionnaires during the course, and student focus groups. Teachers can gather feedback on student learning through classroom assessment techniques, such as minute papers. Tools to gather feedback from students are discussed in detail in Chapter 12 below.

Collaboration with Colleagues. Colleagues can be valuable resources in several types of teaching development activities. Private conversations between trusted colleagues can help teachers deal with pedagogical problems and provide ideas for changes in teaching practices. More senior colleagues can be teaching mentors for junior colleagues. Indeed, some schools have formal systems for assigning a teaching mentor to new faculty members. Colleagues can explore teaching and learning at brownbag lunch programs. Pairs of colleagues can observe one another's classes and review one another's slides, handouts, exercises, and assessments. Peer review for formative assessment purposes is explored in Chapter 12 below.

Teaching Conferences and Workshops. Many law schools sponsor workshops on teaching and learning for their full-time and adjunct faculty members. Effective teachers can organize and present at those workshops. Several institutions sponsor national and regional conferences and workshops on teaching and learning (AALS, ILTL, CALI, SALT, LWI). Teachers looking to improve their effectiveness attend those conferences, or better yet, lead a session.

3. Self-, Peer-, Student-, and Administrator-Assessments of Teaching

Evidence, information, opinions, and data provide the basis for summative and formative assessments of teaching. Four main sources of evidence, information, opinions, and data are teachers themselves, their peers, their students, and administrators. Each of those sources has strengths, weaknesses, and biases.

a. Self-Assessment

Self-assessment should play an important role in the assessment of teaching.[20] Teachers are the best source of information on many aspects of their own teaching:

- The teacher's teaching philosophy and beliefs about teaching and learning;
- The teacher's explanation of all aspects of instructional design at both the course and class session levels — learning objectives, teaching and learning activities, materials, and formative and summative assessment schemes;
- The teacher's rationale and practices for creating a healthy teaching and learning environment; and
- The teacher's efforts at enhancing subject matter expertise and engaging in ongoing teaching development activities.

In addition, teachers are well positioned to gather evidence of student learning outcomes. Teachers' reflection on all aspects of their teaching can be a part of summative assessment of teaching and is a centerpiece of formative assessment of teaching.

Self-assessment of teaching has significant limitations as well. Teachers are not the best source of how students experience the teaching and learning environment, how students react to teachers' instructional delivery, and what teacher behaviors hinder and enhance students' learning. Teachers' self-interest in personnel decisions creates a significant conflict of interest for teachers in summative assessment of teaching. Consequently, while self-assessment is an excellent mechanism for teachers to *report* on their efforts and rationale related to teaching philosophy, instructional design, teaching and learning environment, subject matter expertise, instructional delivery, and ongoing teaching development, teachers' bias makes them a poor source to *evaluate* the effectiveness of their own practices in the context of summative assessment.

b. Peer Review

Peer review can play a significant role in both formative and summative assessments of teaching.[21] Two types of peer review are common: first, observation of teaching (including classroom, clinical, and online settings), and second, review of course documents (including syllabi, course web page, assignments, exercises, slides, videos, podcasts, handouts, exams, and student work products). From these observations and document reviews, peers should be able to assess many components of effective teaching, including student learning outcomes, the teacher's subject matter expertise, the teaching and learning environment, course and class design, instructional delivery, and assessment of students.

Limitations of peer review include problems with validity, reliability, bias, and collegiality. Problems with peer review are especially relevant concerns in summative assessment of teaching. Validity concerns arise when peer reviewers base their assessments more on their own personal views of effective teaching than on a set of accepted standards on what constitutes good teaching. Substantial disagreements between peer reviewers who view the same class or same documents raise reliability issues. Reliability is also a concern if only one or two class sessions are observed. Bias appears in two forms. Once source of bias is the prior interpersonal relationship between the teacher and the peer reviewer, while another source of bias is the influence of underlying societal, cultural issues such as sexism and racism. Finally, peer review can cause hard feelings and hostility among colleagues.

c. Student Ratings and Feedback

As discussed briefly above in the section on ongoing teaching development, feedback from students can play a central role in formative assessment of teaching. Teachers can gather formative feedback from students through questionnaires during the course, student focus groups, classroom assessment techniques, and the numerical and narrative information in student evaluations at the end of the course. Because students have direct experience with a teacher throughout a course, they are well positioned to provide information on instructional delivery, the teaching and learning environment, and some aspects of instructional design, such as the effectiveness of the syllabus and course materials.

The appropriate role of student ratings in summative assessment of teaching is more complex. The higher education literature contains thousands of articles on student ratings of college teaching, including empirical studies and comprehensive reviews of those studies.[22] Summaries of that literature reveal the following about end-of-the-course student ratings of teaching.

- The vast majority of colleges and universities use end-of-the-course student ratings as part of their summative assessment of teaching.
- Student ratings are valid and reliable measures of teaching effectiveness and moderately correlated with independent measures of student learning. This statement is true if the rating instrument was constructed and validated in accordance with rigorous psychometric and statistical procedures. Unfortunately, many institutions employ student ratings instruments that were developed by committees of faculty members, administrators, and students, without psychometric and statistical expertise — those instruments suffer from reliability and validity problems.
- Student ratings of teaching are persistent; their ratings of teaching immediately after the course and post-graduation are consistent.
- Students tend to rate difficult, challenging courses higher than easy courses in which they learn less.
- Students tend to give higher ratings to teachers whom students perceive as likable and expressive.
- Student ratings sometimes depend on the subject of the course; teachers in the humanities tend to get higher ratings than math and science faculty.
- Students tend to rate teachers higher in elective courses and lower in required courses.
- Students tend to rate courses higher as they progress through college (freshmen give lower ratings than sophomores, who give lower rating than juniors, who give lower rating than seniors).
- The relationship between class size and student ratings is mixed. Some studies find no significant difference between student ratings of large and small classes. Other studies find that teachers of small classes tend to get higher ratings.
- The relationship between student ratings of teaching and grades is mixed. Many studies find no relationship between students' actual grades or expected grades and their ratings of teaching. Other studies find a small positive correlation between grades (expected or actual) and ratings of teachers.
- The relationship between gender and student ratings of teaching is mixed. Some studies find that ratings by male and female students are

consistent, but other studies find that one gender or the other gives higher ratings. Likewise, some studies find no significant relationship between the gender of the teacher and student ratings of teaching. Other studies find differences in how female and male instructors are rated; some find that female teachers receive higher ratings and some find that female teachers receive lower ratings.

The legal education literature about student ratings of teaching consists of a few empirical studies and dozens of essays and articles reviewing the higher education literature on student ratings of teaching. The results of empirical studies of student ratings in law schools are generally consistent with the empirical results in the higher education literature.

- Almost all law schools use end-of-the-course student ratings in their summative assessment of teaching. A minority of law schools use student interviews as part of the summative assessment process as well.[23]
- One small study found that teachers tend to get lower student ratings in legal research and writing courses than in other courses they teach.[24]
- One small study found that teachers tend to get lower student ratings in large classes (average class size of 57) compared to small classes (average class size of 13).[25]
- One study found that student ratings in first-year courses (all required courses) were significantly lower than student ratings in upper level courses (mostly elective).[26]

The legal education literature contains narrative reports of gender and racial bias in student ratings of teaching. Qualitative research shows that while some women of color receive high numerical ratings and glowing positive comments, many receive inappropriate comments about their personal appearance and comments containing subtle and direct racism and sexism. Rigorous quantitative empirical study of gender and racial bias in student ratings in legal education has yet to be conducted.[27]

After reviewing the higher education and legal education literature on student ratings of teaching, scholars make a range of recommendations regarding students' role in summative assessment of teaching.[28] Most scholars conclude that student ratings should not be the sole source of information for the summative assessment of teaching. Many scholars recommend that summative assessment of teaching include multiple sources of information, including student ratings, peer review, and self-evaluation. Recommendations about sources of information from students about teaching effectiveness run the gamut from using both the numerical and narrative information from end-of-the-course student ratings, to only using the narrative comments, to using student focus groups instead of or in addition to end-of-the-course student ratings.

d. Administrator Review

Administrators can play a significant role in both formative and summative assessments of teaching. Deans and associate deans can perform reviews similar to peer reviews through observation of teaching and examining course documents. From their observations and document reviews, administrators can assess many components of effective teaching, including the teacher's subject matter expertise, the teaching and learning environment, course and class design, instructional delivery, and assessment of students. Associate deans whose jurisdiction includes outcomes assessment or faculty development may have particular expertise in assessing student learning outcomes or ongoing teaching development activities.

The limitations of administrator reviews are similar to the limitations of peer reviews, including problems with validity, reliability, and bias. Validity problems occur if administrators base their assessments on their personal views of effective teaching rather than the institution's definition of what constitutes good teaching. Reliability is a concern if administrators observe only one or two class sessions. Bias can arise from the prior interpersonal relationship between the teacher and the administrator or from implicit or explicit bias.

4. Key Points in Assessment of Teaching Fundamentals

- Law schools should develop systems for both summative and formative assessments of teaching.
- Law schools should develop clear guidelines concerning the use of information from formative assessment in personnel decisions.
- Components of effective teaching include student learning outcomes, learning theory principles, subject-matter expertise, teaching and learning environment, instructional design, instructional delivery, assessment of students, and ongoing teaching development.

- Law schools should define the components of teaching effectiveness that will be assessed for personnel decisions.
- Sources of evidence, information, opinions, and data for summative and formative assessments of teaching include teachers themselves, peers, students, and administrators; each of those sources has strengths, weaknesses, and biases.
- Law schools should use multiple sources of evidence in summative assessment of teaching.
- Teachers should use multiple sources of information, opinion, and data in formative assessment of teaching.

Endnotes

1. The higher education literature and legal education literature both recognize fundamental distinctions between summative and formative assessment of teaching. The discussion of the purpose, characteristics, and interrelationship of summative and formative assessment is drawn from three sources: PHYLLIS BLUMBERG, ASSESSING AND IMPROVING YOUR TEACHING: STRATEGIES AND RUBRICS FOR FACULTY GROWTH AND STUDENT LEARNING 104–105 (2013); NANCY VAN NOTE CHISM, PEER REVIEW OF TEACHING: A SOURCEBOOK 5–7 (2d ed. 2007) (hereinafter "PEER REVIEW OF TEACHING"); and Paul T. Wangerin, *The Evaluation of Teaching in Law Schools*, 11 J. PROF. LEGAL EDUC. 87, 97–100 (1993).

2. THOMAS A. ANGELO & PATRICIA CROSS, CLASSROOM ASSESSMENT TECHNIQUES: A HANDBOOK FOR COLLEGE TEACHERS 3 (2d ed. 1993) (hereinafter "CLASSROOM ASSESSMENT TECHNIQUES").

3. MICHAEL HUNTER SCHWARTZ, GERALD F. HESS & SOPHIE M. SPARROW, WHAT THE BEST LAW TEACHERS DO 35 (2013) (hereinafter "WHAT THE BEST LAW TEACHERS DO").

4. CLASSROOM ASSESSMENT TECHNIQUES, *supra* note 2, at 3.

5. PATRICIA L. SMITH & TILLMAN J. RAGAN, INSTRUCTIONAL DESIGN 25 (3d. ed. 2005) (1992) (hereinafter "INSTRUCTIONAL DESIGN"). For a comprehensive discussion of learning theories, instructional design principles, and their application to legal education, see Michael Hunter Schwartz, *Teaching Law by Design: How Learning Theory and Instructional Design Can Inform and Reform Law Teaching*, 38 SAN DIEGO L. REV. 347 (2001).

6. The discussion of behaviorism is based on INSTRUCTIONAL DESIGN, *supra* note 5, at 25–26 and Schwartz, *supra* note 5, at 367–371.

7. The discussion of cognitivism is based on INSTRUCTIONAL DESIGN, *supra* note 5, at 26–28; Schwartz, *supra* note 5, at 371–379; and MICHAEL HUNTER SCHWARTZ, SOPHIE M. SPARROW & GERALD F. HESS, TEACHING LAW BY DESIGN: ENGAGING STUDENTS FROM THE SYLLABUS TO THE FINAL EXAM 3–6 (2d ed. 2017) (hereinafter "TEACHING LAW BY DESIGN").

8. The discussion of constructivism is based on INSTRUCTIONAL DESIGN, *supra* note 5, at 19–20; Schwartz, *supra* note 5, at 379–382; and TEACHING LAW BY DESIGN, *supra* note 7, at 6–7.

9. TEACHING LAW BY DESIGN, *supra* note 7, at 11.

10. The discussion of teaching and learning environments is based on TEACHING LAW BY DESIGN, *supra* note 7, at 11–18; WHAT THE BEST LAW TEACHERS DO, *supra* note 3, at 76–122; and Gerald F. Hess, *Heads and Hearts: The Teaching and Learning Environment in Law School*, 52 J. LEGAL EDUC. 75, 87–105 (2002) (hereinafter "*Heads and Hearts*").

11. The discussion of instructional design is based on Gerald F. Hess, *Value of Variety: An Organizing Principle to Enhance Teaching and Learning*, 3 ELON L. REV. 65 (2011) (hereinafter "*Value of Variety*"), and TEACHING LAW BY DESIGN, *supra* note 7, at 33–78, 121–135. For a detailed application of instructional design principles to legal education, see Schwartz, *supra* note 5, at 383–427.

12. The discussion of preparation is based on TEACHING LAW BY DESIGN, *supra* note 7, at 15–18, and WHAT THE BEST LAW TEACHERS DO, *supra* note 3, at 151–176.

13. The discussion of organization is based on TEACHING LAW BY DESIGN, *supra* note 7, at 65–69, 102–119, and WHAT THE BEST LAW TEACHERS DO, *supra* note 3, at 180–183.

14. The discussion of communication is based on TEACHING LAW BY DESIGN, *supra* note 7, at 109, 112; WHAT THE BEST LAW TEACHERS DO, *supra* note 3, at 63–65, 189–190; and BARBARA GROSS DAVIS, TOOLS FOR TEACHING 150–154 (2d ed. 2009) (hereinafter "TOOLS FOR TEACHING").

15. The discussion of interaction is based on WHAT THE BEST LAW TEACHERS DO, *supra* note 3, at 187–194; PEER REVIEW OF TEACHING, *supra* note 1, at 110–116; and *Heads and Hearts*, *supra* note 11, at 104–105.

16. *E.g.*, TEACHING LAW BY DESIGN, *supra* note 7, at 97–135; EXPERIENTIAL EDUCATION IN THE LAW SCHOOL CURRICULUM (Emily Grant, Sandra Simpson, & Kelly Terry eds., 2017); GERALD F. HESS & STEVEN FRIEDLAND, TECHNIQUES FOR TEACHING LAW (1999); GERALD F. HESS, STEVEN L. FRIEDLAND, MICHAEL HUNTER SCHWARTZ & SOPHIE SPARROW, TECHNIQUES FOR TEACHING LAW 2 (2011); ROY STUCKEY ET AL., BEST PRACTICES FOR LEGAL EDUCATION: A VISION AND A ROAD MAP (2007) (hereinafter "BEST PRACTICES FOR LEGAL EDUCATION"); BUILDING ON BEST PRACTICES: TRANSFORMING LEGAL EDUCATION IN A CHANGING WORLD (Deborah Maranville et al., eds., 2015).

17. The discussion of visuals is based on TEACHING LAW BY DESIGN, *supra* note 7, at 71–73, 113–114.

18. The discussion of assessment is based on TEACHING LAW BY DESIGN, *supra* note 7, at 155–183; BEST PRACTICES FOR LEGAL EDUCATION, *supra* note 17, at 175–197; GREGORY S. MUNRO, OUTCOMES ASSESSMENT FOR LAW SCHOOLS 105–110 (2000); *Value of Variety*, *supra* note 11, at 86–91; *Heads and Hearts*, *supra* note 10, at 105–108.

19. The discussion of ongoing teaching development is based on TEACHING LAW BY DESIGN, *supra* note 7, at 169–174, 201–222, and TECHNIQUES FOR TEACHING LAW 2, *supra* note 16, at 309–314.

20. The discussion of self-assessment of teaching is based on PETER SELDIN ET AL., THE TEACHING PORTFOLIO, 10–14, 27–28, 44–50 (4th ed. 2010); PETER SELDIN ET AL., CHANGING PRACTICES IN EVALUATION OF TEACHING, 44–50, 97–113 (1999) (hereinafter "CHANGING PRACTICES IN EVALUATION TEACHING"); and Wangerin, *supra* note 1, at 106–111.

21. The discussion of peer review is based on PEER REVIEW OF TEACHING, *supra* note 1, at 17–25, 54–61, 76–78; CHANGING PRACTICES IN EVALUATION OF TEACHING, *supra* note 20, at 70–73; RAOUL A. ARREOLA, DEVELOPING A COMPREHENSIVE FACULTY EVALUATION SYSTEM 95–97 (3d ed. 2007) (hereinafter "DEVELOPING A COMPREHENSIVE FACULTY EVALUATION SYSTEM"); and Wangerin, *supra* note 1, at 115–116.

22. The discussion of the higher education literature on student ratings of college teaching is based on DEVELOPING A COMPREHENSIVE FACULTY EVALUATION SYSTEM, *supra* note 21, at 98–104; CHANGING PRACTICES IN EVALUATION OF TEACHING, *supra* note 20, at 13–21, 26–28; TOOLS FOR TEACHING, *supra* note 14, at 534–539; Kenneth A. Feldman, *Identifying Exemplary Teachers and Teaching: Evidence from Student Ratings*, *reprinted in* THE SCHOLARSHIP OF TEACHING AND LEARNING IN HIGHER EDUCATION: AN EVIDENCE-BASED PERSPECTIVE 93 (Raymond P. Perry &

John C. Smart eds., 2007); Michael Theall & Kenneth A. Feldman, *Commentary and Update on Feldman's (1997) "Identifying Exemplary Teachers and Teaching: Evidence from Student Ratings*, *in* THE SCHOLARSHIP OF TEACHING AND LEARNING IN HIGHER EDUCATION: AN EVIDENCE-BASED PERSPECTIVE 93, 94–101 (Raymond P. Perry & John C. Smart eds., 2007); Herbert W. Marsh, *Students' Evaluations of University Teaching: Dimensionality, Reliability, Validity, Potential Biases and Usefulness*, *in* THE SCHOLARSHIP OF TEACHING AND LEARNING IN HIGHER EDUCATION: AN EVIDENCE-BASED PERSPECTIVE 319, 334–358 (Raymond P. Perry & John C. Smart eds., 2007); and AMERICAN SOCIOLOGICAL ASS'N, STATEMENT ON STUDENT EVALUATIONS OF TEACHING (September 2019), https://www.asanet.org/sites/default/files/asa_statement_on_student_evaluations_of_teaching_sept52019.pdf (last visited July 15, 2020).

23. Richard L. Able, *Evaluating Evaluations: How Should Law Schools Judge Teaching*, 40 J. LEGAL EDUC. 407, 412–414 (1990) (based on results from 147 ABA-approved law schools responding to a 1989 survey).

24. Melissa Marlow-Shafer, *Student Evaluation of Teacher Performance and the Legal Writing Pathology*, 5 NEW YORK CITY L. REV. 115, 124–126 (2002) (based on survey responses from 21 legal writing directors who taught both Legal Writing and other courses).

25. Nira Hativa, *Teaching Large Law Classes Well: An Outsider's View*, 50 J. LEGAL EDUC. 95, 97 (2000) (based on student evaluations of 14 full-time faculty who taught both a large and small class in the same semester).

26. Melissa J. Marlow, *Blessed Are They Who Teach an Upper-Level Course, for They Shall Earn Higher Student Ratings*, 7. FL. COASTAL L. REV. 553, 561–566 (2006) (based on 20 semesters of student ratings of courses taught by full-time faculty members at a public law school in the Midwest).

27. Arthur Best, *Student Evaluations of Teaching Work Well: Strongly Agree, Agree, Neutral, Disagree, Strongly Disagree*, 38 SOUTHWESTERN L. REV. 1, 5–10 (2008); Judith D. Fischer, *Use and Effects of Student Ratings in Legal Writing Courses: A Plea for Holistic Evaluation of Teaching*, 10 LEGAL WRITING: J. LEGAL WRITING INST. 111, 128–130 (2004); Deborah J. Merritt, *Bias, the Brain, and Student Evaluation of Teaching*, 82 ST. JOHN'S L. REV. 235, 235–238, fn. 209 (2008). MEERA E. DEO, UNEQUAL PROFESSION: RACE AND GENDER IN LEGAL ACADEMIA 68–71 (2019). Deo's *Unequal Profession* is the result of the Diversity in Legal Academia project, an extensive qualitative study of the experiences of women of color in legal academia including barriers to entry, relationships with colleagues and students, tenure and promotion struggles, leadership positions, and work-life balance. It includes qualitative data on student comments on end-of-the-course ratings of teachers who are women of color.

28. The discussion of the role of students in summative assessment of teaching is based on Able, *supra* note 23, at 452–455 (summative assessment of teaching should include narrative comments from students on end-of-the-course rating forms, student interviews, peer review, and self-evaluation); Best, *supra* note 27, at 13–14 (for personnel decisions, law schools should use numerical and narrative information from end-of-the-course student rating forms; end-of-the-course student ratings should not be the sole or major source of information about teaching effectiveness for purposes of personnel decisions; other sources of information include self-evaluation, peer review, and student focus groups); Merritt, *supra* note 27, at 280–285 (summative assessment of teaching should include student focus groups coupled with other sources of information about teaching effectiveness, including self-evaluation, peer reviews, and expert reviews of teaching); Wangerin, *supra* note 1, at 109–117 (summative assessment of teaching systems should include end-of-the-course student ratings coupled with other sources of information such as self-assessment via teaching portfolios, peer review, and expert review of teaching).

CHAPTER ELEVEN

Summative Assessment of Teaching

Chapter 11 has three major subparts:

(1) Characteristics of effective systems for summative assessment of teaching;

(2) Design elements for a summative assessment system; and

(3) Good practices in self-, peer-, and student-assessments of teaching.

1. Characteristics of Effective Systems for Summative Assessment of Teaching

There is no perfect system for summative assessment of teaching. Likewise, no model for a summative assessment system works for all institutions. Instead, an effective system for summative assessment of teaching must be consistent with the culture and values of the institution. Further, summative assessment of teaching in law schools may need to conform to both law school policies and university-wide requirements. Nevertheless, effective summative assessment systems share a number of characteristics,[1] including:

- Clarity and transparency;
- Multiple and varied sources of evidence;
- Fairness and equal treatment;
- Good faith and confidence in the system;
- Education and training for everyone involved in the process;
- Efficiency and sustainability; and
- Review and revision of the system.

Clarity and Transparency. Every aspect of the summative assessment system should be clear and transparent. Clear, written guidelines should address questions such as the following:

- What are the substantive standards defining effective teaching?
- What components of effective teaching will be assessed?
- What are the steps in the assessment process and what deadlines apply?
- Will the candidate, peers, and students be sources of evidence of teaching performance?
- How will evidence of teaching performance be gathered and considered?
- What role will faculty members and administrators have as decision makers?
- Do the same or different standards and procedures apply to decisions regarding tenure, promotion, contract renewal, salary, and other personnel decisions?
- Is there an appeal process for negative decisions?
- If so, what are the steps and deadlines of the appeal process?

Multiple and Varied Sources of Evidence. Teaching is a complex activity. Scholars agree that no single source of evidence is adequate to fairly assess teaching. Effective summative assessment systems rely on multiple sources of information about teaching, including candidates themselves, peers, students, administrators, and outside experts. Those sources can produce varied evidence through teaching portfolios, classroom observations, reviews of course documents (syllabi, materials, assignments, exams), and student ratings of teaching (numerical, narrative, or both).

Fairness and Equal Treatment. It is critical that the summative assessment process is followed carefully and the substantive standards are applied equally for every candidate. Peers and administrators involved in summative assessment should be vigilant in ensuring that bias does not affect the process or ultimate decision.

Good Faith and Confidence. A summative assessment system flourishes only if the faculty members, administrators, and students involved in the process operate in good faith and have confidence in the integrity of the system. One way to get buy-in from faculty, administrators, and students is for them to play significant roles in the development, evaluation, and revision of the assessment program. Clarity, transparency, and fairness in the operation of the assessment system enhance the credibility of the assessment program.

Education and Training. Everyone involved in the summative assessment process can benefit from education and training. Candidates need to know how to assemble effective teaching portfolios or dossiers. Students need to understand the importance of their ratings of teachers, the role the numerical and narrative ratings play in the assessment process, and how to make effective narrative comments. Peer reviewers need training on classroom observations and review of course documents. Administrators and faculty members who make personnel decisions need training on how to evaluate the information they receive from student ratings, candidate self-evaluations, and peer reviews. This chapter includes references to excellent books addressing peer review, self-evaluation, and student ratings in the context of summative assessment of teaching. In addition, education and training could be provided by experts at a university teaching center, educational consultants from outside of the university, and faculty members who develop expertise in summative assessment of teaching.

Efficiency and Sustainability. Developing and operating an effective system for summative assessment of teaching requires significant effort from faculty members and administrators. To be sustainable, the assessment program must be efficient. The time commitment of individual faculty members and administrators must be reasonable in light of their other roles and duties.

Review and Revision. The summative assessment system should be a work in progress, subject to periodic review. Lessons learned in the development, operation, and review of the assessment program should inform appropriate revisions of the system.

2. Design Elements for a Summative Assessment System

Summative assessment of teaching occurs in a variety of personnel decisions, including tenure, promotion, contract renewal, and salary determinations. The substantive standards and processes may be the same for each type of personnel decision or the standards and processes could differ depending on the type of decision. Either way, three basic design elements are common in effective summative assessment systems:[2]

- Definition of effective teaching;
- Sources of evidence of teaching effectiveness; and
- Methods of gathering evidence of teaching effectiveness.

a. Definition of Effective Teaching

The first step in designing a program for summative assessment of teaching is to define the concept of effective teaching. Chapter 10 describes eight components of effective teaching. An institution could use all eight components to define effective teaching, a subset of those components, or different components. It is essential that faculty members and administrators reach a consensus on the components of effective teaching that will be assessed in personnel decisions.

Table 11.1 is an example of an instrument an institution could use to determine which components of effective teaching will be evaluated in the summa-

Table 11.1: Components of Effective Teaching as Part of Summative Assessment

Component of Effective Teaching	Include in Summative Assessment System? (Yes or No)
Student Learning Outcomes (student achievement of institutional, programmatic, and course-level learning outcomes)	
Consistency with Learning Theory Principles (principles of learning from behaviorism, cognitivism, and constructivism)	
Teacher's Subject-Matter Expertise (including legal doctrine, theory, policy, practical application, thinking skills, performance skills, ethical issues, and professionalism)	
Teaching and Learning Environment (respect, expectations, support, passion, inclusion, engagement, collaboration)	
Instructional Design (articulating learning objectives, choosing teaching and learning activities, identifying instructional materials, developing an assessment scheme, preparing a syllabus, and reviewing and revising the design)	
Instructional Delivery (preparation, organization, communication, interaction, methodology, visuals)	
Assessment of Students (formative—specific, positive corrective, prompt feedback summative—multiple, varied, fair)	
Ongoing Teaching Development (reflection, scholarship, feedback from students, collaboration with colleagues, conferences and workshops)	
Other Components?	

tive assessment system. More extensive descriptions of each component would accompany the table.

Institutions could choose to provide more structure to the definition of effective teaching. For example, the components could be weighted—student learning outcomes (20%), consistency with learning theory principles (5%), subject matter expertise (10%), teaching and learning environment (15%), instructional design (15%), instructional delivery (15%), assessment of students (15%), ongoing teaching development (5%).

b. Sources of Evidence of Teaching Effectiveness

The second step in designing a program for summative assessment of teaching is to identify the sources of evidence for each component of effective teaching that will be assessed. Common sources include the candidate, peers, students, and administrators.

The institution will need to further define several of the sources. Peers could include law school colleagues, faculty members in the university but outside of the law school, and faculty members from other institutions. Students could include students who complete ratings of the candidate's teaching while they were in the law school or alumni who complete ratings after graduation. Typical administrators would include the dean or an associate dean of the law school.

For each source of evidence, the institution should identify the components of effective teaching for which the source is appropriate and effective. For example:

- Candidates are capable of producing evidence on all components of effective teaching and may be the best source of evidence for consistency with learning theory principles and ongoing teaching development.
- Peers are capable of producing evidence on all components of effective teaching and may be the best source of evidence for the teacher's subject matter expertise, instructional design, and assessment of students.
- Students are capable of producing evidence of student learning outcomes, teaching and learning environment, instructional delivery, and assessment of students; they may be the best source of information on instructional delivery and the teaching and learning environment.
- Administrators are capable of producing evidence on all components of effective teaching and may be the best source of evidence for student learning outcomes.

Finally, the institution needs to decide, for each component of effective teaching, the source or sources of evidence on which it will rely. This requires a careful balance. On the one hand, thoroughness cuts in favor of multiple sources for each component. But efficiency and sustainability cut in favor of a single source for a component. Table 11.2 is an example of a list of sources of evidence for each component of effective teaching that attempts to reach that balance.

Table 11.2: Sources of Evidence of Effective Teaching

Component of Effective Teaching	Sources of Evidence
Student Learning Outcomes	Candidate Administrator
Consistency with Learning Theory Principles	Candidate
Teacher's Subject-Matter Expertise	Candidate Peers
Teaching and Learning Environment	Students Peers
Instructional Design	Candidate Peers
Instructional Delivery	Students Peers
Assessment of Students	Peers
Ongoing Teaching Development	Candidate

c. Methods of Gathering Evidence of Teaching Effectiveness

The third step in designing a system for summative assessment of teaching is to identify the methods of gathering evidence of teaching effectiveness for each source.

Candidates. A primary purpose of a candidate's teaching portfolio, dossier, or application is for the candidate to gather and reflect upon evidence of teaching effectiveness. Common elements of a teaching portfolio include a statement of teaching philosophy and goals; course syllabi; samples of handouts, exercises, assignments, exams; summaries of student ratings; summaries of peer reviews of teaching and course documents; evidence of student learning; and a description of teaching development activities.

Peers. The peer-review process can generate two types of evidence of teaching effectiveness. First, each peer observation of teaching should result in a completed observation instrument. Likewise, peer review of course documents (syllabi, course web page, assignments, exercises, slides, videos, podcasts, handouts, exams, student work products) should produce completed instruments that guide the reviews.

Students. At most law schools, students complete rating forms at the end of each course. Student ratings typically include both numerical assessment of a variety of aspects of teaching and the course as well as narrative comments. Additional methods of gathering evidence of teaching effectiveness from students include interviews with focus groups of current students or alumni.

Administrators. Deans and associate deans could gather evidence of teaching effectiveness via observations of teaching and reviews of course documents in the same manner as peer review described above. Administrators can provide evidence of student learning generated in the school's institutional and programmatic assessment programs.

For each component of effective teaching that will be part of the summative assessment scheme, the institution should identify the methods for gathering evidence. Again, decisions concerning how many sources of evidence to use should balance thoroughness, efficiency, and sustainability. Table 11.3 is an example of an assessment scheme that seeks to strike that balance.

Table 11.3: Methods of Gathering Evidence of Effective Teaching

Component of Effective Teaching	Methods of Gathering Evidence
Student Learning Outcomes	Teaching portfolio Results of institutional, programmatic, and course-level learning outcomes assessment
Consistency with Learning Theory Principles	Teaching portfolio
Teacher's Subject-Matter Expertise	Teaching portfolio Peer review—class observations and review of documents
Teaching and Learning Environment	Student ratings—numerical and narrative Peer review—class observations
Instructional Design	Teaching portfolio Peer review of course documents
Instructional Delivery	Student ratings—numerical and narrative Peer review—class observations
Assessment of Students	Teaching portfolio Peer review of course documents
Ongoing Teaching Development	Teaching portfolio

3. Good Practices in Self-, Peer-, and Student-Assessments of Teaching

Self-, peer-, and student-assessments of teaching are major elements of an effective scheme for summative assessment of teaching. Good practices can maximize the strengths and minimize the weaknesses and bias of each source of evidence of teaching effectiveness.

a. Good Practices in Self-Assessment of Teaching: Portfolios

The higher education and legal education literature endorse the use of teaching portfolios as part of a scheme for summative assessment of teaching.[3] An excellent resource is Peter Seldin's *The Teaching Portfolio: A Practical Guide to Improved Performance and Promotion/Tenure Decisions*, which includes detailed discussions of the construction and evaluation of teaching portfolios in the context of summative assessment of teaching as well as numerous samples of teaching portfolios, including one developed by a law school teacher.

In the context of summative assessment, the purpose of a teaching portfolio is to demonstrate the effectiveness of the teacher. In the narrative sections, the teacher provides detailed description, analysis, and reflection on all aspects of teaching. An appendix provides documentation and evidence supporting the narrative. The portfolio contents should reflect careful selection of documentation of teaching effectiveness rather than an exhaustive compilation of all documents related to teaching performance.

The contents of a teaching portfolio depend upon the type of personnel decision, the components of effective teaching that the institution will assess, the sources of evidence of teaching effectiveness that the institution will consider, and the methods of gathering evidence that the institution will use. Consequently, there is no single set of contents applicable to all institutions and all personnel decisions. Each institution will need to tailor its list of contents. The following list of contents is typical; it is based on the assumption that the institution is using the components of effective teaching, sources, and methods set out in Table 11.3 above.

Teaching Portfolio Narrative Sections

1. Description of teaching responsibilities
2. Teacher's philosophy of teaching and learning
3. Instructional design of courses

4. Teaching methodologies and strategies
5. Teaching materials — electronic and paper
6. Formative and summative assessment of students
7. Evidence of student learning
8. Student ratings of teaching — summary and reflection
9. Peer observations of teaching — summary and reflection
10. Peer review of teaching documents — summary and reflection
11. Ongoing teaching development — activities and goals
12. Ongoing development of subject matter expertise
13. Teaching awards and recognition

Teaching Portfolio Appendices

1. Representative course syllabi
2. Samples of teaching materials — handouts, slides, exercises, etc.
3. Samples of assessments — exams, graded assignments, rubrics, etc.
4. Samples of graded student work product — exams, papers, performances
5. Video of teaching
6. Student ratings of teaching
7. Peer observation reports
8. Peer review of teaching documents
9. Scholarship of teaching and learning
10. Documentation of ongoing teaching development
11. Documentation of teaching awards and recognition

A variety of good practices, from the initiation of a teaching portfolio program to the process of evaluating portfolios, can enhance the likelihood that teaching portfolios will be an important part of an effective program for summative assessment of teaching.

Administrative Support. To launch and maintain a teaching portfolio program, law school deans and associate deans, as well as university administrators involved in personnel decisions, need to publicly support the program. Administrators likely will need education on the purposes, construction process, and value of teaching portfolios. Administrators must commit the necessary resources to launch and maintain the program.

Faculty Support. Most faculty members will also need education on the purposes, construction process, and value of teaching portfolios. To build faculty support, faculty members should have major roles in the development of the portfolio program.

Pilot Program. It may take a year or two to develop and test a portfolio program. Volunteer faculty members can develop draft portfolios. Administrators and faculty members should test the operation of the program, including the development of guidance on how to prepare and evaluate portfolios.

Clear Guidelines. The success and fairness of the teaching portfolio program depends in part on clear guidelines for faculty members and administrators. The guidelines should identify the required contents and maximum length of the narrative section and appendices.

Workshops for Faculty. The institution should conduct workshops periodically to train faculty members on how to develop and evaluate teaching portfolios.

Models. The institution should make available to faculty members several examples of high quality portfolios to serve as models.

Mentors. The institution should provide mentors to help faculty members develop effective portfolios. Mentors should be well versed on the portfolio process and have the interpersonal skills to develop an effective mentoring relationship with faculty members. For faculty members who prefer to prepare a portfolio without a mentor, Seldin's *The Teaching Portfolio* provides a list of self-mentoring questions.[4]

Portfolio Evaluation. The process and standards for evaluating teaching portfolios should be clear and comprehensive. The higher education literature contains examples of evaluation instruments, which an institution can use as a starting point for developing an appropriate portfolio evaluation system.[5]

b. Good Practices in Peer-Assessment of Teaching

The higher education and legal education literature endorse the use of peer review as part of a scheme for summative assessment of teaching.[6] An excellent resource is Nancy Van Note Chism's *Peer Review of Teaching: A Sourcebook*, which contains detailed discussions of the development and operation of peer review in the context of summative assessment of teaching as well as numerous sample instruments for classroom observations and reviews of teaching documents.

The details of peer review in summative assessment of teaching will vary based on the type of personnel decision, the institution's definition of effective teaching, the sources of evidence the institution will use, and the relevant methods of gathering evidence. Each institution will need to design its own peer-review scheme. The following ten good practices will apply to most peer-review systems.

1) Build Support of Administrators and Faculty

Law school deans and associate deans, university administrators involved in personnel decisions, and most faculty members need education on the purposes, value, strengths, and weaknesses of peer review for summative assessment of teaching. Administrators need to publicly support the program and commit the necessary resources to initiate and maintain it. Key faculty members need to express their support and their willingness to expend the effort necessary to make the program succeed.

2) Develop a Peer-Review Statement and Protocol

Successful peer-review programs feature clear plans and guidelines. A peer-review statement should address foundational issues underlying the program, such as the purpose of peer review in summative assessment of teaching, the relationship between a formative and summative peer-review program, and basic values of the peer-review program (*e.g.*, fairness, trust, sustainability). A peer-review protocol should establish clear guidelines for all important aspects of the system, including the components of effective teaching assessed via peer review, the selection and training of peer reviewers, the number of reviews, teaching observation process and instruments, teaching document-review process and instruments, and peer-review reports.

3) Selection of Peer Reviewers

The protocol should delineate who is eligible to serve as a peer reviewer. Faculty members from the law school? From the university outside of the law school? From other institutions? Must the reviewers be of a certain rank? What type of expertise is required? Must some of the reviewers have subject matter expertise, such as teachers or scholars in the subject areas the candidate teaches? Must some of the reviewers have expertise in the types of courses the candidate teaches, such as online, hybrid, clinical, or legal research and writing courses? Should reviewers include faculty with particular expertise in instructional design or the scholarship of teaching and learning? The protocol should include limits on the frequency of a faculty member's eligibility to serve as a peer reviewer in order to ensure that the burden of this service is shared relatively equally among all faculty members.

The protocol should also describe the process of selecting reviewers. Are the reviewers chosen by the administration? By a rank, promotion, and tenure committee? Does the candidate have input into the selection of the reviewers? Some institutions designate a pool of potential reviewers, allow the candidate to identify a number of preferred reviewers (six, for example), and then task the administration or personnel committee with choosing the final list of reviewers (three, for example) from those identified by the candidate.

Fairness to the candidate and highly qualified reviewers should be hallmarks of the peer eligibility rules and the peer selection process.

4) Components of Effective Teaching Assessed via Peer Review

As noted above, peers are capable of producing evidence on many components of effective teaching and may be the best source of evidence for the teacher's subject-matter expertise, instructional design, and assessment of students. For the peer-review system to be reasonable and sustainable, peer review should not be expected to assess all components of teaching effectiveness. The protocol should clearly identify the components that will be assessed via peer review.

5) Training Peer Reviewers

Training of reviewers is an important part of an effective peer-review program. Topics of the training could include the role of peer review in summative assessment of teaching, fairness and ethical issues, the process for classroom observations and document reviews, completing the teaching observation and document-review instruments, and writing final reports. Training could take place in a workshop with mock classroom reviews using videos of teaching and sample documents (syllabi, handouts, slides, exams) for mock reviews. An institution could develop a training packet, such as a video and accompanying workbook for peer reviewers to view. Facilitators for this training could be experts from a university teaching center, consultants from outside of the university, or faculty members who have developed expertise in peer review of teaching.

6) Number of Reviews

The Protocol should establish guidelines for the number of teaching observations, the number of peers who will observe teaching, the number of peers who will review teaching documents, and the type and number of documents to review. The strong consensus is that multiple classes should be observed and multiple peers should observe classes. Scholars recommend from two to four reviewers and from two to ten total classes observed. The observation of many classes by many peers and the review of many documents by several peers enhance the validity and fairness of the peer-review process. However, peer reviews take considerable time and effort, so a system with numerous reviews and reviewers may not be reasonable and sustainable. Each institution needs to find an appropriate balance.

7) Teaching Observation Process

The protocol should establish whether the teaching observations will be announced, unannounced, or a combination of the two. Announced visits allow the peers and teacher to schedule the visit for an appropriate class session and to have a pre-visit meeting to facilitate the observation. Announced visits also allow teachers to thoroughly prepare for class and to put forward their best teaching. Unannounced visits can create fear and distrust and can result in visits on days when there is little to observe, such as days dominated by an exam or extended video. On the other hand, unannounced visits allow assessment of the teacher's preparation and instructional delivery for a typical (not specially prepared) class.

The protocol should clearly delineate the teaching observation procedure. A three-step process is common.

- **Pre-Observation Meeting.** For announced visits, the teacher and peer reviewer should meet in advance of the class. This meeting allows the teacher to describe the instructional design for the class (learning objectives, instructional methods, materials, student preparation expectation) and to put the class into the context of the course as a whole.
- **Observation of Teaching.** The Protocol should establish guidelines for the length of the observation — a minimum of 50 minutes is typical. The observation should be guided by an observation instrument that the peer reviewer is expected to complete.

- **Post-Observation Meeting.** The teacher and peer reviewer should meet after the class. In summative assessment of teaching, the purpose of the post-observation meeting is not to provide feedback; the purpose is to allow the teacher to add clarification that may help the peer reviewers understand what they observed and to respond to questions the peer reviewers may have about the class.

8) Teaching Document-Review Process

The protocol should specify the types of course documents subject to peer review, such as syllabi, course web pages, assignments, exercises, slides, videos, podcasts, handouts, exams, and student work products. The documents could be included in the candidate's teaching portfolio or could be supplied by the candidate if the institution does not use portfolios. The protocol should provide guidelines on the number of documents that the candidate should submit and the number of documents that the peers should select for review, if less than all of the documents.

9) Teaching Observation and Document-Review Instruments

Both peer observations of teaching and peer review of course documents should be guided by instruments that the peer reviewers complete as part of the process. The instruments should be developed by administrators and faculty members, perhaps with the assistance of an expert from the university's teaching and learning center or from another institution. The instruments should reflect the components of effective teaching that the institution decides to assess via peer review. The instruments should be tested and revised before being employed in the summative assessment process.

Three types of peer-review instruments are common. First, the instrument could be in a narrative format with a set of question-prompts and space for the reviewer to note responses to the questions. Second, the instrument could be a set of statements with a scaled rating (such as a numerical scale with anchor words, ranging from (1) Strongly Agree to (5) Strongly Disagree). Third, the instrument could be an extensive checklist of items that relate to an aspect of effective teaching, such as organization, clarity, and rapport with students. The scaled ratings instrument and checklist could also include space for narrative comments.

Chism's *Peer Review of Teaching* includes numerous peer-review instruments that an institution can use as a starting point for developing its own instruments. Chism's teaching observation instruments include a pre-observation conference form, a narrative prompt form, a checklist form, and a scaled rating form.[7] Chism's document-review instruments include forms for peer review of syllabi, course packs and text books, bibliographies, presentation slides, handouts, multimedia materials, exams, exercises, and teacher comments on student work.[8] Chism also includes forms for peer review of online courses.[9]

10) Peer-Review Reports

The protocol should set out a process for generating peer-review reports that are consistent in form across reviewers. The completed instruments for each class observation and document review could constitute the peer-review reports or could serve as the basis for a consolidated peer-review report. Either way, the candidate should have the opportunity to comment on the drafts of the completed instruments and consolidated report before they become final.

c. Good Practices in Student-Assessment of Teaching

The higher education and legal education literature identify student ratings of teaching as the most common source of evidence in summative assessment of teaching.[10] An excellent resource is Raoul Arreola's *Developing a Comprehensive Faculty Evaluation System*, which includes extensive discussions of the strengths and weaknesses of student ratings systems, developing a student ratings instrument, potential student ratings items, examples of commercial student ratings instruments, administering a student ratings system, and reporting and interpreting student ratings results.

1) Developing a Student Ratings Instrument

A valid, reliable student ratings instrument is essential to a fair system for summative assessment of teaching. The development of such an instrument requires professional expertise in statistics and psychological measurement. Student ratings instruments that have not undergone rigorous analysis and testing are likely to have dubious validity and reliability.

An institution could develop its own student ratings system with a consultant who has psychometric expertise. Arreola describes a multi-phase process for developing a valid, reliable student ratings instrument:[11]

- Determine what components of effective teaching that the student ratings form will assess;
- Write or select the potential items (statements or questions) to include in the instrument (Arreola includes a catalog of 525 potential items);[12]
- Develop a response scale (*e.g.*, Strongly Agree, Agree, Neither Agree nor Disagree, Disagree, Strongly Disagree);
- Conduct a field trial to gather data on each potential item (the trial may include many items and should gather at least 200 responses on each potential item);
- Conduct a factor-analysis study to determine the reliability and validity of each item (whether each item measures the component of effective teaching that it is intended to measure);
- Develop subscales to produce separate scores on each component of effective teaching measured by the instrument;
- Refine the form based on the factor analysis;
- Organize the items in a logical sequence in the final instrument.

Arreola notes that the development of the student ratings instrument will take at least a year and that it will take several years of using the instrument for the institution to accumulate the data necessary to create meaningful norms for interpreting the results.

A second option is for an institution to adopt a commercially available student ratings instrument that has been professionally developed and validated. Arreola reviews well-known commercial instruments including the Aleamoni Course/Instructor Evaluation Questionnaire (CIEQ) and Kansas State University's IDEA system.[13]

2) Administering Student Ratings Instruments

Each institution must develop a process for administering student ratings instruments. A threshold issue is whether the student ratings instrument will be paper or electronic. Higher education institutions have decades of experience in administering paper student ratings instruments. Some researchers have found that online ratings systems have several advantages over paper instruments, including ease of administration, longer and more thoughtful student responses, reduced processing time and cost, and more accurate data collection. Others caution that online student ratings systems may reduce response rates and have not been thoroughly studied.

A well designed process should be transparent, uniform, and fair. The system should lead to a response rate of at least 67% so that the results are more likely to be representative of the entire class. The following practices can help an institution meet these goals.

Communicate Regularly with Students. The dean or an associate dean should maintain regular communication with students about the student ratings system. The deans should make clear to students the purpose and importance of student ratings, how the data will be used in personnel decisions, the need for a robust response rate, the anonymity of students who respond, and that faculty members will not receive the results of the ratings until they have submitted final grades for the course.

Develop a Uniform Process for Administering Student Ratings. The process for administering student ratings should be uniform and applied to all courses. For paper ratings forms administered in class, the process should include the following:

- During what time period should the ratings be administered (*e.g.*, the last two weeks of the course)?
- During what time in class will students complete the form (*e.g.*, 10 minutes at the beginning of class)?
- Who will hand out the forms, read the instructions, collect the completed forms, and deliver the completed forms (*e.g.*, a student, a staff person)?
- Will the faculty member leave the room during the time when students complete the ratings (yes)?

For online student ratings, students need to know where to access the ratings instrument, the time period during which students can complete the form, and the mechanics of completing the form.

Prepare Instructions. For both paper and electronic rating systems, students should receive uniform instructions, including a script that informs students of the purpose and importance of student ratings, how the data will be used in personnel decisions, the need for a robust response rate, the anonymity of students who respond, and that faculty members will not receive the results of the ratings until they have submitted final grades for the course.

Use Procedures to Get a Robust Response Rate. For paper ratings, an effective means of increasing response rates is to administer the ratings at the beginning of a class period and give students sufficient time to complete the forms, rather than administering ratings at the end of the class period or allowing students to take the forms home and return them later. Likewise, students could be given the opportunity to complete online ratings at the beginning of a class period in addition to being able to complete the form outside of class. If technically possible, the institution could require students to complete course evaluations in order to receive their grades.

3) Reporting and Interpreting Student Ratings Results

A comprehensive report of student rating results for a course would include the following:

- The response rate;
- For narrative response items, all of the responses if they are part of the summative assessment scheme;
- For each item with a numerical rating scale:
    - The frequency distribution (the number and percentage of students choosing each item);
    - The median, mean, or both;
    - The standard deviation;
    - Appropriate comparative medians, means, or both (for the same course, for all first-year courses, for all law school courses).

Administrators involved in summative assessment of teaching and all faculty members should receive training in interpreting the results of student ratings. They need to understand the meaning and value of frequency distributions, means, medians, standard deviations, and comparative data. They need guidance on the significance of differences in mean scores for an item; for example, what is the significance in a mean of 4.1 on an item for a given course and a mean of 4.3 for the same item in the comparative score for all courses? A written summary of the training should accompany each student ratings report or be easily available to all faculty and administrators.

4) Using Student Focus Groups

Some scholars recommend that student focus groups supplement or replace end-of-the-course student ratings of teaching effectiveness.[14] Interviews of students can promote a more deliberative process and more thoughtful responses than completing student rating forms. To develop a focus group system for summative assessment of teaching, an institution must address a number of issues:

- How will students be selected to participate in focus groups?
- What will be the size of the focus groups?
- Will one or more than one focus group be interviewed for each course?
- Who will facilitate the focus groups?
- How will facilitators be trained?
- What process will be used to develop and test an instrument for facilitators to use with the focus groups?
- How will the results of the focus groups be compiled and reported?

Student focus groups can enhance the process of summative assessment of teaching, but they require a significant commitment of time and resources to develop and administer.

Endnotes

1. The discussion of characteristics of effective systems for summative assessment of teaching is based on Peter Seldin et al., Changing Practices in Evaluation of Teaching, 162–176, 213–225 (1999) (hereinafter "Changing Practices in Evaluation of Teaching"), and Nancy Van Note Chism, Peer Review of Teaching: A Sourcebook 7–8, 26–38, 66–70 (2d ed. 2007) (hereinafter "Peer Review of Teaching").

2. The discussion of design elements is based on Raoul A. Arreola, Developing a Comprehensive Faculty Evaluation System, 17–25, 47–50, 59–68 (3d ed. 2007) (hereinafter "Developing a Comprehensive Faculty Evaluation System"); Changing Practices in Evaluation of Teaching, *supra* note 1, at 1–23; and Peer Review of Teaching, *supra* note 1, at 50–56, 170–172.

3. The discussion of teaching portfolios is based on PETER SELDIN ET AL., THE TEACHING PORTFOLIO: A PRACTICAL GUIDE TO IMPROVED PERFORMANCE AND PROMOTION/TENURE DECISIONS, 3–50, 234–244 (4th ed. 2010) (hereinafter "THE TEACHING PORTFOLIO"); CHANGING PRACTICES IN EVALUATION OF TEACHING, *supra* note 1, at 162–182; PEER REVIEW OF TEACHING, *supra* note 1, at 168–185; Judith D. Fischer, *Use and Effects of Student Ratings in Legal Writing Courses: A Plea for Holistic Evaluation of Teaching*, 10 LEGAL WRITING: J. LEGAL WRITING INST. 159–160 (2004); and Paul T. Wangerin, *The Evaluation of Teaching in Law Schools*, 11 J. PROF. LEGAL EDUC. 109–111 (1993).

4. THE TEACHING PORTFOLIO, *supra* note 3, at 32–34.

5. *Id.* at 41–50; PEER REVIEW OF TEACHING, *supra* note 1, at 181–185.

6. The discussion of peer review is based on PEER REVIEW OF TEACHING, *supra* note 1, at 26–119; CHANGING PRACTICES IN EVALUATION OF TEACHING, *supra* note 1, at 70–96; Fischer, *supra* note 3, at 160–161; and Wangerin, *supra* note 3, at 115–117.

7. PEER REVIEW OF TEACHING, *supra* note 1, at 105–116.

8. *Id.* at 82–97.

9. *Id.* at 147–152.

10. The discussion of student ratings of teaching in the context of summative assessment is based on DEVELOPING A COMPREHENSIVE FACULTY EVALUATION SYSTEM, *supra* note 2, at 98–169; CHANGING PRACTICES IN EVALUATION OF TEACHING, *supra* note 1, at 28–44; BARBARA GROSS DAVIS, TOOLS FOR TEACHING 537–550 (2d ed. 2009); and Richard L. Able, *Evaluating Evaluations: How Should Law Schools Judge Teaching*, 40 J. LEGAL EDUC. 407, 412–414 (1990).

11. DEVELOPING A COMPREHENSIVE FACULTY EVALUATION SYSTEM, *supra* note 2, at 111–116.

12. *Id.* at 125–138.

13. *Id.* at 139–161.

14. The discussion of student focus groups is based on Able, *supra* note 10, at 453–454, and Deborah J. Merritt, *Bias, the Brain, and Student Evaluation of Teaching*, 82 ST. JOHN'S L. REV. 235, 280–283 (2008).

CHAPTER TWELVE

Formative Assessment of Teaching

Chapter 12 addresses formative assessment of teaching in five sections:

(1) Teaching-Development Model, Activities, and Plans;

(2) Self-Assessment and Reflection;

(3) Feedback from Students;

(4) Peer Review and Consultations; and

(5) Fostering Ongoing Teaching Development.

1. Teaching-Development Model, Activities, and Plans

Formative assessment of teaching is an integral part of the process of ongoing teaching development. The most effective teachers are made, not born. They strive to evolve and develop as teachers throughout their careers.

a. Teaching-Development Model

Teaching development can cycle through several stages: instructional awareness, formative feedback, pedagogical knowledge, implementation, and assessment.[1] Throughout their careers, effective teachers will go through many teaching-development cycles.

Instructional Awareness. One step in ongoing development is for teachers to better understand their own teaching philosophy and practice. What do teachers believe about the goals of legal education and their roles as teachers? What assumptions do they make about teaching and learning? What type of environment do they foster in the classroom? What verbal and nonverbal behaviors do teachers exhibit in their interactions with students in and out of the classroom? Are teachers' practices consistent with their teaching philosophy?

Figure 12.1: Ongoing Teaching Development

Pedagogical Knowledge. Deeper understanding of student learning and teaching methods can help teachers become more effective. Teachers can gain valuable insights from scholarship about learning theory, student motivation, and factors that enhance and inhibit learning. The literature on teaching methods, instructional design, educational technology, and assessment should inform teachers' choices about appropriate adjustments in their teaching.

Formative Feedback. Formative feedback is critical to improving teaching and learning. To make effective changes in teaching, teachers need to evaluate the strengths and weaknesses of their current practices. Teachers need to assess the effects of their current teaching methods on students' motivation and learning outcomes. Teachers can gather that feedback from themselves, students, and colleagues.

Implementation. Teaching improvement occurs through significant changes in teachers' teaching philosophy, attitudes, and behavior. Those changes could affect the teaching and learning environment, instructional design, teaching methods, and formative and summative assessment of students. To be most effective, the changes should be incremental and systematic rather than wholesale and sporadic. A good start in teaching improvement would entail implementing one or two small changes throughout a semester. Small changes made each semester can accumulate to make substantial differences in teaching and learning after several years.

Assessment. The final stage is for teachers to evaluate the effectiveness of their teaching-development efforts. Did the changes result in a more thoughtful, coherent teaching philosophy? Did the knowledge of teaching and learning principles becomes more sophisticated? Did teachers' passion for teaching and confidence in their teaching increase? Did teachers' communication and relationships with students become healthier? What effect did the changes in teachers' attitudes and practices have on student motivation? Perhaps most importantly, did the changes result in more and deeper student learning? Sources of information for answering these questions include teachers themselves, peers, and students. Answers to these questions form the basis for the next cycle of teaching development.

b. Teaching-Development Activities

Chapter 11 identified five categories of ongoing teaching-development activities: (1) reflection, (2) scholarship, (3) feedback from students, (4) collaboration with colleagues, and (5) conferences and workshops. Table 12.1 specifies potential teaching-development activities for each category.[2]

Table 12.1: Ongoing Teaching-Development Activities

Reflection	• Self-assessment—completing the same course evaluation instrument that students complete • Self-assessment—taking inventories regarding teaching and learning principles and practices • Preparing a teaching portfolio • Keeping a teaching journal • Building a reflective practice • Reviewing a video of own teaching
Scholarship	• Reading scholarship on teaching and learning—books, articles, newsletters, websites, blogs • Producing scholarship on teaching and learning
Feedback from Students	• Reviewing and analyzing results of student ratings • Gathering feedback from students during the course • Using student assessment techniques during the course • Reviewing student performance and learning outcomes during and after the course • Meeting with student focus groups

continued on next page

Table 12.1: Ongoing Teaching-Development Activities *continued*

Collaboration with Colleagues	• Discussing teaching and learning with colleagues • Small-Group Instructional Diagnosis • Participating in collaborative peer observations of teaching • Participating in collaborative peer review of course documents
Conferences and Workshops	• Attending teaching and learning workshops at own institution • Designing and presenting teaching and learning workshops • Attending regional and national conferences on teaching and learning • Presenting at teaching and learning conferences

It would be rare for any teacher to engage in all of these ongoing teaching-development activities, even over the course of a career. But all teachers should be able to identify some teaching-development activities that appeal to them.

c. Teaching-Development Action Plans

A teaching-development action plan is a device to help teachers engage in ongoing teaching development in an incremental, systematic way. Teachers could prepare an action plan each year to guide their ongoing development. Table 12.2 is a questionnaire to help teachers develop an action plan tailored to their specific teaching-development needs.

Table 12.2: Teaching-Development Action Plan Questionnaire

1. Identify two or three aspects of your teaching you would most like to improve during the next year.
2. What teaching-development activities do you think would most effectively address those aspects of your teaching?
3. What teaching-development activities would most help you increase your awareness of your own teaching philosophy and practices?
4. What teaching-development activities would most help you increase your knowledge of teaching and learning principles?
5. What teaching-development activities would most help you increase your confidence in your teaching?

6. What teaching-development activities would most help you increase your enthusiasm and passion for teaching?
7. What teaching-development activities would most help you implement changes in your teaching practices?
8. What teaching-development activities would most help you gather evidence of student learning?
9. Identify three teaching-development activities you commit to employing during the next year.
10. Identify ways to measure the effectiveness of the three teaching-development activities that you will employ.

The next three sections of this chapter explore in detail formative assessment of teaching. Continued development as teachers depends in large part on formative self-assessment, feedback from students, and peer review.

2. Self-Assessment and Reflection

Teachers can engage in formative self-assessment of teaching through a variety of self-evaluation techniques and reflection practices.

- Completing the student rating instrument for each course;
- Completing the peer review instruments for course documents;
- Completing teaching inventories;
- Reviewing a video of their teaching;
- Building a reflective practice;
- Keeping a teaching journal; and
- Constructing a teaching portfolio.

These activities can help teachers increase their instructional awareness, provide feedback on the effectiveness of teachers' current practices, and suggest incremental changes to implement in the future.

a. Completing the Student Ratings Instrument

For each course, teachers can complete the same instrument that the students will complete at the end of the course. Teachers can benefit from completing the instrument once during the course and again at the end of the course. Completing the instrument during the course can help teachers take stock of the course and make appropriate adjustments. After completing the instrument at the end of the course, teachers can compare their responses to the students' responses. Areas in which the teachers' and students' responses differ significantly are ripe for further study and reflection.

b. Completing Peer-Review Instruments for Course Documents

For each course, teachers can complete instruments to assess the effectiveness of course documents, including syllabi, course packs, textbooks, presentation slides, handouts, multimedia materials, exams, exercises, and teacher comments on student work. Teachers can use the same instruments that the institution employs in the peer review process. If the institution does not use those instruments or if teachers want to supplement those instruments, the higher education literature contains many sample instruments to review course documents.[3] Table 12.3 is an example of an instrument for review of exams.

Table 12.3: Instrument for Self- or Peer-Review of Exams

Comment on the following aspects of the exam:
Type of exam
Clarity of directions
Clarity of exam questions
Clarity of grading criteria
Match of exam content to course goals
Appropriate level of challenge
Appropriate length
Levels of thinking, analysis, practice skills tested
Legibility and layout
Proofreading
Other

c. Completing Teaching Inventories

Teaching inventories can help teachers self-assess a range of teaching behaviors.[4] Inventories adapted to legal education help teachers self-assess their teaching in light of seven empirically derived principles for enhancing learning:[5]

- Encouraging student-faculty contact;
- Fostering cooperation among students;
- Encouraging active learning;
- Giving prompt feedback;
- Emphasizing time on task;
- Communicating high expectations; and
- Respecting diverse talents and ways of learning.

All of those inventories are available in Appendix 11.1 of *Teaching Law by* Design (2d ed. 2017). Table 12.4 is a portion of one of those inventories.

Table 12.4: Teaching Inventory

Articulate Clear, High Expectations	
Assess your teaching practices on each item with the following scale: **(1)** Very often, **(2)** Often, **(3)** Occasionally, **(4)** Rarely, **(5)** Never	
____	I articulate specific goals (content, skills, values) for each class session and my course as a whole.
____	I clearly communicate my expectations to students for each class, each graded event, and the course as a whole.
____	I involve students in setting expectations for themselves and the course.
____	My expectations for students are reasonable and achievable.
____	I provide feedback on students' performance so that they understand the expectations.
____	I make myself available to help students achieve my expectations.

***

Teachers could create their own inventories based on all or some of the eight components of effective teaching described in Chapter 10:

- Student Learning Outcomes,
- Learning Theory Principles,
- Subject-Matter Expertise,
- Teaching and Learning Environment,
- Instructional Design,

- Instructional Delivery,
- Assessment of Students, and
- Ongoing Teaching Development.

The inventory could consist of the teacher's narrative for each component or teachers could develop a set of subcomponents to guide self-assessment.

d. Reviewing Video of Teaching

A video of a class session is an excellent tool for self-assessment of many aspects of instructional delivery.[6] Video provides accurate oral and visual feedback on verbal and nonverbal communication, interactions with students, questioning techniques, visual impact of slides and board work, clarity, organization, and flow. While reviewing a video, teachers can gather detailed feedback. For example, teachers could write down every question they asked during the class and then analyze the levels of thinking that each question addressed. Or teachers can create a log of the class, noting what is happening and who is speaking at minute intervals throughout the class. Teachers can get broad feedback by completing a peer observation instrument or a checklist while reviewing the video. The instrument could be the one the institution uses in peer observations or one of the instruments available in the teaching and learning literature.[7]

e. Building a Reflective Practice

Reflection is an important part of formative assessment of teaching.[8] Critical self-reflection can help teachers increase their instructional awareness, develop a teaching rationale, and make informed changes in teaching practices. Most teachers have tacit assumptions about teaching and learning, patterns of behavior, and underlying motivations that profoundly affect their teaching. Reflection helps teachers to identify those assumptions, behaviors, and motivations and then to assess how they are hindering or enhancing their teaching effectiveness. Reflective teachers can articulate a coherent rationale that explains the strategies, attitudes, and behaviors that result in their success in facilitating student learning. That rationale can increase confidence, credibility, and responsiveness to new teaching challenges. Instructional awareness and a thoughtful teaching rationale put teachers in a position to make informed changes in their attitudes, behaviors, and teaching practices. Reflective teachers engage in a continuous process of reviewing their experience, challenging their own ideas and assumptions, and implementing changes designed to broaden and deepen student learning in their courses.

An excellent resource for legal educators who desire to build a reflective practice is *A Teacher's Reflection Book* by Jean Koh Peters and Mark Weisberg. Peters and Weisberg define reflection as "an intentional, non-judgmental review of experience" which can become "purposeful, lifelong learning from experience, through witnessing that experience, examining it, illuminating and exploring it."[9] They recommend three elements of reflection:

- **A Focal Point.** Reflection should have a clear starting point—a thoughtful prompt,[10] a reading, a critical incident in one's teaching, etc.
- **Experience.** All types of teaching experiences can be rich material for reflection. Whether the experience is negative or positive, reflection helps teachers process the experience, understand why it went well or poorly, and plan how to move forward.
- **Nonjudgment.** An attitude of nonjudgment focuses reflection on inquiry and fact-finding rather than blame and critique. A nonjudgmental reflection on a teaching event could include several steps: (1) recall in detail what happened, (2) identify key moments in the event, (3) recall more details for each critical moment, (4) identify your interpretation of what happened and why, and (5) brainstorm alternative explanations.

f. Keeping a Teaching Journal

Keeping a teaching journal is an excellent way for teachers to engage in formative self-assessment, reflection, and ongoing development.[11] The process of producing a teaching journal is simple and flexible—the only critical requirement is that teachers write regularly about their teaching experiences. Journaling helps teachers record events and ideas, plan instruction, clarify assumptions, analyze problems, engage in critical reflection, and pursue lifelong learning.

Recording. A teaching journal can serve as a recording device in which teachers memorialize events, ideas, feelings, problems, successes, and strategies for improvement. Teachers who keep a journal will have a comprehensive, accurate account of their experience during a term. That record becomes the basis for teachers' reflection, analysis, planning, and growth.

Planning. A teaching journal can be a helpful planning tool. Journal entries can set teaching and learning goals for an entire course, a unit, or an individual class session. Other entries can explore teaching methods appropriate for achieving those goals. Reading back through journal entries from the last time a teacher taught a course (what went well, what did not, new ideas to try) can help the teacher redesign the course.

Clarifying Assumptions. Journal writing can help teachers make explicit their assumptions and beliefs about teaching and learning. Then teachers can assess whether they need to revise those assumptions and beliefs based on their recent teaching experiences.

Analyzing Problems. A teaching journal is a place for teachers to engage in problem-solving. The teacher can articulate the problem (*e.g.*, low student engagement and effort on an exercise), identify key facts and emotions involved in the problem, and brainstorm solutions. Journaling can help teachers deal with the fear, failure, disappointment, and struggles that can be part of their teaching experience.

Reflecting. The process of keeping a journal can create the time and space for reflection. Journaling can help teachers organize their thinking and gain perspective on events that can be chaotic at the time they occur. The journal is a place for teachers to systematically assess strengths and weaknesses and to engage in critical thinking about teaching and learning.

Lifelong Learning. The process of recording, describing, analyzing, and evaluating experiences actively involves teachers in their own education. Journaling utilizes the connection between writing and learning. It facilitates the process of teachers making connections between their existing knowledge and new ideas. Journal writing is tangible evidence of a teacher's commitment to ongoing development and lifelong learning.

A key to success in keeping a teaching journal is for the process to be a joy, not a chore. Ultimately, each teacher must find a method that works. Suggestions for successful journaling include: find a place to write that is comfortable and free of interruptions; schedule a time for writing (*e.g.*, twice a week for 20 minutes or after each class for 10 minutes); treat journaling as a professional commitment; choose a format that feels right, such as a bound journal book, artist's sketchbook, tablet, or computer.

g. Teaching Portfolio

A teaching portfolio can be a powerful tool for formative assessment of teaching.[12] The portfolio contains evidence, reflection, and self-evaluation.

Chapter 11 discussed the use of portfolios in personnel decisions. The purpose of teaching portfolios in summative assessment is for the candidate to present evidence demonstrating teaching effectiveness. On the other hand, the purpose of a teaching portfolio in formative assessment is for the teacher to reflect on evidence in order to improve teaching effectiveness.

The contents of a teaching portfolio for formative assessment should be flexible and adaptable to the needs of each individual teacher. For example, a teacher could prepare a portfolio that contains all thirteen elements of a narrative section and all eleven appendices of the portfolio described in Chapter 11. That type of portfolio would contain evidence, reflections, and self-evaluation regarding all of the teacher's courses. Or a teacher could prepare a streamlined portfolio aimed at a particular course. For example, a course portfolio could contain the following eight elements:

(1) A brief description of the course and the students;

(2) A teaching philosophy for the course;

(3) The course design (a description of the course goals, methods, materials, assessment scheme);

(4) Self-assessment of the course design, environment, delivery, and instructional innovations;

(5) Evidence of student learning in the course;

(6) Reflections on student ratings (numerical and narrative), peer observations, and peer review of course documents;

(7) An action plan for improving teaching and learning in the course; and

(8) Selected documents (*e.g.*, syllabus, handouts, slides, exercises, web page, exams, quizzes, graded student work product, video of teaching, student ratings, peer review reports).

3. Feedback from Students

Students can provide formative feedback on both teaching and learning. Student feedback on teaching and learning can take place during the course, allowing teachers to make mid-course adjustments to improve their effectiveness. Student feedback at the end of the course can help teachers improve teaching and learning in future courses. Mechanisms for gathering feedback from students on teaching include end-of-the-course student ratings, teacher-designed questionnaires, and student focus groups. To gather feedback on student learning, teachers can use alumni focus groups, classroom assessment techniques, and course-level outcomes assessment.

a. Student Ratings at the End of the Course

As noted in Chapter 11, almost all law schools have students complete ratings instruments at the end of each course. Empirical research confirms that almost all law teachers review the results of those student ratings after the course. But law teachers rate their review of end-of-the-course student evaluations as only somewhat effective in increasing their instructional awareness, pedagogical knowledge, confidence, enthusiasm for teaching, and implementation of changes in their teaching practices.[13] A set of good practices may help institutions and teachers use student rating results more effectively to enhance teaching effectiveness.[14]

Teach Faculty How to Interpret Numerical Results. As noted in Chapter 11 regarding summative assessment of teaching, faculty members need training in interpreting the numerical results of student ratings, including the meaning and usefulness of frequency distributions, means, medians, standard deviations, and comparative data. Teachers need to understand what differences in scores are significant enough to warrant attention in future iterations of the course.

Teach Students How to Make Narrative Comments. Educate students on the value of their narrative comments for purposes of formative feedback. Teach students how to make meaningful comments—"more variety in teaching methods would help keep me interested" rather than "this course is boring." Make clear to students that nasty comments—"worst teacher ever"—are hurtful and unprofessional.

Prompt Faculty Members to Make Formative Use of Student Ratings. Deans could establish an expectation that teachers address their student ratings as part of teachers' annual reports to the dean. For example, one dean asks faculty members to "briefly reflect on what you have learned from your review of your most recent student evaluations and any changes you plan on making (or have already made) as a result of this student feedback."[15]

Help Teachers Make Effective Use of Student Ratings. Many teachers find their review of student ratings to be stressful. Often teachers focus on low scores and negative comments, while underplaying high scores and positive comments. As a result, teachers may be deterred from making effective formative use of their student ratings. An institution could conduct a workshop or prepare a memorandum (or both) on how teachers can use student ratings in formative assessment. Suggestions to teachers could include the following:

- Look at the numerical scores and skim the narrative comments to get a general sense of students' reaction to the course.
- Return to the numerical scores to analyze the results. Compare the scores on each item to previous ratings of the course and to comparative data for comparable courses or all courses. Create a table to help summarize the comparisons. Pay attention to significant differences (not minor deviations) in the scores.
- Return to the narrative comments. Identify themes in writing. Note several categories of positive comments. Identify one or two areas where multiple students made negative comments or suggested changes.
- Based on the analysis of numerical scores and the narrative themes, identify one or two areas to address in future courses. Make incremental changes rather than major revisions.
- Have a colleague review the student ratings to help identify trends, themes, and potential adjustments in the course.

b. Teacher-Designed Feedback Questionnaires

Teachers can design short questionnaires to gather feedback from students on teaching effectiveness during the course.[16] This method of soliciting formative feedback is simple and flexible. The questionnaires can be in paper or electronic formats. They can address any aspect of teaching, including teaching methods, exercises, materials, classroom environment, or instructional delivery. The questionnaire could focus on a specific teaching issue or could address teaching in the course more holistically. Table 12.5 provides examples of teacher-designed questionnaires.

Table 12.5: Examples of Teacher-Designed Questionnaires

Example 1 For the Climate Change simulation, please rate the following: Clarity of the instructions: ____ **(1)** Very clear **(2)** Somewhat clear **(3)** Unclear Level of challenge:____ **(1)** High **(2)** Medium **(3)** Low Comments about any aspect of the simulation:
Example 2 Please rate your level of preparation for most class sessions in this course:_____ **(1)** High **(2)** Medium **(3)** Low What suggestions do you have to motivate students to prepare well for class?
Example 3 What teaching and learning methods have been *most* effective for you in this course? What teaching and learning methods have been *least* effective for you in this course? What other teaching and learning methods should we try in this course?

The questionnaire process should be efficient. Teachers should explain to their students the formative purpose of the questionnaires. Students can complete the questionnaire in a few minutes in class. After class, teachers review and summarize the students' responses. In the next class, teachers report to students the themes in their responses and inform students of a change they intend to implement as a result of the students' feedback. The questionnaire process not only leads to appropriate changes in teaching behavior, it demonstrates respect for students, enhancing the teaching and learning environment.

c. Student Focus Groups

Teachers can gather formative feedback from students through a variety of types of focus groups. One simple method is to use 20 minutes of class time to gather feedback from students in small groups. Teachers can ask the groups to create three lists of teaching activities and behaviors: (1) those the teacher should continue doing, (2) those the teacher should stop doing, and (3) those the teacher should start doing. Students should include a brief reason or explanation for each item on their lists. The students can then share the lists with the class or give the lists to the teacher who will report back during the next class.[17]

Teachers can convene student focus groups outside of class to provide feedback. Teachers can ask for student volunteers to meet with the teacher to discuss general aspects of the teacher's effectiveness, such as course structure, the teaching and learning environment, assignments, materials, teaching methods, and assessment methods. Or the meeting could focus on a particular issue or dilemma.[18]

A more structured focus group format is a student advisory team (SAT).[19] An SAT is a group of students who meet periodically with the teacher throughout the course. The students monitor the course through their own experience, solicit comments from all students in the class on the effectiveness of current teaching methods, and make suggestions to improve teaching and learning in the course. The teacher's role is to listen to the SAT's feedback and suggestions and to respond appropriately, which could include implementing a reasonable suggestion during the course, working with the team to modify the suggestion, implementing the suggestion the next time the course is offered, or explaining why the teacher will not implement the suggestion. Empirical research supports the use of SATs in law school. SAT members report that their participation improved their attitudes toward the course (94%), themselves as learners (82%), the teacher (94%), and law school (82%). Most team members believed that the SAT process improved the course (94%), their learning (82%), and the teacher's effectiveness (92%).

d. Alumni Focus Groups

Teachers can receive valuable feedback on learning from alumni who took the teacher's course in law school. A group of alumni with three to ten years of experience after graduation from law school can offer insights into lasting learning. What knowledge, skills, and values did they learn in the course? What knowledge, skills, and values from the course have been most helpful in their professional work? What knowledge, skills, and values do they wish they had learned in the course? Alumni responses to questions like these can help teachers make appropriate adjustments in course design and delivery to foster lasting learning.

e. Classroom Assessment Techniques

Classroom assessment aims to improve student learning and teachers' effectiveness. The classic resource is *Classroom Assessment Techniques* by Thomas Angelo and Patricia Cross.[20] Classroom assessment emphasizes the link between teaching, learning, and formative feedback. One significant way to improve student learning is to improve teaching. To improve their effectiveness, teachers need feedback on students' progress in achieving course learning objectives. Likewise, to improve their learning, students need formative feedback throughout the course.[21]

Two techniques for gathering feedback from students on teachers' effectiveness described above — student advisory teams and teacher-designed questionnaires — are both contained in *Classroom Assessment Techniques.*[22] The focus in this section is the use of classroom assessment techniques (CATs) to gather specific feedback on student learning. *Classroom Assessment Techniques* describes in detail dozens of ways teachers can discover how well their students are learning key knowledge, thinking skills, and values.

Table 12.6 briefly explains three CATs.[23] The process is similar for all three. The students complete the CAT designed to assess their learning of an important aspect of the course. The teacher reviews the students' responses. During the next class, the teacher reports back to students about their learning and makes appropriate instructional adjustments.

Table 12.6: Examples of Classroom Assessment Techniques

Focused List	During the last ten minutes of class that focused on important content or skill in the course (*e.g.*, "hostile work environment," "diversity jurisdiction," "oral advocacy") ask students to identify and briefly explain five fundamental concepts relevant to the concept or skill. Student responses could be on a sheet of paper or posted on the course website. Or students could create their lists at the beginning of class and revise them throughout the class.

Minute Paper	This CAT is popular, simple, and flexible. During the last five minutes of class, the teacher asks students to respond to a prompt on a sheet of paper or by posting on the course website. Examples of prompts include: • Identify and briefly define the one or two most important concept(s) you learned in class today. • Identify the aspect(s) of drafting effective complaints that is (are) still unclear to you. • Identify the most essential contents of an Environmental Impact Statement. Or the teacher could have students complete the minute paper at the beginning of the class, scan the results, and adjust the focus of the class session accordingly.
Concept Maps	Concept maps are diagrams that show relationships among concepts, theories, or processes. For example, a teacher could ask students to produce a concept map outside of class on an important topic in the course (*e.g.*, "lawyers' duties to clients," "equitable defenses in civil litigation," "compensatory damages in torts"). During the class, students review the maps two other students completed. During the last five minutes of class, students edit their maps before turning them in.

f. Student Learning Outcomes

Every student performance in a course is an opportunity for teachers to assess student learning and make appropriate adjustments in instruction. Quizzes, exams, papers, drafting exercises, oral arguments, presentations — graded or ungraded — reveal whether and how well students are learning important skills, doctrine, theory, and professional values. Teachers may decide to adjust instruction immediately based on what students learned or did not learn. Teachers can record the areas where student learning was strong and weak in order to revise aspects of course design or instructional delivery the next time they teach the course.

4. Peer Review and Consultation

Peers can be an excellent source of formative feedback for teachers. A peer could be a colleague at the law school, a faculty member from the university teaching and learning center, or an educational consultant from another institution, and the review can take a variety of forms.

a. Small-Group Instructional Diagnosis (SGID)

Colleagues can help one another gather formative feedback from students through Small Group Instructional Diagnosis (SGID).[24] The SGID process has three steps. First, the teacher and a colleague meet to discuss the course and the types of feedback the teacher would like to receive. Based on that discussion, the teacher and colleague draft appropriate prompts to use with students. For example, "What most helps you learn in this course?" "What hinders your learning in this course?" "What changes would improve this course?" "What would help you better prepare for class?" "When are you most engaged in this course?" When are you least engaged in this course?" The teacher and colleague choose two or three prompts.

In the second step, the teacher explains to the students the purpose of the SGID process. The teacher leaves class 20-30 minutes early. The colleague acts as a facilitator with the students. The colleague divides students into small groups of three to six students. Each small group discusses the prompts and creates a list that represents the group's consensus responses to each prompt. At this point, the colleague could collect the group's responses and dismiss the class. Or each group could report its responses and the colleague could record those responses and lead a discussion to try to achieve class-wide consensus on the responses to the prompts.

In the third step, the teacher and colleague meet again. The colleague reports the students' responses. The teacher and colleague discuss appropriate responses to the students' feedback, including any changes in the course that the teacher intends to make based on the students' feedback. Finally, the teacher reports back to the students, informing them of the teacher's responses to their feedback.

The SGID process is flexible. Teachers can adjust the process to meet their ongoing teaching-development needs. For example, the SGID process can be even more collaborative if two colleagues agree to engage in a reciprocal process in which they act as facilitators with one another's students. Colleagues who engage in the SGID process learn quite a bit about teaching effectiveness in both the role of teacher and facilitator.

b. Peer Observation of Teaching

Colleagues can help one another improve teaching effectiveness through peer observation and formative feedback. This section presents seven ideas to maximize the benefits of peer observation of teaching.

1) Characteristics of Effective Peer-Observation Programs

In *Collaborative Peer Review*, Larry Keig and Michael Waggoner review ten peer-review programs at colleges and universities and identify common elements of successful programs.[25] The programs begin with the premise that all teachers can improve their effectiveness; the programs are not remedial. Participation in the program is voluntary. Participants decide for themselves the aspects of teaching they would like to assess and the process for doing so. Classroom visits are reciprocal (colleagues switch roles as observer and observed) and occur multiple times during a semester. The results of the observations are confidential and separate from the process for summative assessment of teaching.

2) Roles of Administrators and Faculty Members

The dean or an associate dean should champion the formative peer-review program and support its development. Administrators can help set high expectations for teaching effectiveness and for the formative peer-review process. The deans can provide resources for peer review and free up time for faculty members to participate. The colleague who will review a teacher's class needs to be collaborative, not judgmental. The colleague's tasks include gathering the type of feedback the teacher wants to receive, helping the teacher process that feedback, and working with the teacher in making appropriate changes in instruction. Teachers whose classes will be reviewed need to welcome peer review, actively engage in designing the process to meet their ongoing teaching-development needs, and be open to both positive and negative feedback.[26]

3) Three-Step Process for Peer Observation and Feedback

A three-step process for peer observation and feedback is typical. The process is similar to the three-step process described above for small-group instructional diagnosis. Step 1 is a pre-observation conference in which the teacher and colleague discuss goals for the course and for the class session, materials, expectations for student preparation, teaching methods for the class, and, most importantly, the specific types of feedback the teacher would like the colleague to provide. In Step 2, the colleague observes the class and gathers the feedback. In Step 3, the post-observation conference, the teacher and colleague discuss the feedback, assess strengths and weaknesses of the class, and explore alternative methods to improve future teaching effectiveness and student learning.[27]

4) Reciprocal Peer Review

As noted above, one characteristic of effective peer-review programs is that the class observations are reciprocal — pairs of colleagues view each other's teaching. The reciprocal arrangement creates mutual vulnerability and shared responsibility. Two colleagues working together throughout the semester or year can develop deep levels of trust and respect. They become invested in improving each other's teaching.[28]

5) Effective Formative Feedback

Effective formative feedback after classroom observations is prompt, tailored, descriptive, and followed by strategizing. The post-observation conference should happen while the class is still fresh in the minds of the teacher and colleague — shortly after class, later that day, or the next day. The post-observation conference should focus on the feedback the teacher requested so that it is tailored to the needs of the teacher. The tailored feedback can be supplemented with other insights the colleague gleaned from observing the class. The feedback should be descriptive, not judgmental. For example, "Your questions were very effective" is judgmental; "Your questions focused on analysis, synthesis, and creative thinking" is descriptive. Likewise, "Your instructions for the small group activity were problematic" is judgmental; "Approximately 50% of the small groups seemed confused by the instructions for the activity" is descriptive. Finally, feedback should be the impetus for the teacher and colleague to discuss teaching and learning more deeply and to brainstorm potential instructional adjustments to make teaching and learning more effective.[29]

6) Generating Data Through Class Observations

One way that teachers can reap major benefits from class observation is to ask the colleague to collect data during the class. The data should focus on important aspects of teaching and learning in the class that the teacher cannot keep track of while teaching the class. For example, the colleague could keep track of the students who speak in class. How many different students spoke? How many males? How many females? How many students of color? Many teachers are surprised by this data. Or the colleague could copy everything the teacher writes on the board during the class. After class, the teacher and colleague could analyze the clarity and usefulness of the board work. Likewise the colleague could note what the teacher and the students are doing at minute intervals during the class. The teacher and colleague can use that data to assess students' engagement throughout the class and the relative amounts of teacher-talk and student-talk during the class.[30]

7) Class-Observation Instruments

Class-observation instruments can focus the feedback gathered during class. A teacher may want the colleague to complete the same class-observation instrument that the school uses for summative assessment of teaching. This process can help teachers identify strengths to build upon and weaknesses to address before summative assessment occurs. Or the teacher and colleague could use class-observation instruments available in the literature as sources of ideas for the types of feedback the teacher may want to receive or as a starting point for developing an instrument tailored to the teacher's ongoing development needs.[31]

c. Peer Feedback on Course Documents

Peer feedback on course documents is a valuable and underutilized aspect of formative peer review.[32] Colleagues can provide one another feedback on a wide variety of course materials, including syllabi, slides, handouts, exercises, course web page, assignments, readings, exams, and assessment of student work products. Peer review of course materials has several advantages. Colleagues are well positioned to assess course materials, which reveal much about course design and delivery. Reviews of course materials are unobtrusive; no classes need to be interrupted. The reviews can take place at a time and place convenient for the colleague.

The process for peer review of course materials is similar to the process for class observations. Teachers identify the documents for review and the types of feedback they hope to receive. A colleague reviews the documents, perhaps guided by a review instrument. Then the teacher and colleague meet to discuss the feedback and explore appropriate instructional improvements. The process can be especially valuable if the teacher and colleague review one another's course documents and work together throughout a semester.

Different types of course documents lend themselves to peer feedback on several aspects of teaching effectiveness.

- **Syllabi.** Review of syllabi is an excellent vehicle for feedback on course design — learning objectives, materials, teaching and learning activities, and the scheme for assessment of student learning. In addition, review of syllabi can provide insight into teaching philosophy, the teaching and learning environment, and the teacher's written communication with students.

- **Slides and Handouts.** Reviews of these documents can get at important aspects of instructional delivery, including clarity and student engagement.
- **Assignments and Exercises.** Reviews of assignments and exercises can focus on clarity of the instructions, active learning, and the level of expectations the teacher has for students.
- **Course Web Page, Videos, and Podcasts.** Reviews of these electronic course materials can provide a window into expectations for student learning outside of the classroom.
- **Exams and Quizzes.** Reviews of drafts of exams and quizzes before they are administered can help identify unintended ambiguity, errors, and lack of clarity in grading criteria that the teacher can fix before using them with students. Reviews of exams and quizzes can focus on the levels of thinking and skill students must exhibit to succeed on the assessment.
- **Feedback on Student Work Product.** Colleagues can review one another's feedback to students on exams, quizzes, writing assignments, and performances. These reviews can focus on formative feedback to students, summative assessment of student performance, or both.

Instruments can help maximize the value of reviews of course documents, just as instruments help focus classroom observations. The teacher may want the colleague to use the same instruments the school employs in the summative assessment of teaching protocol. Or the teacher and colleague could use the many instruments available in the literature to guide the reviews of materials.[33]

d. Individual Coaching

Empirical research in college and law school supports individual coaching as a means of improving teaching effectiveness. Law school faculty members who worked with a consultant increased their pedagogical awareness, increased their knowledge of teaching and learning principles, and made changes in their teaching practices.[34] Student ratings of university teachers improved after they worked on their teaching for a semester with a colleague who was recognized as an excellent teacher.[35]

The teacher and colleague/coach/consultant can engage in a four-phase process to improve teaching effectiveness.[36]

- **Data collection.** The consultant interviews the teacher about the teacher's course goals, methods, and materials. The consultant and teacher discuss the teacher's concerns about teaching and consultation objectives. The consultant gathers information through a self-assessment completed by the teacher, classroom observation, review of materials, student teaching evaluations, and formative feedback from students.
- **Data analysis.** The consultant organizes and summarizes the data. The teacher and consultant examine the data summary to determine the teacher's strengths and weaknesses. They identify specific areas of the teacher's instruction to address.
- **Improvement strategy.** The teacher and consultant agree on an objective for change in the teacher's behavior or attitude. The consultant acts as a resource to help the teacher choose an improvement strategy, select new methods to try, or identify appropriate training.
- **Feedback.** The consultant observes the teacher's instructional changes and provides feedback on their effectiveness. The consultant helps the teacher make appropriate refinements in the improvement strategies.

5. Fostering Ongoing Teaching Development

Some faculty members will engage regularly in formative assessment of teaching. These teachers' intrinsic motivation spurs them to pursue ongoing development as teachers. Other faculty members need additional incentives and support to encourage them to consistently strive to improve their teaching. After all, faculty members have many professional demands on their time, including expectations that they produce significant scholarship and perform service to their institutions and communities.

Law schools can foster a culture of ongoing teaching development. In *Fifty Ways to Promote Teaching and Learning*, the authors describe many institutional and administrative support approaches to improve teaching and learning in law schools.[37] Table 12.7 identifies fourteen of those approaches.

Table 12.7: Institutional and Administrative Approaches to Foster a Culture of Ongoing Teaching Development

1. Provide financial support for faculty members to participate in teaching and learning conferences.
2. Host teaching and learning conferences at the law school.
3. Hold faculty retreats, workshops, and lunches on teaching and learning.
4. Fund sabbaticals that focus on teaching and learning.
5. Assign significant value to teaching effectiveness in tenure and promotion decisions.
6. Value teaching effectiveness in annual evaluation and salary decisions.
7. Provide teaching mentors to junior faculty members.
8. Appoint an associate dean for excellence in teaching and learning.
9. Value scholarship on teaching and learning.
10. Fund statistical experts to support empirical research on teaching and learning.
11. Provide library resources and librarian time to support teaching and learning.
12. Confer a variety of annual teaching awards.
13. Provide course release and scheduling flexibility for teaching innovation or mentoring.
14. Support adjunct faculty members with teaching mentors, peer review, and workshops on teaching and learning.

It is unlikely that all of these approaches will be a good match for any law school. But every law school should be able to identify some of these approaches and other ideas to foster a culture of ongoing teaching development.

Endnotes

1. The discussion of the ongoing teaching-development model is based on MICHAEL HUNTER SCHWARTZ, SOPHIE M. SPARROW & GERALD F. HESS, TEACHING LAW BY DESIGN: ENGAGING STUDENTS FROM THE SYLLABUS TO THE FINAL EXAM 202–203 (2d ed. 2017) (hereinafter "TEACHING LAW BY DESIGN"), and Gerald F. Hess, *Improving Teaching and Learning in Law School: Faculty Development Research, Principles, and Programs*, 12 WIDENER L. REV. 443, 444–446 (2006) (hereinafter "*Improving Teaching and Learning in Law School*").

2. For an empirical study of law teachers' engagement in twenty-two ongoing teaching-development activities and the effectiveness of those activities, see Gerald F. Hess & Sophie M. Sparrow, *What Helps Law Teachers Develop as Teachers: An Empirical Study*, 14 WIDENER L. REV. 149 (2008).

3. *E.g.*, NANCY VAN NOTE CHISM, PEER REVIEW OF TEACHING: A SOURCEBOOK, 82–97 (2d ed. 2007) (hereinafter "PEER REVIEW OF TEACHING"), and LARRY KEIG & MICHAEL D. WAGGONER, COLLABORATIVE PEER REVIEW: THE ROLE OF FACULTY IN IMPROVING COLLEGE TEACHING 61–62 (1994) (hereinafter "COLLABORATIVE PEER REVIEW"). Table 12.3 is based on these sources.

4. The discussion of teaching inventories is based in part on TEACHING LAW BY DESIGN, *supra* note 1, at 205, 300–303.

5. See volume 49, number 3 of the *Journal of Legal Education* for a series of articles on Seven Principles of Good Practice in Legal Education.

6. For tips on recording and viewing a video of teaching, see TEACHING LAW BY DESIGN, *supra* note 1, at 216–217, and BARBARA GROSS DAVIS, TOOLS FOR TEACHING 472–474 (2d ed. 2009) (hereinafter "TOOLS FOR TEACHING").

7. *E.g.*, PEER REVIEW OF TEACHING, *supra* note 3, at 106–116; COLLABORATIVE PEER REVIEW, *supra* note 3, at 46–49; TOOLS FOR TEACHING, *supra* note 6, at 475–477.

8. The discussion of reflection is based on JEAN KOH PETERS & MARK WEISBERG, A TEACHER'S REFLECTION BOOK: EXERCISES, STORIES, INVITATIONS 25–59 (2011) (hereinafter "A TEACHER'S REFLECTION BOOK"), and Gerald F. Hess, *Learning to Think Like a Teacher: Reflective Journals for Legal Educators*, 38 GONZ. L. REV. 129, 136–137 (2002) (hereinafter "*Learning to Think Like a Teacher*").

9. A TEACHER'S REFLECTION BOOK, *supra* note 8, at 26.

10. For a list of reflection prompts, see TEACHING LAW BY DESIGN, *supra* note 1, at 304–306, and *Learning to Think Like a Teacher*, *supra* note 8, at 148–153.

11. The discussion of teaching journals is based on *Learning to Think Like a Teacher*, *supra* note 8, at 139–153, and TEACHING LAW BY DESIGN, *supra* note 1, at 206–207.

12. The discussion of teaching portfolios for formative assessment is based on PETER SELDIN ET AL., THE TEACHING PORTFOLIO: A PRACTICAL GUIDE TO IMPROVED PERFORMANCE AND PROMOTION/TENURE DECISIONS 8–9 (4th ed. 2010), and TOOLS FOR TEACHING, *supra* note 6, at 481–485. For an example of teaching portfolios for ongoing development in legal education, see Susan R. Dailey, *Integrating Theory and Practice Through Teacher Portfolios*, 4 LEGAL WRITING: J. LEGAL WRITING INST. 149 (1998).

13. Hess & Sparrow, *supra* note 2, at 152–159.

14. The discussion of good practices for using feedback in student rating results to enhance teaching effectiveness is based on TEACHING LAW BY DESIGN, *supra* note 1, at 208–09; PETER SELDIN ET AL., CHANGING PRACTICES IN EVALUATION OF TEACHING 45–60 (1999); and *Improving Teaching and Learning in Law School*, *supra* note 1, at 455.

15. *Improving Teaching and Learning in Law School*, *supra* note 1, at 455.

16. The discussion of teacher-designed questionnaires is based on TEACHING LAW BY DESIGN, *supra* note 1, at 209–10, and TOOLS FOR TEACHING, *supra* note 6, at 461–464, 467–468.

17. TOOLS FOR TEACHING, *supra* note 6, at 465.

18. *Id.* at 466.

19. The discussion of student advisory teams is based on TEACHING LAW BY DESIGN, *supra* note 1, at 210–212, and Gerald F. Hess, *Student Involvement in Improving Law Teaching*, 67 UMKC L. REV. 344, 352–364 (1998).

20. THOMAS A. ANGELO & K. PATRICIA CROSS, CLASSROOM ASSESSMENT TECHNIQUES: A HANDBOOK FOR COLLEGE TEACHERS (2d ed. 1993).

21. *Id.* at 7–9.

22. *Id.* at 330–342.

23. *Id.* at 126–131 (focus lists), 148–153 (minute papers), and 197–202 (concept maps).

24. The discussion of small-group instructional diagnosis is based on TOOLS FOR TEACHING, *supra* note 6, at 465–466, and GREGORY S. MUNRO, OUTCOMES ASSESSMENT FOR LAW SCHOOLS 136–137 (2000).

25. COLLABORATIVE PEER REVIEW, *supra* note 3, at 73, 95.

26. The discussion of roles in the peer-review process is based on PEER REVIEW OF TEACHING, *supra* note 3, at 66–69.

27. *Improving Teaching and Learning in Law School*, *supra* note 1, at 458–459.

28. Teaching Law by Design, *supra* note 1, at 213.
29. Peer Review of Teaching, *supra* note 3, at 70–72.
30. Teaching Law by Design, *supra* note 1, at 213.
31. Peer Review of Teaching, *supra* note 3, at 105–116 (pre-observation instrument and several types of class observation instruments); Collaborative Peer Review, *supra* note 3, at 45–49 (pre-observation conference guide, observation guide, post-observation conference guide).
32. The discussion of formative peer review of course documents is based on Peer Review of Teaching, *supra* note 3, at 76–79, and Collaborative Peer Review, *supra* note 3, at 59–69.
33. Peer Review of Teaching, *supra* note 3, at 82–97 (instruments for review of syllabi, readings, slides, handouts, multimedia materials, exams, exercises, and comments on student work); Collaborative Peer Review, *supra* note 3, at 61–62, 67 (guides for reviews of syllabi, readings, tests, papers, and feedback on student work).
34. Hess & Sparrow, *supra* note 2, at 167.
35. *Improving Teaching and Learning in Law School*, *supra* note 1, at 466.
36. Teaching Law by Design, *supra* note 1, at 215.
37. Gerald F. Hess, Michael Hunter Schwartz, & Nancy Levit, *Fifty Ways to Promote Teaching and Learning*, 67 J. Legal Educ. 696 (2018).

APPENDIX

Sample Institutional Assessment Plans

University of Arkansas at Little Rock William H. Bowen School of Law Outcomes Assessment Plan

Introduction

Under ABA Standard 315,

> The dean and the faculty of a law school shall conduct ongoing evaluation of the law school's program of legal education, learning outcomes, and assessment methods; and shall use the results of this evaluation to determine the degree of student attainment of competency in the learning outcomes and to make appropriate changes to improve the curriculum.

Interpretation 315-1 explains the expected process more:

> Examples of methods that may be used to measure the degree to which students have attained competency in the school's student learning outcomes include review of the records the law school maintains to measure individual student achievement pursuant to Standard 314; evaluation of student learning portfolios; student evaluation of the sufficiency of their education; student performance in capstone courses or other courses that appropriately assess a variety of skills and knowledge; bar exam passage rates; placement rates; surveys of attorneys, judges, and alumni; and assessment of student performance by judges, attorneys, or law professors from other schools. The methods used to measure the degree of student achievement of learning outcomes are likely to differ from school to school and law schools are not required by this standard to use any particular methods.

Finally, in June 2015, the ABA issued a Guidance Memo that provides a timeline for implementing Standard 315 and the other new ABA standards relating to outcomes. That memo states:

> Site teams visiting schools in the 2016-17 academic year and thereafter will be asked to report on the progress schools are making in establishing learning outcomes and in developing an assessment plan. Schools will be expected to show steady work and progress toward the adoption of a full set of learning outcomes. Those outcomes should be in place by the end of the 2017-2018 year. Schools must have adopted an assessment plan and be able to demonstrate that they are implementing it by the end of the 2018-2019 academic year.

Bowen is ahead of the curve in terms of our outcomes and curriculum mapping, and we have done some outcomes assessment, including the 2013 Hanover survey and the graduating student survey we conducted in spring 2016. We do not yet have, however, an assessment plan. By way of background, an assessment plan details when an educational institution will assess its success as to each of its learning outcomes and how it will do so. The pages that follow are a proposed plan.

A few additional details are worth noting. First, higher education experts distinguish between direct evidence that students have attained an outcome and indirect evidence. Direct evidence involves assessing actual student performance on tests, papers, and other work. In looking at direct evidence, the law school is evaluating whether the student performance is at a level the law school regards as minimally competent. For example, the law school could evaluate the quality of the writing in students' final versions of their papers for the upper-level writing requirement to determine whether students possess minimal writing competency. Indirect evidence involves looking at survey data. For example, the recent survey of graduating students asked the students about the degree to which they believed they had learned some of the skills, knowledge, and values identified in the law school's list of outcomes.

Second, the law school will need to define for itself what constitutes competency for each of its outcomes. For most of our outcomes, that definition of competency would involve developing rubrics like the one attached to this proposal and deciding what level on the scale constitutes minimum competency.[1] For example, as to our legal analysis and reasoning outcome, the assessment committee (and, ultimately, the faculty) might decide that our minimal competency level would be reflected in scores of at least 3 or at least 4 for both categories of the legal analysis and reasoning portion of the rubric. **The assessment committee, as it engages in the assessment process each time for each outcome, will need to decide and propose to the faculty the level of performance it believes reflects minimal competency on the relevant rubric.**

In a few instances, we already have done some of the work in defining specific criteria for our outcomes. For example, as to our problem solving outcome, we have stated, in effect, that effective problem solving includes "identifying and diagnosing problems; generating alternative solutions and strategies; developing and implementing plans of action; and keeping the planning process open to new information and ideas." While this list would need further elaboration to be effective as a rubric to assess student work projects, it is a good start.

---

[1] At a recent conference, faculty of the Boston University Law School presented the attached rubric for evaluating upper-level papers. It appeared that the BU faculty decided that minimum competency was a score of a 3.

Third, no educational accreditor expects an educational institution to be so successful that 100% of the students achieve attainment of any outcome. The law school will need to make decisions about the goal percentage of attainment as to each of its outcomes and sub-outcomes. **The assessment committee, as it engages in the assessment process each time for each outcome, will need to decide and propose to the faculty the percentage of students it believes should be meeting the minimal competency standard.**

The purpose of engaging in these evaluations is to determine whether the students are learning or whether changes might be needed to the law school's curriculum, teaching methods, or assessment methods. For example, if only 60% of our students' upper-level writing papers reflected the desired level of success as to the legal analysis and reasoning skill, the law school might decide the problem lies in how we teach our upper-level writing courses and propose reforms aimed at improving how we teach our upper-level writing courses, such as providing more practice and feedback. Alternatively, the law school might decide that the students should be learning more before they get to their upper-level writing courses and decide that students should get more writing practice and feedback throughout the curriculum, such as by adopting a writing-across-the-curriculum rule.

Finally, it is important to note that law schools will not lose their accreditation simply because their students are not achieving the law school's desired level of performance as to any particular outcome. As long as a law school is engaging in systematic assessment and using the resulting data to improve the law school's teaching methods, curriculum, and assessment practices, the law school will be doing what the ABA wants.

Outcome and Sub-Outcomes	Direct Evidence of Attainment	Indirect Evidence of Attainment
KNOWLEDGE. Every graduate should have knowledge and understanding of the following at a level sufficient to practice ethically as a lawyer and to pass the bar examination in any United States jurisdiction: 1. The organization, hierarchy, and relationships of legal systems; 2. The sources of primary law and the ways they relate to one another; 3. The nature of legal rules and institutions; 4. The fundamental sources and tools of legal research; 5. The principles of the fundamental areas of American substantive law, including civil procedure, constitutional law, contracts, criminal law and procedure, evidence, property, and torts; 6. The nature, sources, and content of ethical standards applicable to lawyers and the practice of law in the United States.	1. Bar exam results • MEE • MBE • MPT 2. Post-Tests in Upper-Level Specialized Legal Research Courses 3. MPRE Results (If we can obtain; if we can't obtain MPRE, review sample of final exams from Legal Profession)	1. Data from 2013 Hanover Employer Survey 2. Data from Spring 2016 Student Survey 3. Data from Summer 2021 Follow-up Employer Survey 4. LSSSE[2] data (Current questions 3a, 10a, 10b)
SKILL 1. Within a specific or discrete subject matter, to engage in effective problem solving by: a. identifying and diagnosing problems; b. generating alternative solutions and strategies; c. developing and implementing plans of action; and d. keeping the planning process open to new information and ideas.	1. Final Assessment in Clinic, Externship, or Practicum by supervisor 2. MPT results from bar exam	1. Data from 2013 Hanover Employer Survey 2. LSSSE data (Current questions 3d, 3e, 10l) 3. Data from Summer 2021 Follow-up Employer Survey

[2] "LSSSE" is the acronym for the Law School Survey of Student Engagement.

SKILL 2. To comprehend legal texts and apply the legal principles extracted from the texts to new factual circumstances by: a. comprehending a legal text, such as a case, a statute, an administrative rule, a secondary source, or a contract; b. comprehending a series of legal texts and synthesizing them into a coherent legal narrative, including the ability both to harmonize apparently conflicting authorities and to recognize genuinely conflicting authorities; and c. applying governing legal principles to new factual situations, including the abilities to spot issues, to formulate issues, to develop potential legal solutions, and to assess their validity.	1. Review of Random Sample of Upper-Level Writing Papers by Assessment Committee 2. MPT results from bar exam 3. MEE results from bar exam	1. Data from 2013 Hanover Employer Survey 2. LSSSE data (Current questions 3b, 3c, 10e) 3. Data from Summer 2021 Follow-up Employer Survey
SKILL 3. To conduct effective and efficient legal research by developing a research strategy, identifying potentially relevant sources of law, locating legal texts that provide the governing legal principles for a factual situation, and understanding the role that legal reasoning plays in legal research.	1. Post-Tests in Upper-Level Specialized Legal Research Courses 2. Review of Random Sample of Upper-Level Writing Papers by Assessment Committee	1. Data from 2013 Hanover Employer Survey 2. Data from Spring 2016 Student Survey 3. LSSSE data (Current question 10g) 4. Data from Summer 2021 Follow-up Employer Survey
SKILL 4. To communicate effectively orally and in writing by presenting material in a clear, concise, well-organized, and professional manner that is appropriate to the audience and circumstances.	1. Review of Random Sample of Upper-Level Writing Papers by Assessment Committee	1. Data from 2013 Hanover Employer Survey 2. LSSSE data (Current questions

a. For all communication, to use active listening, empathy, and emotional intelligence. b. For written communication, to write 1) an effective objective memorandum predicting the resolution of one or more legal issues; 2) effective trial and appellate briefs advocating a position for a client; and 3) a legally effective document other than in the litigation context.	2. Review of Random Sample of RWA I Objective Memos by Assessment Comm. 2. Review of Random Sample of RWA II Appellate Briefs by Assessment Comm. 3. Review of Random Sample of Settlement Agreements Written in Lawyering Skills I by Assessment Comm.	10c, 10d) 3. Data from Summer 2021 Follow-up Employer Survey
SKILL 5. To work cooperatively as part of a team.	1. Review of Random Sample of Peer Team Member Evaluations in Property I and II by Assessment Committee	1. Data from 2013 Hanover Employer Survey 2. LSSSE data (Current question 10h) 3. Data from Summer 2021 Follow-up Employer Survey
SKILL 6. To practice effectively by: a. recognizing and resolving potential ethical issues; b. developing systems and procedures to ensure the efficient allocation of time, effort, and resources, and the timely performance and completion of work; and c. facilitating effective working relationships.	1. Review of Random Sample of Peer Team Member Evaluations in Property I and II by Assessment Committee 2. MPRE Results (If we can obtain; if we can't obtain, review sample of final exams from Legal	1. Data from 2013 Hanover Employer Survey 2. LSSSE data (Current question 10h) 3. Data from Summer 2021 Follow-up Employer Survey

	Profession)	4. Data from Spring 2019 Follow-up Student Survey (question on time-management)
VALUE 1. As a member of a profession dedicated to the service of clients, a commitment to professionalism and to the rules of professional responsibility, including: a. attaining and maintaining a level of competence in the lawyer's own field(s) of practice; b. representing clients in a competent manner; c. increasing the lawyer's knowledge of the law and improving the lawyer's practice skills; and d. other aspects of professionalism, including honesty, integrity, reliability, respect for others, diligence and hard work, maturity, and judgment.	Not Applicable.	1. Data from Spring 2016 Student Survey 2. LSSSE data (Current questions 10i, 10n) 3. Data from Spring 2019 Follow-up Student Survey
VALUE 2. As a member of a profession that bears special responsibilities for the quality of justice, a commitment to: a. promoting justice, fairness, and morality in the lawyer's practice in harmony with the lawyer's ethical duties to clients; b. contributing to the profession's fulfillment of its responsibility to ensure that adequate legal services are provided to those who cannot afford to pay for them; c. contributing to the profession's fulfillment of its responsibility to enhance the capacity of law and legal institutions to do justice; and d. showing respect for all people.	Not Applicable.	1. Data from Spring 2016 Student Survey 2. LSSSE data (Current questions 5b, 7d, 10n) 3. Data from Cultural Proficiency Survey in PWL Class 4. Data from Spring 2019 Follow-up Student Survey

VALUE 3. As a member of a self-governing profession, a commitment to: a. participating in activities designed to improve the profession; b. assisting in the training and preparation of new lawyers; and c. striving to rid the profession of prejudice based on race, religion, national or ethnic origin, gender, sexual orientation, disability, age, or socio-economic status, and to rectify the effects of those prejudices.	Not Applicable.	1. Data from Spring 2016 Student Survey 2. LSSSE data (Current question 10k) 3. Data from Cultural Proficiency Survey in PWL Class 4. Data from Spring 2019 Follow-up Student Survey
VALUE 4. As a member of a learned profession, a commitment to selecting and maintaining employment that will allow the lawyer to develop as a professional and to pursue the lawyer's professional and personal goals.	Not Applicable.	1. Data from Spring 2016 Student Survey 2. LSSSE data (Current question 10m) 3. Data from Spring 2019 Follow-up Student Survey

OUTCOMES ASSESSMENT SCHEDULE (ASSUMING 2024 ABA SITE VISIT)

OUTCOME	2016-2017	2017-2018	2018-2019	2019-2020	2020-2021	2021-2022	2022-2023	2023-2024
KNOWLEDGE. Requisite knowledge and understanding of subparts 1-6.	X			X			X	X
SKILL 1. Problem-solving.							X	
SKILL 2. Comprehending legal texts and applying legal principles to new factual circumstances.		X						
SKILL 3. Conducting effective and efficient legal research.		X						
SKILL 4. Communicating effectively orally and in writing.			X					
SKILL 5. Working cooperatively as part of a team.					X			
SKILL 6. Recognizing and resolving potential ethical issues; developing time-management procedures; facilitating effective working relationships.						X		
VALUE 1. Commitment to professionalism and the rules of professional responsibility.				X				
VALUE 2. Special responsibilities for quality of justice.				X				
VALUE 3. Improving the profession; striving to rid the profession of prejudice.				X				
VALUE 4. Selecting and maintaining employment that allows lawyer to develop as professional and pursue lawyer's professional and personal goals.				X				

Washburn University School of Law
Assessment Plan

PROGRAM ASSESSMENT PLAN ~ 2017-18 through present

This document only needs to be updated when changes are made.

UNIT	LAW
Department (if applicable)	
Degree/Program	JD
Date Prepared	November 20, 2017
Date Revised	April 10, 2020

PROGRAM MISSION

Cell will expand to accommodate text.

Washburn Law has a multi-faceted mission:

Teaching and Student Development – Washburn Law provides an outstanding legal education for future leaders in our society. We combine innovative teaching approaches with individualized and focused attention in a collegial and collaborative learning environment. We ensure that our graduates have acquired the knowledge, skills, and values necessary to serve their clients and provide leadership in their local, national, and global communities. Washburn Law proactively assists in placing students on the path to success in a wide range of possible careers.

Scholarship – Washburn Law is committed to the development of scholarship. We recognize that scholarship not only informs and enriches our teaching, but also influences academic, judicial, and professional discourse on a wide range of legal issues, thereby contributing to the world of ideas and the development of the law and a more just society.

Service – Washburn Law's faculty, staff, and students build on a strong tradition of service, contributing in various ways to enhancing the strength, integrity, and dynamism of the legal system and the rule of law, at the local, national, and international levels.

Diversity – Washburn Law contributes to the development of a more diverse legal profession, and to the fostering of the principles of equality in our society more broadly, by striving to create a law school community that is itself diverse, inclusive, and sensitive to the diversity-related issues in law and society.

PROGRAM STUDENT LEARNING OUTCOMES (PSLO)

Upon completion of the program:

PSLO 1	Graduates will demonstrate knowledge of the law and the legal system.
PSLO 2	Graduates will demonstrate analytical and problem-solving skills.
PSLO 3	Graduates will communicate effectively.
PSLO 4	Graduates will demonstrate competency in legal practice skills.
PSLO 5	Graduates will possess the requisite skills to recognize and resolve dilemmas in an ethical and professional manner.
PSLO 6	Graduates will demonstrate knowledge of the importance of service to the profession and to the community at large, both nationally and internationally.

PROGRAM ASSESSMENT PLAN ~ 2017-18 through present

This document only needs to be updated when changes are made.

CURRICULUM MAP (Alignment)

List all courses required for program majors and indicate, where applicable, (using the following key) the PSLO with which they are associated.

T = Taught
X = Taught and Assessed
A = Assessed

If the program has more than 6 PSLO, "Copy and Paste" rows from this table below the existing table, beginning with the row numbering the PSLO.

Required Courses	PSLO 1	PSLO 2	PSLO 3	PSLO 4	PSLO 5	PSLO 6
Con Law I	X	X				
Contracts	X	X				
Civ Pro	X	X				
LARWI	X	X	X	X		
Criminal Law	X	X	X			
Property	X	X				
Torts	X	X				
LARWII	X	X	X	X		
Evidence	X	X				
Prof. Resp.	X	X			X	
Con Law II	X	X	X			
Civ Pro II	X	X				
Crim Pro	X	X	X			
Perspectives						X
Upper Level Writing			X	X		
Upper Level Oral			X			
Skills Requirement				X		

PROGRAM ASSESSMENT PLAN ~ 2017-18 through present

This document only needs to be updated when changes are made.

ASSESSMENT MEASURES (Method)

Indicate (*mark with an X*) the type of assessment used to evaluate each PSLO.
Check as many boxes as apply.
Programs should use at least 2 direct measures for each PSLO.

If the program has more than 6 PSLO, "Copy and Paste" rows from this table below the existing table, beginning with the row numbering the PSLO.

	PSLO 1	PSLO 2	PSLO 3	PSLO 4	PSLO 5	PSLO 6
DIRECT						
Bar Exam	X					
Upper Level Writing Rubric	X	X	X	X		
Upper Level Oral Rubric	X	X	X	X		
MPRE Exam					X	
Externship Supervisor Eval Forms	X	X	X	X	X	
Clinic Supervisor Eval Forms	X	X	X	X	X	
Perspectives Rubric						X
Pro Bono Hours						X
INDIRECT						
Alumni Survey	X	X	X	X	X	X
Employer Survey	X	X	X	X	X	X
3L Survey (with LSSSE questions)	X	X	X	X	X	X

THRESHOLD OF STUDENT SUCCESS

For each PSLO, list each measure separately and indicate the threshold of student achievement considered acceptable.
(example: 75% of students will receive B or better) **- see Assessment Plan Guide for additional instructions.**

Hit :Tab" in the last cell to add another row. Cells will expand to accommodate text.

PSLO	MEASURE	THRESHOLD
1	Bar Exam	90% ultimate bar pass rate (the two-year number reported to ABA)
	Bar Exam	75% pass rate for first time takers in the previous calendar year
	ULW Rubric	80% of students average 70% of total points
	ULO Rubric	80% of students average 70% of total points
	Externship Supervisor Eval Form	Q1: average > 4
	Clinic Supervisor Eval Form	Q1: average > 4
	Alumni Survey	Average score >4
	Employer Survey	Average score >4
	3L Survey	Average score >4
2	ULW Rubric	80% of students average 70% of total points
	ULO Rubric	80% of students average 70% of total points
	Externship Supervisor Eval Form	Q2: average > 4

PROGRAM ASSESSMENT PLAN ~ 2017-18 through present

This document only needs to be updated when changes are made.

	Clinic Supervisor Eval Form	Q2: average > 4
	Alumni Survey	Average score >4
	Employer Survey	Average score >4
	3L Survey	Average score >4
3	ULW Rubric	80% of students average 70% of total points
	ULO Rubric	80% of students average 70% of total points
	Externship Supervisor Eval Form	Qs 4-6: average > 4
	Clinic Supervisor Eval Form	Qs 4-6: average > 4
	Alumni Survey	Average score >4
	Employer Survey	Average score >4
	3L Survey	Average score >4
4	Externship Supervisor Eval Form	Q7: average > 4
	Clinic Supervisor Eval Form	Q7: average > 4
	Alumni Survey	Average score >4
	Employer Survey	Average score >4
	3L Survey	Average score >4
5	MPRE Exam	80% of takers in previous calendar year pass (self-reported)
	Externship Supervisor Eval Form	Q8: average > 4
	Clinic Supervisor Eval Form	Q8: average > 4
	Alumni Survey	Average score >4
	Employer Survey	Average score >4
	3L Survey	Average score >4
6	Perspectives Rubric	80% of students average 70% of points
	Pro Bono Certification	50% of graduates have over 15 pro bono hours
	Alumni Survey	Average score >4
	Employer Survey	Average score >4
	3L Survey	Average score >4

DATA COLLECTION CALENDAR

Indicate how often assessment data are collected for each PSLO.
S=every semester
Y=every year
2=every other year
3=every 3 years, (etc.)
O-Other (please explain)
If the program has more than 6 PSLO, hit "Tab" in the last cell to add another row.

	Frequency of Data Collection
PSLO 1	3
PSLO 2	3
PSLO 3	3
PSLO 4	3
PSLO 5	3
PSLO 6	3

PROGRAM ASSESSMENT PLAN ~ 2017-18 through present

This document only needs to be updated when changes are made.

ANALYSIS AND REPORTING CALENDAR

Indicate (*mark with an X*) the years in which each PSLO was/will be analyzed and reported.
Cycle will repeat after Year 6.
If the program has more than 6 PSLO, "Copy and Paste" rows from this table below the existing table, beginning with the row numbering the PSLO.

	PSLO 1	PSLO 2	PSLO 3	PSLO 4	PSLO 5	PSLO 6
Year 1/2018-19	X					
Year 2/2019-20		X				
Year 3/2020-21			X			
Year 4/2021-22	X			X		
Year 5/2022-23		X			X	
Year 6/2023-24			X			X
Year 7/2024-25	X			X		

If field experiences are a significant part of the program, explicitly address how validity and reliability of the evaluation instrument is ensured.
Cell will expand to accommodate text.

N/A

STAKEHOLDER INVOLVEMENT

Describe how stakeholders (faculty, students, alumni, advisory boards, community, etc.) are involved in the development, implementation, periodic review and continuous improvement of the Assessment Plan.
Cell will expand to accommodate text.

Many of our assessment measures involve surveys to solicit input from the students themselves, from recent alum, and from employers of our graduates. Additionally, we plan to circulate results with our faculty and to discuss the results at a faculty meeting.

PROGRAM ASSESSMENT PLAN ~ 2017-18 through present

This document only needs to be updated when changes are made.

PROGRAM ASSESSMENT PLAN REVIEW CYCLE

Indicate (*mark with an X in column 2*) the year(s) in which this Program Assessment Plan will be reviewed and indicate in column 3 (when applicable) when changes are made and addressed in the appropriate year's annual report.

Cycle repeats after Year 6.

	Program Assessment Plan Review	Were changes made and addressed in the Annual Report? Yes or No (update when applicable)
Year 0/2017-18	X	Plan initially developed and implementation begun.
Year 1/2018-19	X	Plan revised, began data collection for PSLO1
Year 2/2019-20	X	Plan updated, gathered and evaluated data for PSLO1, began data collection for PSLO2

Index

Thanks to Jade Morgan, Washburn University School of Law Class of 2022, for her help with this Index.